A.C. Croft

Managing
a Public Relations Firm
for Growth and Profit
Second Edition

Pre-publication
REVIEWS,
COMMENTARIES,
EVALUATIONS . . .

"Croft's unerring focus on PR firm profitability and how to maximize and sustain it sets him apart from other authors in this field. He does not allow PR firm leaders the luxury of excuses for why they are not more profitable. Instead, he provides specific guidelines, formulas, and caveats for success. We adopted his client profitability formula and benefited mightily."

John Bliss, MS
Principal,
Bliss, Gouverneur & Associates, Inc.

"This is the perfect sequel to Croft's first book. The original has become a ready reference manual for our management team regarding compensation, profitability, and management of our growing firm. After the first decade of focusing on being excellent practitioners we decided it was time for our firm to become profitable. We credit the combination of Croft's counsel and his book with helping us achieve 300 percent profitable growth."

John Rosica
Founder, Rosica Strategic Public Relations

"If you run a public relations firm and want it to succeed, you must read this book! The first edition was terrific, and this is even better. It doesn't miss a thing."

David M. Grant
President, LVM Group, Inc.

More pre-publication
REVIEWS, COMMENTARIES, EVALUATIONS . . .

"**A**.C. Croft has done it again! In his latest edition of *Managing a Public Relations Firm for Growth and Profit* he mixes it up with a unique combination of how-to and real-life case studies. His book covers important agency issues ranging from managing time and people to planning the future of your firm, all in the highly readable fashion. If you are a longtime agency principal or a soon-to-be PR agency founder, this is the definitive guidebook, to be read with a highlighter and a beginner's mind. Guaranteed, years from now it will be your most well-worn, dog-eared reference text."

Sheri Benjamin
Founder, The Benjamin Group Inc.

"**M**anaging a Public Relations Firm for Growth and Profit, Second Edition is a must-read for anyone currently running an agency or thinking about opening their own. It is also a must-read for agency account executives looking to rise to the top. From identifying agency strengths to systematic prospecting to time management to billing to tracking profitability—it's all between the covers of this book. After 18 years of owning and managing a 45-person agency, I will continue to use this book as an ongoing reference to guide me through the challenges that arise in growing a successful business. A must-read for everybody in the public relations agency business (except my competition)."

Michael Layne
Marx Layne & Company

"**A**.C. Croft is right. Public relations firm owners love to win. His latest edition is a playbook covering management fundamentals, updated for the way the game is won today. The all-new chapter on the rise of procurement provides insights into understanding the procurement mentality as well as great advice on how to emerge financially unscathed. The chapter on the anatomy of an agency search is a familiar story that even seasoned agency owners should reread every year. In fact, all firm owners would do well to routinely reacquaint themselves with the many valuable management doctrines recorded in this insightful work."

Gary Myers, MA
President and CEO,
Gary Myers & Associations, LLC;
Founder and former president,
Morgan & Myers

"**W**hereas many PR firm consultants focus primarily on getting new accounts and servicing client business, Al Croft's 'sweet spot' is in helping PR firm principals run their businesses and make a profit. We began working with him years ago, and the principles he preached then are still the foundation for how we operate our firm. His advice has always been candid, consistent, and on target, and his book reflects this."

Cathy G. Ackermann
President and CEO
Ackermann Public Relations & Marketing

Managing
a Public Relations Firm
for Growth and Profit

Second Edition

THE HAWORTH PRESS
Titles of related interest

Transforming New Technologies into Cash Flow: Creating Market-Focused Strategic Paths for Business-to-Business Companies by Roger More

Lifestyle Market Segmentation by Dennis J. Cahill

Handbook of Niche Marketing: Principles and Practice by Tevfik Dalgic

Marketing Research: Text and Cases, Second Edition by Bruce Wrenn, Robert E. Stevens, and David L. Loudon

Principles of Advertising: A Global Perspective, Second Edition by Monle Lee and Carla Johnson

The Concise Handbook of Management: A Practitioner's Approach by Jonathan T. Scott

Marketing Planning Guide, Third Edition by Robert E. Stevens, David L. Loudon, Bruce Wrenn, and Phylis Mansfield

The Book on Management by Bob Kimball

Internal Relationship Management: Linking Human Resources to Marketing Performance edited by Michael D. Hartline and David Bejou

Strategic Management: Formulation, Implementation, and Control in a Dynamic Environment by Abbass F. Alkhafaji

Using Public Relations Strategies to Promote Your Nonprofit Organization by Ruth Ellen Kinzey

4 × 4 Leadership and the Purpose of the Firm by H. H. Bradshaw

Managing a Public Relations Firm for Growth and Profit

Second Edition

A. C. Croft

Best Business Books®
An Imprint of The Haworth Press, Inc.
New York • London • Oxford

For more information on this book or to order, visit
http://www.haworthpress.com/store/product.asp?sku=5561

or call 1-800-HAWORTH (800-429-6784) in the United States and Canada
or (607) 722-5857 outside the United States and Canada

or contact orders@HaworthPress.com

Published by

Best Business Books®, an imprint of The Haworth Press, Inc., 10 Alice Street, Binghamton, NY
13904-1580.

PUBLISHER'S NOTE
The development, preparation, and publication of this work has been undertaken with great care.
However, the Publisher, employees, editors, and agents of The Haworth Press are not responsible
for any errors contained herein or for consequences that may ensue from use of materials or information contained in this work. The Haworth Press is committed to the dissemination of ideas and information according to the highest standards of intellectual freedom and the free exchange of ideas.
Statements made and opinions expressed in this publication do not necessarily reflect the views of
the Publisher, Directors, management, or staff of The Haworth Press, Inc., or an endorsement by
them.

First edition published 1996

Cover design by Kerry E. Mack.

Photo of Phil Mirabito, Pierpont Communications, © Gittings & Lorfing, 1999. Reprinted by permission.

Library of Congress Cataloging-in-Publication Data

Croft, A. C.
    Managing a public relations firm for growth and profit / A.C. Croft.—2nd ed.
        p. cm.
    Includes bibliographical references and index.
    ISBN-13: 978-0-7890-2864-8 (hard : alk. paper)
    ISBN-10: 0-7890-2864-6 (hard : alk. paper)
    ISBN-13: 978-0-7890-2865-5 (soft : alk. paper)
    ISBN-10: 0-7890-2865-4 (soft : alk. paper)
    1. Public relations firms—Management. I. Title.
HD59.C755 2006
659.2'068—dc22
                                                                        2005019820

CONTENTS

ABOUT THE AUTHOR

A.C. Croft, President of A.C. Croft & Associates Inc., is a public relations management consultant specializing in training, evaluation, and critical and conceptual thinking. He provides confidential planning, evaluation, and counseling services to small and midsize national public relations firms. Mr. Croft has more than 25 years' experience in national public relations firms, including 15 years in senior management, and formed his management consulting practice in 1987. Formerly he was senior vice president and Midwest general manager of Bozell Public Relations, one of the country's largest public relations firms. A widely published author, Mr. Croft has written for such publications as *PRSA Strategist*, the *Holmes Report*, *PR Week*, *Bank Marketing*, *Marketing Week*, *Public Relations Journal*, *Communication Briefings*, *Advertising Age*, and *Sales and Management Marketing*. He has also served as a contributing editor for *Public Relations Quarterly*, and is currently editor of *Management Strategies*. Mr. Croft is a frequent speaker to professional organizations, including annual conferences of the Public Relations Society of America, and he conducts in-house account management seminars for public relations firms. In addition, he hosts the Sedona Round Table, a three-day workshop for public relations firms held each fall in Sedona, Arizona. The Public Relations Society of America has awarded Mr. Croft two Silver Anvils, the highest recognition in the public relations profession.

Foreword

Some have thought of public relations as a craft. Others have viewed it as a profession. Still others define PR as applied social science. Al Croft looks at public relations as a service of value and as a business. And nobody knows more than Al about the business of public relations.

Like most of his peers, he was thrust into the business of managing a public relations firm. But unlike some of us who were dragged kicking and screaming from "doing PR" to running a business, Al made it his business to master the principles of good management and apply them to public relations.

In this book, he shares his wealth of knowledge about public relations management, drawing on his long experience running successful public relations operations.

To achieve success in running a public relations business, managers must satisfy the sometimes contradictory needs of at least three diverse audiences. They must provide exemplary service to clients. They must provide expansive career opportunities to employees. And they must return a reasonable profit to the guy who owns the place.

Public relations entrepreneurs are a funny lot. While owners of other kinds of businesses are unabashedly in it for all they can take out of it, your typical PR firm owner often has been satisfied by the freedom to run his own business, often substituting psychic income for dollars and cents. He or she is genuinely turned on by doing good work and getting results for clients. All too often, they have been more motivated by the thrill of winning new business and the satisfaction of serving important clients than by enhancing their firm's bottom line.

I have worked for PR firms that performed excellent work for prestigious companies for years despite the fact that these accounts were marginally if at all profitable. The rationale was that these clients

doi:10.1300/5561_a

were a ticket to attracting new clients, wear and tear on staff and the absence of profit not withstanding to the contrary.

It's no wonder that employees of PR firms that overservice and undercharge clients for their work complain that they are overworked and underpaid. You cannot build a ball club with stressed-out players. An agency needs a staff motivated by the opportunities to share the goodies as well as the fun. The boss who may think he can do it all now can't continue to be a one-man band as the firm grows.

The times are changing. The renewed emphasis clients are placing on doing what it takes to maximize profits isn't lost on PR firms. Many formerly independent PR shops are now owned by other entities such as advertising agencies, holding companies, and larger PR firms. Their casual ways of doing business have given way to strict adherence to the systems and processes imposed by their new parents. They find themselves valued as much or more for their contributions to the P&L than the quality of their work. It's a rude shock for former paternalistic owners to learn just how serious the new owners are about their volume and earnings expectations. Many of the old owners have found it uncomfortable to operate under a new order and have been replaced by professional managers who are accustomed to managing the bottom line.

This new breed of entrepreneurs is more serious about the business of the business than were their predecessors. They are in business to make money, and they want to see their hard work rewarded. It follows that they are doing what it takes to manage for profitable growth. Some plan to cash out at some point in time and are bent on making their firms attractive to potential buyers. Others wouldn't think of working for someone else ever. Still, they are taking steps to generate rewards that are commensurate with their efforts.

Whatever their motivation, it's no coincidence that many of these bright young agency owners are students of Al Croft. He has worked with management of scores of agencies around the country to help them manage their business profitably and has conducted seminars for their account managers on how to manage their accounts more efficiently.

His *Management Strategies* newsletter is must reading for his owner-subscribers. His annual Sedona Round Table enables a select group of PR firm principals to learn from Al and one another. I have been privileged to be a Round Table faculty member and have come away absorbing as much as I have imparted.

Now, he has given us the ultimate "how to" book in PR firm management. I would have given anything to have a book like this when I started up the public relations operation for the international giant Foote Cone & Belding.

I had spent half a career managing accounts while somebody else managed the business. I had to learn the business of public relations from scratch, and it wasn't easy. The ad folks tried to help, but their business is substantially different from public relations. Their accounting systems were based on the then-sacrosanct commission system that doesn't apply to PR. Accounts were staffed by armies of handsomely rewarded vice presidents, account directors, account supervisors, and other executives that no PR account could afford. The abundant overhead charges easily absorbed by the ad side were devastating to our business.

By trial and error, hook or crook, and an understanding management, we learned how to run a profitable business. So intrigued with our success was the then CEO that he started the PR acquisition craze of the 1970s. But that's another story.

If you are now running or planning to run a PR firm, I guarantee you that *Managing a Public Relations Firm for Growth and Profit* will save untold hours of pain and misery and reinventing the wheel. Al has put together an altogether remarkable book that you will refer to time and time again.

Al covers all the bases. He happens to be a skilled communicator as well as a student of management. His book is clear, concise, easy to understand, and easy to apply. He spells it all out: How to market and manage your firm. What to do. What not to do. What kind of clients to work for and what kind to avoid. How to make money. And how to lose it.

He even provides some of the basic forms and documents you will need, such as sample letters of agreement and resource allocation matrices.

Running a firm today has become much more complicated, but the computer has come to the rescue. Al tells you how to harness technology to help you track vital processes such as staff utilization, performance against projections, budget status, and cash flow.

Al doesn't limit his content to the particulars of the PR business. He offers his readers very valuable suggestions on such subjects as time management and paper management that can be shared with a spouse, a friend, or even a client in another service business.

As a reader bonus, each chapter is supplemented by succinct real-world wisdom from the chiefs of twenty successful public relations firms.

Al has directed his book to small and midsized firms. I predict that those who apply the wisdom of the ages embodied in this book to their business won't be small or midsized for long.

A long time ago, I took a college course from a professor who wrote a book called *Write That Book*. I urged Al Croft to write this book because it's needed and because nobody could do it better. I think you will agree.

Thomas L. Harris
APR Fellow PRSA

Preface

As with the original edition of *Managing a Public Relations Firm for Growth and Profit,* published in 1996, this second edition is aimed at helping you learn to manage a public relations firm . . . for growth and profit. It will tell you what you need to know to start a PR firm and make it go!

This is not simply a replay of the first edition; rather, all the text has been edited and updated and a great deal of fresh material, including three new chapters, added. The manuscript for this edition has about 60 percent more pages than the original. After all, a lot has happened in the agency business since the first edition's manuscript went to the publisher late in 1994.

But I digress; this is about you and your PR firm (or the one you plan to or long to start).

Perhaps, you have already made the leap and have at least a few employees and several paying clients. You may even have been in business for a number of years and consider your firm successful.

However, occasionally, or even consistently, you may suffer a disquieting sense that, after an initial spurt of business, your firm is now sitting on dead center, gaining few new clients, or even losing business that is not being replaced. Or you may experience a nagging disenchantment with your financial rewards compared to the hours you invest.

This book will help you correct such problems by demonstrating (1) how to market, promote, and sell your firm to attract, win, and hold the kind of clients you want and (2) how to manage your firm so that it is productive and profitable and has a long-range future.

If you are a second-level agency manager or a corporate PR executive toying with the idea of firm management or ownership, you will learn how to avoid duplicating the mistakes of those who have gone before you.

Senior management of national firms who read this book will be comforted by recognizing practices, precepts, and philosophies that they have espoused all their professional lives. Most of what works for the 500-employee agency works equally well for the five-man (or woman) firm.

You also will find brief profiles of 19 seasoned and successful PR firm principals. These are not chief executive officers of mammoth international endeavors. Rather, they each founded a midsized firm currently generating somewhere between $1 million and $10 million a year in fee income. In one case, the original owner now caries the title of "founder" after a carefully planned sale of his firm to two of his senior executives.

There are several thousand such independent firms operating in the United States and Canada, not to mention probably a similar number in foreign ports. Each of the firms has grown in the image of its owner/principal. Some of the firms are generalists, working for a variety of clients; others specialize in one or more specific market niches. Some firms are fast moving, fast growing; others are laid-back with more moderate growth. In these cases, growth should not necessarily be taken as the only mark of success but merely as an indication of the path chosen by the principal.

You would do well to listen as the principals talk about their early mistakes and heed the advice they offer.

Interestingly, of the 18 agency principals profiled in the first edition, only 10 appear in this edition. The others have sold their firms to another larger firm and retired, their firms have gone out of business, or they chose not to appear in this edition. Several of the original 18 firms have morphed into newer versions because of either economic problems or changes in ownership. Ten new principals are profiled here.

I should also note that I have endeavored not to be chauvinistic. I was an early and enthusiastic supporter of equal pay and equal assignments for women. However, I draw the line at constantly writing "he or she" to demonstrate my nonchauvinism. So please understand that when I write "he," it is the literary shortcut to "he and/or she."

This book is based on my experience over the most recent 18 years as a consultant to PR firm principals and for the 25 years before that as either an employee or a principal of three medium-sized and very successful PR agencies. (Although the agencies I ran were divisions or subsidiaries of large national advertising and public relations firms,

I operated them independently. And sometimes suffered for that affront.)

I am indebted to two friends for their willingness to read the first edition of this effort and tell me whether it made sense. John Charleston, chairman/cofounder of Charleston/Orwig, Hartland, Wisconsin, is a former Wisconsin colleague and one of the finest writers I have ever encountered. Mike Walker, president, The Walker Agency, Scottsdale, Arizona, started his successful boutique firm with his wife at their dining room table 23 years ago after being unceremoniously relieved of his PR responsibilities at a Fortune 500 corporation. I thank them for their insight and encouragement.

I also thank Tom Harris—author, university professor, jazz enthusiast, consultant, former vice chairman of Golin/Harris Communications, long-time faculty for the Sedona Round Table, and friend of more than 30 years—who first encouraged me to write this book.

And to my wife, Irene, who shares the responsibility for A.C. Croft and Associates: How did I ever get along before I met you 35 years ago?

If this book lights a path for you through the maze of public relations firm management, I will be pleased. My final thanks goes to all those who have walked that path with no light and who have stumbled in the dark. I learned from you.

PART I:
INTRODUCTION—THE REAL WORLD OF PUBLIC RELATIONS FIRM MANAGEMENT

Chapter 1

What Is a Public Relations Firm?

If you are reading this (and I assume that you are reading it, otherwise, why are you looking at the page?), you are probably in one of two situations: (1) you are thinking about or want to become the owner or manager of a public relations firm or (2) you are already the owner or manager of a PR firm.

If you are not already the owner/manager/principal of a firm, you are probably either working for a PR firm at some level of supervision or management or are a corporate PR executive (or were until recently working for one of these organizations). If you have experience in the agency business, most of what follows should make sense. You probably know a lot of it already. If your experience is limited to corporations or not-for-profit organizations, you are in for a real learning adventure.

True, both an agency principal and a corporate PR executive need to be consummate communication professionals and able counselors. However, beyond the professional area, their responsibilities are about as similar as a rattlesnake's bite and a lover's kiss.

Corporations are pretty much alike. (Okay, so maybe some of them are different.) However, about the only thing standard in the agency business is that there are very few standards. Hardly any agency operates exactly like any other agency. If the agency business has one major business weakness, it is this lack of standards. If this book contributes to the establishment and acceptance of more operating standards, the author will have achieved a major goal.

The majority of the dollars in the agency business funnel into about fifteen mega international agencies, most of which are owned by holding companies. On the other hand, there are several thousand small PR firms, with an average six to seven employees, operating at various levels of success. Weber Shandwick Worldwide, the largest agency in the

doi:10.1300/5561_01

3

world, had more than $400 million in annual fee income and 2,800 employees according to a recent edition of a national directory of PR firms.

At this writing, it's hard to get a fix on the current status of the majority of the international firms owned by holding companies because of reporting restrictions imposed by Congress in 2002 via the Sarbanes-Oxley Act. For current rankings of independent PR firms, including annual fee income and staff size, see the annual directories published by *PR Week* and the J.R. O'Dwyer Company.

Agencies measure their size—and their stature—by their "net fee income." This is the amount of revenue that a firm earns from its clients through staff time hourly charges and markup or commissions earned on purchased items. Sometimes, if a firm wants to look bigger than it actually is, it will report "billings." Billings are the total amount invoiced to clients by a firm, including staff time, markups, and the cost of material or services that the agency buys in behalf of its clients and then bills back to them, usually with a markup added.

The 17.65 percent markup commonly added to out-of-pocket costs by PR firms is derived from the 15 percent commission that advertising agencies historically earn on purchased advertising space or time. Stick with me, this gets complicated. If an advertising agency is charged $100 for an ad that it has purchased in behalf of a client, it sends the client a bill for $100 but only pays the media $85—the real cost of the ad—thus earning a 15 percent commission. If a PR firm buys printing worth $85, it is actually only billed $85 by the printer. To earn the same real dollar commission, it then adds 17.65 percent of $85—$15—and sends the client a bill for $100. Remember that formula; there will be a pop quiz on Tuesday.

Just to make sure that everyone is running on the same track, let's talk about a PR firm's function and purpose. They are different and often provide a source of conflict to agency principals.

A public relations firm has only one function: to serve its clients to the best of its ability and in their best interests at all times. Sometimes, this means telling the client that he or she is wrong and refusing to do the client's bidding.

An ancient piece of PR industry lore says that public relations practitioners should go to work every day prepared to resign rather than compromise their principles or ethics in their employer's behalf. The same wisdom holds true for public relations firms.

Every company or institution has the right to have its side of the story told to and examined and judged by the public. However, no agency has the option or right to color the truth or delete facts to make the story better or shine a purer light on its client.

Agencies should be prepared to resign an attractive piece of business rather than place their integrity, credibility, and reputation in harm's way.

In some cases, particularly when the article or news release describes a company's past, present, or future financial condition, the agency can be held as responsible as the client for communicating untruthful information. More than one firm has faced legal attention for wittingly or unwittingly playing with the truth. In one case, a number of years ago, the owner of a prominent Midwest firm, accused of distributing misleading information about a client, was forced to resign from the Public Relations Society of America, the industry's largest professional organization, rather than face an ethics tribunal.

On the other hand, a PR firm also has only one purpose: to achieve and maintain levels of income and profit that will ensure a reasonable financial return to its owners and fair and competitive compensation to its employees.

The client needs the best possible service, and the agency needs the highest possible income and profit. Therein lies a potential for conflict that every agency principal will encounter sooner or later and that must be managed with a win-win approach and results. Standards of ethics, integrity, and credibility must guide your actions.

"Account management"—the responsibility umbrella under which every agency practitioner functions—has been defined as "bringing the agency's management, professional and creative services to bear against a client's problems and opportunities so that we serve the client with maximum effectiveness while also generating maximum income and profit for the agency." No small chore!

A PR firm has only one thing to sell. Its basic product is the time that employees invest in behalf of the firm's clients. "Results" are hazy; a "maybe" kind of thing can't be promised or really measured in a way that satisfies everyone. "Time" is rock hard solid; you either invest it wisely or you squander it. You can track it and measure it.

Such a system requires a great deal of trust—trust by the firm's principal/s that employees not only will invest the proper amount of time in the client's behalf (ideally, neither more nor less than the budget calls for) but also will record that time honestly, frugally, and accurately.

In return for his financial support, the client is asked to trust that the invoice from his agency is a fair and accurate representation of the time invested in his behalf as well as an honest accounting of the expenses and out-of-pocket purchases made by the agency in his behalf. When this trust evaporates—for whatever reason—ugly situations can develop, such as the recent case when the Los Angeles city controller accused Fleishman-Hillard of overbilling the city more than $4 million over a six-year period.

This emphasis on the use and value of time is unique to service organizations such as legal, accounting, and public relations firms. The importance and relevance of time places heavy responsibilities on a PR firm's professional employees. It can, if not handled carefully, unduly emphasize the need for productivity and profit rather than the need for top-notch client service and satisfaction. Of course, if the agency's level and degree of client service does not translate into results that can be measured in terms of client satisfaction, the agency's longevity will be severely endangered.

This emphasis on time creates oft-strange jargon; "billability" is hard to say, but everyone in the agency business knows what it means (i.e., the ability of an individual to bill a large portion of his or her on-the-job time to clients). Practitioners' value to an agency may be judged by how "billable" they are.

A PR firm becomes profitable by (1) serving its clients well; (2) controlling its costs (salaries and overhead); and (3) charging fair, competitive hourly rates.

Historically, agencies used a simple multiple of hourly salary costs—three to four times salary costs—to set hourly rates. However, such a basic approach fails to cover modern and continually rising technology and health care costs. Today, many firms establish hourly rates—or project cost estimates or fees based on them—by using a formula that divides the sum of an individual's salary and benefits costs, a share of the firm's overhead, and the desired profit percentage by the number of hours that the individual is expected to bill annually. (More on this formula later.)

IS IT A FIRM OR AN AGENCY?

There are two types of public relations firms: those that are independent—owned and managed by a single individual, a partnership, or a group of individuals—and those that are a department, division, or subsidiary of a national PR firm, holding company, or advertising agency.

Some PR practitioners insist that there are public relations *firms* and advertising *agencies*. Many of the same souls who insist that only *firm* be used also frown on abbreviating public relations as *PR*. Owners and employees commonly refer to their "agency" except in more formal situations, such as a new business presentation, when they may discuss their "firm's" capabilities and exploits. To acquire new public relations representation, corporations conduct "agency searches."

However, the Public Relations Society of America formerly insisted that *firm* be used in all Society communications, evidently feeling that *agency* is somehow disparaging to its members. On the other hand, everybody understands when you say, "I've been in the agency business for X years." Nobody says, "I've been in the firm business for X years." I tend to use *firm* and *agency* interchangeably, and I don't mind *PR*. Use whichever term you're comfortable with and that fits the situation. Don't worry about the semantics.

ON BEING SUCCESSFUL

There are agencies that are successful: growing and profitable. And those that are not. Being either independent or subordinate has little relationship to whether your firm is successful. However, as a member of a corporate group of firms, you may be required to carry a hefty corporate overhead burden on your books over which you will have no control but which will impact on your bottom line if you manage a profit center.

On the other hand, as part of a multioffice/agency corporate family, you will have the corporate bank account as backup. As an independent, you will be largely on your own financially with the ever-pressing need to meet your monthly "nut" (minimum cash outlay including salaries and rent as well as all other nonrebillable out-of-pocket costs).

As a corporate entity, you will have the strength and varied resources of a large national firm available to you and your clients. As an independent, you can offer prospects fast turnaround and consistent counseling by senior personnel.

YOUR BASIC RESPONSIBILITIES

To ensure that your firm is successful (i.e., growing and profitable with a staff of highly competent professionals and a bevy of satisfied, prompt-paying clients) at a minimum you must meet the following six basic responsibilities:

1. *Listen to the voices and tides impacting on your clients.* What is the media saying? What public movements are gaining credence and momentum? What nascent trends are evident? Who is more or less important than a year ago?
2. *Report and interpret what you hear.* Will burgeoning public opinion create a problem for your client; what will be the timing, dimensions, and scope of the problem? What disruptions can media comment, public opinion, or popular movements create in such areas as product acceptance, employee productivity, or share value?
3. *Recommend policies and programs that relate corporate and public interests.* Develop programs to soothe and solve environmental concerns while protecting the organization's bottom line. Develop training or retraining programs to meet minority or senior citizen needs, compensate for economic cut backs, and/or produce upgraded skills for technology jobs.
4. *Communicate honestly and fully in anticipation of and in response to the voices and tides.* Deliver your client's messages concisely, coherently, and consistently to critical audiences and markets as broadly and precisely as necessary and possible.
5. *Prove that your effort moved mountains.* With the help of benchmarks, demonstrate that your communication campaign influenced public behavior, fostered product acceptance, promulgated new ideas, calmed negative opinion, dampened a fire storm, stimulated audience reaction, and reached the eyes and ears of those who control your client's life or death.
6. *Get your bills out on time.* Never let a client owe you money longer than thirty days. It's called "cash flow"!

And you will need it. Coupling wisdom and vision with finely tuned abilities to listen, interpret, respond, communicate, and demonstrate—not to mention collect what's owed you—will generate and ensure your clients' attention and confidence. And guarantee your firm's success.

MARKETING AND MANAGING YOUR FIRM

No matter what your firm's corporate status, high quality, professional client service, obviously, is essential to success. However, you will find little discussion in these pages of client service or general public relations theory and philosophy. Dozens of other books do that most admirably. Here, except for one brief chapter, we will assume the quality of your client service. And concentrate on tips, instructions, philosophies, theories, and guidance to help you market and manage your firm.

But first, what kind of person must you be to function well as the king of the hill in your agency?

PROFILE 1: CATHY ACKERMANN

President, Ackermann Public Relations
Knoxville, Tennessee

After serving as director of corporate marketing for the 1982 World's Fair, Ackermann founded the area's first full-service communications firm. The agency's first year's income of $250,000 grew to $4 million 20 years later.

However, fast expansion during the firm's early years and a lack of administrative systems took their toll. "I was having too much fun being a practitioner and wasn't paying enough attention to the business side," Ackermann says.

After a couple years, we said, "We're working too hard not to make more money." That drove us to put systems in place. We tightened everything that had to do with the financial side of the business. For example, every month, I look in detail at such things as the financial statement, cash flow, gross profit, billable hours, and accounts receivable. I also examine individual staff productivity and client profitability.

Currently, the firm's key practice areas include health care, technology, real estate development, tourism and entertainment, consumer products, and manufacturing. The firm also offers branding studies and Web site design. Ackermann PR has offices in Dallas, Texas, and Washington, DC, in addition to their headquarters in Knoxville, Tennessee, and is ranked by *PR Week* as a top 100 PR firm.

Ackerman's advice to a new agency principal or someone thinking about starting a PR firm: "Love the business. Otherwise, go to work for someone else."

Chapter 2

What Is an Agency Principal?

Individuals who lead PR firms may be the owner, manager, partner, managing partner, president, chairman, director, general manager, or some other semantic differentiation. However titled, they are *the principal,* the "first in rank, authority, and importance," according to my dictionary. Thereby, instead of strewing personal titles haphazardly through these pages, I will simply refer to all firm leaders as principals.

In addition to having a title, a larger office than anyone else, perhaps a leased car, and other perks, what is an agency principal?

To manage a successful public relations firm—independent agency, division, or local office of a larger firm—you, the agency principal, need both entrepreneurial and professional strengths and skills as well as marketing and management interest and ability. You (and your staff members) must be able to skillfully and positively manage the potential conflict between your clients' need for the best possible service and your firm's need for the most-possible income and profits.

To manage these dual responsibilities, you may need to choose between being an account executive or an agency manager, i.e., do the work or manage it. This can be a tough choice, particularly if you favor hands-on client work over administrative chores and have convinced yourself that you must focus 100 percent of your time and attention on client service. This could be a mistake!

Certainly, clients need and want access to senior practitioners for planning and counsel. They bristle when agency principals are featured in a new business presentation and then are replaced by junior professionals in day-to-day service.

In small agencies, the principal may not enjoy the luxury of backup senior professionals. You may need to be very active in client contact and program implementation. Complicating matters is the fact

doi:10.1300/5561_02

that many principals enjoy the creative and professional challenges of account work and find it difficult to step aside.

It also can be comforting to ignore management problems such as slow cash flow, client or staff defections, and other business disasters by staying immersed in direct client work. (The old "head in the sand" trick.)

Entrepreneurs in general are not particularly well-known for down-to-earth business acumen and management skills. Witness the well-documented cases of corporate entrepreneurs who have founded high visibility companies only to be forced out as the company grows because of their lack of sound management skills. These same weaknesses often cause problems for PR firms.

Neglecting the administrative and management needs of your agency is as dangerous as neglecting your clients' needs. Further, the more your firm grows, the more your attention must be directed toward managing the business. The truth is, "The business of the business is as important as serving the client," says Cathy Ackermann, president, Ackermann Public Relations, a thriving Knoxville, Tennessee, and Dallas, Texas, firm.

PROFESSIONAL EXPERIENCE AND SKILLS

What kind of experience do you need to own or manage a successful PR firm? Let's begin with the obvious. Most individuals who start their own PR firm or become the manager of a national firm's local office are solid, experienced professional public relations practitioners who have excellent planning, writing, media relations, and client relations skills.

However, like every rule, there are exceptions to this one. For example, there was the insurance executive who inherited his mother's PR firm and succeeded in this new field. There are the corporate planning executive and the officer of a software manufacturer who teamed with their PR professional wives to create flourishing technology firms.

There are no rules or statistics covering the minimum number of years' experience required to become a firm principal. However, personal experience and observation tell me that you should have at least three to five years experience as an underling before seeking or attaining the top rung or going out on your own. Five to eight years of agency or corporate experience makes the leap into the bullring that much more comfortable.

Some agency principals arrive directly from corporate backgrounds, either to scratch a nascent entrepreneurial itch or because they were down-sized out of an executive position. However, individuals with an agency background will have an easier time accepting and adapting to the pressures of agency leadership than a corporate emigrant.

There are subtle differences between the personality and motivation of individuals who naturally belong in a corporate atmosphere and those whose light burns brightest at the helm of an agency. I have long felt that if you were to stack 100 PR practitioners in a room, 45 of them would naturally lean toward corporate employment, 45 would function well in the agency business, and the other 10 could be successful switch hitters.

Why so? Doesn't the agency principal have the same professional responsibilities as his corporate counterpart? Don't both individuals strive to develop and implement public relations programs that meet client/employer objectives and produce excellent results? Of course. However, two distinct and unique needs set every agency principal apart from a corporate PR executive.

Agency principals (and staff members as well) are driven by a dominating and sometimes demonic need to be "billable"; to be productive; to bill the majority of their time to clients at a profitable hourly rate. (At this writing, it's been 18 years since I filled out my last agency time sheet and became a consultant to PR firms. And yet, I still feel guilty when confronted during working hours by moments when there is absolutely nothing I have to do.) Concerned agency principals/professionals also strive to reduce client costs by whisking through assignments in the shortest possible time consistent with good quality.

In addition, agency principals face the prospect that, sooner or later, every client is likely to either cut budgets or disappear for reasons totally out of the principal's control. To simply maintain cash flow equilibrium, much less grow the firm, you must constantly seek additional business either by increasing income from current clients through new assignments or by winning new clients, generally under competitive conditions.

These demands focus extreme pressure on the agency principal, pressure not likely to be matched in a corporate venue. As a result, corporate PR executives entering the agency world often encounter severe culture shock. (In a reverse twist, many experienced agency principals would likely feel a sense of emotional jet lag if they tried to pare down to a more moderate corporate pace.)

No matter what their backgrounds, successful agency principals have one thing in common. They are very smart people who thrive under the heat and glare of PR firm leadership.

PERSONAL DEDICATION AND RESILIENCY

Successful agency principals must be dedicated to 60- to 80-hour-plus workweeks, few or no vacations, and slim pay checks when times are tough. (And that's the good news.) You must be able to accommodate (without resorting to violence) overbearing, incompetent, inconsiderate clients (who hopefully and thankfully will be few in number). You must accept gracefully that not every employee will be as competent as you expect. Many are likely to do things differently from you. This is not necessarily a bad thing. Few will be as dedicated to your agency's future as you.

To cope comfortably with such adversity, you must be supremely confident of your own personal strengths and professional capabilities. Conversely, you also must be so comfortable in your ego that you have no problem recognizing, admitting, and accepting gaps in your experience or abilities. And in taking steps to fill such gaps, you must possess in massive quantities the capacity to bounce back, to pick yourself up off the floor of defeat or despair one more time. And then do it again. You must recognize that not every client will approve your best recommendation or applaud your best effort for reasons that you may never understand. You must accept that a prospect's failure to return your phone call does not mean that he or she hates you. You must not be insulted when the prospect does not know who you are after you've sent him several letters and have left phone messages for a month. And you must recognize that losing a new business competition does not mean that your firm is less competent than the winner.

MANAGEMENT INTEREST AND SKILLS

She leads a high-flying specialty PR firm that is one of the most innovative and best known in its market. And yet it has high staff turnover and low profits. She sits at her desk during a quick lunch break in an all-day meeting and silently screams, "I hate to manage!"

The very creative juices and counseling strengths that make many PR firm principals so successful as public relations advisors and generate heady client enthusiasm often conspire to weaken the firm's management structure and bottom line health. The sense of excitement and risk-taking vigor that drives an entrepreneur toward seemingly unreachable goals often drives employees wacky. They long for consistency and rhythm in the workplace while the entrepreneur quickly tires of routine and longs for new directions to explore and new heights to scale.

While the firm is young and emerging from its cocoon, the principal's lack of business management interest and ability may not be noticeable or harmful. But give the firm a little success, a little growth, more staff members and it begins to cry for management structure and direction.

And then you, the entrepreneur, must either become a manager, find a senior backup who can fill the management void . . . or expect possible employee turmoil and a bottom line that does not reflect your best interests.

Example: A southern firm led by an affable entrepreneur with extensive community contacts and professional respect struggled with before-tax profits barely into one digit. Two years after the entrepreneur sensed the problem and recruited a senior practitioner as his chief operating officer, before-tax profits had risen to 15 percent. And a substantial new employee bonus program was in place.

MARKETING AND SALES INTEREST AND SKILLS

An old agency axiom contends that there is no problem that a little new business will not fix.

Somewhere in this world, there may be a public relations agency to whose bosom clients rush with desperate need and mindless trust. An agency for whom a competitive new business "pitch"—a stand-up oral conflict in which your opponents may be three to six other equally hungry firms—is unknown, for whom all the new business that can be handled rolls in as easily and uninvited as if forwarded by the Good Witch of the North. During the boom times of the 1990s, that was often the case. Agencies often had the luxury of turning away business, particularly in the technology field. But, no more.

For the most part, badly needed new business—new clients to flush away despair and restore confidence—will not follow some magical automatic directional finder to your front door. It must be sought out, chased after, and often fought for.

New clients must be pursued with purpose and consistency and stamina and bravery. Cold calls—perhaps the most dreaded part of any shy principal's day—must be made to unresponsive prospects. Your quest for additional business must be organized to take best advantage of your firm's strengths as well as open up opportunities in new fields. And you must seek new business while you are the busiest fighting fires and otherwise meeting current clients' needs. Because despite your best efforts, your best client may not be with you tomorrow . . . and must be replaced.

TAKE THE GOOD WITH THE BAD

In your life as an agency principal, there will be good days and bad days. Hopefully, more of the former than the latter.

On good days, you will rejoice in the independence of not reporting to anyone (except your banker) or perhaps only to a distant executive. There is tremendous satisfaction in knowing that if anything good happens, it probably happened because of something you did, either directly or by training or motivating someone else.

The satisfaction of leading a group of loyal, skilled, enthusiastic people is hard to match. (Consider the emotion generated when thirty-some people applauded as this writer exited an elevator on crutches after a month-long surgical recuperation. This is lumps-in-the-throat stuff.)

You will wallow happily in new business triumphs. A long-sought prospect who phones to say "We've decided to go with your firm" will light a fire in your heart and spark exultation of the highest order. Time for a staff party! (Always, always celebrate wins. There will be enough times when you cannot celebrate.)

The good days also bring peer recognition, days when your firm is ranked high or higher than previously on a list of local or national PR agencies. Or you win an industry award. (I still remember that Saturday morning—a lot of years ago—when the Public Relations Society of America called my Milwaukee home from New York to say that our firm had won a coveted Silver Anvil for a public affairs program in behalf of Harley-Davidson Manufacturing Company.)

Clients may even find reason or occasion to compliment your firm's work. Cherish these occasions!

If you apply the right client service, new business, and agency management principles, the opportunity for financial gain is excellent—despite the sweat you will manufacture each month as you worry through the cyclical nature of the agency business. It is not unheard of for even small firm principals to take home more than $200,000 annually in salary alone, not to mention benefits and perks.

Ahh, but the bad hair days! Come they will. Sometimes with such frequency and intensity that you will plead mournfully "I need something good to happen!" or "I need a win!"

Small firm principals who migrate from large national firms sometimes spend many of their days yearning for the large clients with big budgets and extensive ambitions whom they formerly served. Now, their client list may consist largely of local companies whose small budgets are matched only by their lack of PR sophistication.

Many times, unsophisticated clients are also unprofitable because of the excessive demands that they make on your time combined with your willingness to let them do this if only to help keep the lights burning.

One of the reasons you will need to keep the lights burning is so that you can see to work while you're putting in all the extra hours that will be needed. Managing the business and wooing possible new business will take many of your daylight hours. That leaves the other side of the clock for client work that must be completed, including meeting unrealistic deadlines.

One of the reasons you may have trouble meeting client deadlines is because of a shortage of really competent people, particularly at the salary levels that you will be able to afford when your firm is young (and because most university PR graduates know how to solve the Three Mile Island crisis, but they do not know how to write a new product release or make up a media list).

Your monthly "numbers" will be the cause of some of your worst days. If you are the manager of a unit of someone else's firm, you may only have to answer tough questions when earnings fall short of objectives.

But when your name is on the door, it's a different story. When client budgets are cut (count on it; they will be), expected new clients do not come in when you expect them (prospects' priorities will never be the same as yours), and the monthly nut exceeds the cash in your bank account, calamity will ring its bell. Then your short-range solution may be an American Express card or your home in hock for a bank loan.

Why go through all this when maybe you could get—or keep—a cushy corporate job? Because, in the first place, if you are a true agency person, you will be bored out of your skull in the corporate political arena. Second, being an agency principal gives you far more opportunities to win than lose.

And winning is what the game is all about, whether it is a media coup in behalf of a client, beating another firm in a heated competition for a new piece of business, generating the blackest possible bottom line, or watching a talented but raw young account executive develop into a polished and competent professional.

If you are good at your job, the days that you win will sustain you in the days that you don't. But if you are not good, if you do not have strong professional, entrepreneurial, and management interests and capabilities, then you might better save time and stick your head in the oven in the beginning. Because the end result will be the same.

THE NEW BUSINESS GAME

Aside from ensuring a high level of client service, the days of a successful PR firm principal—your days—will be filled with marketing your firm for growth and managing your firm for profit.

First, marketing your firm for growth—that weird, frustrating, and eminently satisfying process also known as "new business development."

Unlike other contact sports, it is not how you play this game, but whether you win or lose.

PR FIRM PRINCIPALS I HAVE KNOWN

Here are five agency principals you probably know. Their agencies usually have high staff and client turnover, may have trouble with cash flow, and often have a profit problem.

The Great I Am

He intends to build a PR firm in his own image, hire only people who are his intellectual equal, and deal only with the most senior client executives. He has the last word (often the first and only word) on how best to serve clients, knows the best/only way to write or do anything, and does not really want arguments, discussion, or ideas from anyone. He has no real second in command because he can't stand to give up the authority. Employee and industry gossips say his modus operandi is "My way or the highway."

The Whirling Dervish

Sometimes called "the mad entrepreneur," he has the interest attention span of a sand flea (and is about as irritating to those who have to live with his shifting winds). No sooner does a business direction/ endeavor show signs of stability and maybe paying off than boredom sets in and he is off on a different tangent pursuing a new more challenging opportunity. Staff members are left gasping in his dust, trying to figure out which way he'll go next and how to keep from being tossed on their ear by the turbulence.

The Corporate King

He's never quite gotten used to the idea that he no longer works for a big corporation with deep pockets. (There are few of those around these days, anyway.) He feels it's very important that his agency be located in the high-rent district, have an exotic decor, costly furnishing, and ultra-state-of-the-art electronics. He's one of the last remaining agency executives still justifying a private secretary because it gives him a sense of status and style (and really boosts his ego). Chances are his bottom line shows lots of red.

The Sweat Hog

This one seemingly never sleeps and likes nothing better than to grind employees into grit with regular 70- to 80-hour weeks. He thinks employees are not really earning their keep unless they consistently bill 200 hours a month, handle nine different clients (all small), and bring in an auspicious new client every other month. He doesn't pay too well either. Founder of the original "sweatshop."

Clients Love Me

He can't keep his hands out of the soup but ignores stove mainte-nance. Still writes client speeches but doesn't charge his full rate. Otherwise, clients couldn't afford him. He's easily bored or is "too busy" to pay attention to his agency's numbers. He couldn't care less about writing a business plan for the firm or establishing good operat-ing and accounting systems. Often, he spreads himself too thin, bills more hours than everyone else—and irritates all of them—trying to serve all the clients he thinks "love" him and won't work with anyone else.

Make sure you don't see one of these guys staring back at you in the mirror.

THINGS YOU SHOULD NEVER SAY

As a principal, there will likely come times when temptation gets a handle on your mouth. When that happens, never say any of the fol-lowing:

- *To your receptionist*—"Tell him I'm in a meeting" to head off an unknown or unwelcome telephone caller. (Especially when the caller might represent a piece of business.)
- *To a client*—"We will absolutely have it on your desk by 9:00 a.m. tomorrow." (Especially when you know there's no chance at all that you can deliver on the promise.)
- *To a client*—"ABC isn't the best printer, but he's the cheapest. So I recommend we go with him." (Especially when you're re-sponsible for the job's quality.)
- *To a client*—"It looks like we're going to be overbudget. Sorry I didn't say something sooner." (Especially when you've known about the overage for some time but were afraid to tell the cli-ent.)
- *To employees*—"There won't be any layoffs even if we lose our biggest client." (Especially when you know the client is gone

and you're already figuring out who you can do without until you can pull in some more business.)

- *To a prospect*—"Your current agency (or PR director) isn't doing a very good job for you." (Especially if you have any hope of winning the business.)
- *To a vendor*—"I need you to eat ten percent of your bill because we underestimated the job." (Especially if you want the vendor to produce the best quality and be interested in working with you again.)
- *To a vendor*—"I need you to eat ten percent of your bill because we underestimated the job. But you can hide it in the next big job we do for this client." (Especially if you don't want to get caught packing a bill and lose the client as well as the respect of a good vendor.)
- *To a client*—"I'm sorry. Joe really messed up this job. I'm letting him go." (Especially when you were the one who made the mistake or had the final responsibility.)
- *To a client*—"I'm sorry Joe can't get along with you. I'm letting him go. I'm going to take over your business personally." (Especially when you know a saint couldn't get along with this client longer than about seven minutes. And you probably won't have his business much longer anyway.)
- *To an employee*—"I'm sorry. This isn't working out. Today is your last day." (Especially if you've never done anything to train the employee or counsel him on ways to improve his performance. And have assigned him work that he's not qualified to do. And have never kept a written record of your dissatisfaction with the employee's performance and may face a wrongful discharge legal accusation.)

THE PR AGENCY PRINCIPAL'S PRAYER

When all else fails, try this:

Dear Lord, grant me the will to keep this thing going without pay, thanks, or time off. Help me smile gratefully at my clients, even those I'd like to kill, when they finally pay their bill. Give me the excuses I need to put off my creditors one more month. Please keep my equipment working; save me from high repair bills. Smarten up my employees so that they're interested in doing the kind of work I need them to do when I need them to do it. And, last but not least, help me to understand why I wanted to do all this to begin with. (Unknown agency principal)

PROFILE 2: RICHARD BLEWITT

President, Rowan & Blewitt
Washington, DC

Backed by 15 years of newspaper and chemical industry PR experience and armed with a retainer-plus-hours contract from his former employer, Rich Blewitt and partner TV newscaster Ford Rowan opened an issues and crisis management firm in 1984. (Blewitt was one of the few corporate PR executives to beat *60 Minutes'* Mike Wallace to the draw when Wallace drew a bead on Velsicol Corporation, Blewitt's former employer.) The firm stayed independent until 1999, when it sold to Interpublic Group of Companies.

In addition to developing and helping implement strategies on sensitive issues for such clients as Ford Motor, General Motors, Bic, and Household International, the firm offers crisis and media training.

The niche firm is very low profile. "Our clients like it that way," says Blewitt. "They like the fact that we do not normally list our clients or publicize the sensitive work that we do." The firm participates in few competitive presentations. "Our work comes from referrals from top management to top management."

Blewitt's number-one frustration is the volatile nature of crisis counseling. To balance this volatility, the firm uses a "value-added" pricing strategy that calls for a premium fee.

In 2003, the firm had revenue of $11 million with 20 employees divided between its Northern Virginia and Long Island offices. It has a global network of consultants, as well as access to the IPG multiple functions and offices when necessary. Blewitt says,

This business is like an accordion; you have to be able to expand quickly (surge capacity) when you get the call for help; and you have to be able to collapse it as quickly when the crisis is over, thus the need for a large consulting pool versus employees.

PART II:
MARKETING YOUR FIRM
FOR GROWTH

Chapter 3

Anatomy of an Agency Search:
How the Game Is Played

THE BEGINNING

Every week, somewhere in the United States, invitations to a unique tribal mating dance are issued to public relations firms by corporations and institutions. Corporations call this dance an "agency search." PR firms call it a "new business pitch."

It is a dance in which the partners may never have met but during which they exchange intimate details of their business lives. It can result in a relationship that is long range and mutually fulfilling or short range and mutually disastrous. It also can determine whether a corporation achieves its public relations objectives and whether a public relations firm grows and prospers.

This is the story of a hypothetical agency search from the viewpoints of The Company and The Agency.

THE SITUATION

ABC Inc. is a large, well-established company with nationally advertised brand names and a reputation for solid, growth-oriented management. The Company recently completed a dramatic and comprehensive recapitalization and restructuring to avoid a hostile takeover. The successful takeover defense resulted in a substantial debt load that will require ABC Inc. to cut costs, lay off a number of employees, and sell several subsidiaries.

The Company needs to communicate the strength and goals of the "new" ABC Inc. to employees, shareholders, customers, vendors, and the financial and banking communities. Jan Jones, ABC director

doi:10.1300/5561_03

of public relations, recommends that a public relations firm with national capabilities be retained. Because the Company has never used a national public relations firm and she is not familiar with the PR agency community, Jones also recommends that the Company retain a management consultant to coordinate the search for a competent and compatible firm. Management agrees.

THE SEARCH

The Company

March 1- March 4: Jan Jones and the consultant meet with key ABC executives to discuss the Company's public relations objectives and the agency search process. The consultant suggests that the Company talk to no more than six agencies to not only provide a variety of choices for the ABC Review Committee but to make it easier for the Committee to identify and remember each firm's distinctive character under the pressure of competitive agency presentations.

March 15: The consultant submits a draft of the Request for Proposal (RFP) that will be given to counseling firms as the basis for their presentations. The RFP contains an outline of the Company's history; a description of the takeover battle and the resulting recapitalization and restructuring; a review of the objectives and target audiences for the planned public relations program; a description of criteria to be used in evaluating prospective agencies; a preliminary timetable for the search process; and a list of recommended agencies. The consultant also supplies an outline of the recommended agencies' credentials and capabilities and explains the rationale for each firm's selection. (One ABC executive questions the absence of a national "name" agency from the list. He accepts the consultant's reasoning that the agency's strength and reputation lie primarily in consumer product marketing, not in the communication areas that will be required in this assignment.)

March 21: The approved RFP, inviting competitive presentations, is sent to six agencies. One of the national firms on the list declines to participate because of a client conflict in another office. Another firm with strong credentials is invited to compete. The final six agencies include the local offices of three international organizations, two independent firms, and, at the request of the Company, the public relations department of the Company's advertising agency.

The Agency

March 22: Agency general manager Bob Smith receives the RFP and calls the consultant to express his appreciation for the opportunity and to arrange a briefing meeting (offered in the RFP) with Jan Jones and other ABC executives. He also reviews the RFP with two of the Agency's senior executives, and they develop questions to be asked during the briefing meeting.

One of the firm's executives begins to gather accounts of the takeover battle from local newspapers and business publications and from a national database resource.

March 30: Bob Smith and his two senior executives meet with Jan Jones and ABC marketing and financial officers. Bob also asks for a brief, get-acquainted meeting with the ABC president and CEO, who will be part of the Review Committee.

The Company

March 28-April 1: Five of the agencies on the list meet with Company executives. The public relations department of the Company's advertising agency does not request a briefing. Rather, the head of the Company's advertising agency calls ABC's vice president of marketing, indicates his interest in being considered for the public relations assignment, and says that his agency probably knows the Company well enough that they don't need to take anyone's time in a meeting.

Based on the briefing meetings, the ABC executives form opinions about the five agencies and begin to consciously rank the firms in terms of their ability to meet ABC needs. They are very impressed with the personalities and professionalism of two of the firms' executives and respond positively to the astute questions asked.

An ABC executive wonders out loud whether the final agency choice will match the ranking that is already shaping up.

The Agency

April 2-April 25: All six agencies will present in their offices on April 26 and 27. The Company Review Committee will visit each of the firms' offices to get a feel for agency ambiance as well as to observe staff activity levels. Dates and times for the six presentations are drawn at random. The Agency will present at 10:00 a.m., April 27. Their representatives will be allowed one hour for the presentation, with an additional half hour for Review Committee questions. Bob Smith is not particularly pleased with his time slot because agency industry lore says it's better to present to a prospect either first or last to ensure memorability. However, he would rather present in the morning than after lunch when the prospects' attention span may be affected by full stomachs, tired posteriors, or information overload.

The Agency begins to prepare its presentation. A staff member thoroughly researches the Company, its industry, markets, audiences, and market share, and the details of the takeover battle and resulting recapitalization and restructuring. A telephone survey is conducted of editors, industry leaders, financial analysts, and bankers to determine their awareness of the takeover defeat and their understanding and attitude toward the Company's status following the takeover attempt.

A small group of Agency executives and senior staff members brainstorm public relations approaches to the Company's needs, and Bob Smith begins to gather case histories on other successful Agency campaigns that will show the ability to solve similar problems. He meets briefly with the ABC president and gets a slightly different impression of the CEO's goals than was gained from the briefing. He calls Jan Jones for a clarification and asks some additional questions that arose in the brainstorming session.

Bob begins to draft the presentation script, leading with a situation analysis, the results of the Agency's preliminary research, and a brief description of the Agency's capabilities. Most of the presentation will be devoted to recommendations for a public relations program to meet the Company's goals. He times the script as closely as possible to 55 minutes.

The draft script is reviewed and revised and a rough run-through of the presentation is held for timing. Bob decides that since the Company is rather conservative and has never worked with a major public relations firm, a "dog and pony show" with elaborate computer-generated audio and visuals will not be appropriate. Instead, he opts for an attractive flip chart outlining points that the presentation team will make. A short videotape of television news placements for other clients will be shown during the Agency capabilities section. Agency presenters will use the flip chart as a guide rather than as a script to be read.

April 26: Tomorrow's the pitch! The script and flip chart are completed. The presentation team, including Bob Smith, the account supervisor, and the account executive who will be assigned to the business, rehearse several times to polish their delivery and make sure they will be able to stay within the allotted hour. Several senior staff members sit in on the final rehearsal to comment and pose questions that the Review Committee may ask. It's decided that Bob Smith will answer all questions directly but that other members of the team should feel free to add appropriate comments.

A typo on one PowerPoint slide is discovered and corrected. There is a discussion of appropriate dress for the presentation: What should the female account supervisor wear? Does it matter whether Bob Smith and the account executive wear the same color suit? The office manager is asked to have coffee, tea, and rolls available. The staff is alerted to clean up messy offices.

A secretary begins to print and assemble copies of the presentation script for the Review Committee. Special binders have been obtained with the Agency's and the Company's names and logotypes embossed in gold. Everyone agrees that they are as ready as they are going to get.

Mid-afternoon! The consultant calls and asks if the Agency's presentation can be moved up to 9:00 a.m. the next morning so that the Company CEO can have additional time for an important lunch meeting. Bob Smith agrees and informs the Agency team.

A few minutes later, a new piece of information comes in from a source who was not available earlier. It needs to be included in the presentation. One page of the flip chart must be changed. And since the new information goes in the up-front, situation-analysis section of the script, all the following pages will have to be renumbered and reprinted. Bless word processors and laser printers! (The secretary cancels an after-work date.) Inserting the new information will not run the presentation overtime, if one of the case histories is trimmed.

Another rehearsal is held in the evening to make sure that the new material is handled properly and that the timing is still within one hour. Everyone goes home late but feeling that the additional information makes the presentation stronger.

The Company

April 26: The Review Committee meets at 8:00 a.m. to be briefed on the criteria that the management consultant has suggested they apply in evaluating each agency. Information on each agency's address, executive staff, background, and experience is distributed. (A list of the Review Committee's names and titles was sent previously to each agency.) The consultant, who has an extensive agency management background, has developed a list of questions that committee members may want to ask the agencies.

The Review Committee arrives at the first agency, one of the international firms, 15 minutes late and is taken on a tour of the premises before the presentation. Some office doors are closed, prompting one committee member to wonder whether the offices are vacant or occupied by busy people who do not want to be distracted.

There is some shuffling in the conference room as committee members are asked to take seats that place them on one side of the table facing five agency staff members. The presentation is opened by the firm's president, who has come in from agency headquarters. He expresses his pleasure at being considered by ABC Inc., introduces the other staff members, and shows a 15 minute videotape of the firm's national capabilities. (One member of the committee is impressed by the fact that the national president has come in for the presentation; another wonders whether the president's presence indicates a lack of confidence in the local management.)

The president is followed by the local general manager, who describes the firm's emphasis on research and creativity and covers a couple of quick case histories of local office accomplishments. An account supervisor, assisted by two account executives, launches into a series of public relations recommendations that include positioning the Company CEO as a highly visible corporate spokesperson. (The CEO, who hates to speak publicly, winces inwardly.) The agency finishes 10 minutes over the allotted time. Copies of the presentation book are passed out, and the firm's president asks for questions.

The Review Committee is silent, waiting for the Company president to lead off. His question takes the general manager off guard and requires about 10 minutes to answer. There is more silence. A committee member glances at the list of questions provided by the consultant and picks one. Another committee member follows suit, and two other executives ask questions of their own.

One executive turns to the budget page in the back of the presentation book. He underlines the total recommended dollar figure and shows it to another executive, whose eyes widen in alarm. The general manager catches the gesture and quickly explains that the budget represents only a "Chinese menu" that will be finalized after priorities are set and financial parameters established.

Committee members thank the agency for its time and interest. The consultant asks that the Review Committee be permitted to use the conference room for 15 minutes while they complete the 15-category, 150-point, Qualification Audit that he has prepared.

The agency's general manager and visiting president wait in the lobby to bid the committee members good-bye and thank them for coming. As the elevator doors close, a passing account executive asks, "How'd it go?"

"Pretty good, I think," the general manager says.

"Yeah," says the president. "No one threw up."

The Review Committee visits two more firms after lunch, tours premises that are similar to the first agency's (except that there are no closed office doors), and listens intently to the presenters. Some committee members always ask the same questions.

As the Review Committee leaves the last presentation of the day, there is a consensus that one of the firms has taken an early lead. An executive jokes, "Why don't we just pick them and forget about sitting through tomorrow?"

The Agency

April 27: Bob Smith and his team arrive at 8:00 a.m. to make sure that everything is in order. The account executive discovers that, somehow, the pages in the presentation book are out of order. The three hurry to rearrange all the books.

The first member of the Review Committee arrives at 8:45 just as the receptionist is setting out the small sign that reads, "Welcome ABC Inc." By 9:05, all the committee members are present.

After a tour of the office (Bob is thankful that most of the staff members are at their desks despite the earlier schedule), Bob welcomes the guests, introduces the other two members of his team, notes that everything that will be said is covered in writing, and invites questions during the presentation.

The account supervisor discusses the Agency's analysis of the Company's situation and describes the results of the survey. The last-minute piece of information from an important financial analyst stirs a discussion among the committee members. Bob uses this discussion to lead into a description of other work the Agency has done that was aimed at the financial community. This stimulates several more questions. Bob decides to eliminate the rest of the capabilities section and the videotaped TV news clips because they are running long. He introduces the account executive.

Even though this is only the second time the account executive has participated in a new business pitch (only he knows how nervous he really is), he handles his presentation smoothly, segueing from Agency recommendations that respond to the Committee's obvious interest in the financial community to other aspects of the recommended program. Also recognizing that the presentation may go overtime, he manages to shave some minutes without losing his place in the flip chart outline.

Because of the discussion and questions, Bob's conclusion, including "We're ready to go to work tomorrow," goes slightly over the allotted 60 minutes. The Company president leaves, but the rest of the committee members ask questions for another 17 minutes and spend 15 minutes completing the Qualification Audit.

Bob agrees with the supervisor and account executive that, despite all the problems, the presentation went well. He congratulates the account executive on his professional delivery and for being able to shorten his part of the presentation so smoothly.

The Company

April 27: The last two presentations are uneventful but uneven. One of the firms offers a number of creative ideas that are not related to strategies linked to the Company's objectives. The public relations director of the Company's advertising agency, who has drawn the last time slot, recommends activities that appear to be based primarily on the Company's marketing program. The Company's marketing vice president comments later that he had been surprised when the firm passed up the opportunity to meet with Company executives.

The Agency

April 28: Bob Smith messengers a letter to all the members of the Review Committee that briefly reviews the Agency's presentation and emphasizes its ability to help reach and influence the financial community. He works on another new business pitch that will take place within the next week.

Staff members ask how the presentation went and when the prospect will make a decision. Bob answers, "Pretty well, I think. They asked a lot of questions," and "I don't know. Soon, I hope." (He remembers, "Good news comes by the telephone; bad news comes by the mail.")

The Company

May 10: The Review Committee meets to select an agency. (The CEO has been out of town all the previous week.) In the meantime, three of the six committee members, including the CEO, have read all the presentation books supplied by the competing firms.

The consultant has tabulated all the Qualification Audits completed by the committee and arrived at an average score for each firm. The committee discusses the six presentations while the president does not comment. Discussion centers primarily on three questions: how interested the agency appeared to be in the Company's business; how smart they were about the Company and its needs and how well their recommendations relate to those needs; and whether the agency representatives' personalities appear to match the Company's culture. For the most part, the committee agrees that all the agencies appear to be professional and personable. However, the committee is particularly impressed with the expertise and enthusiasm displayed by one agency's general manager and account executive and the creative and strategic strengths of their recommendations.

Concern about the high cost of one agency's recommendations is mentioned. An executive notes that he upgraded his opinion of one firm after reading the firm's presentation book. One firm is criticized for offering a plethora of creative ideas not supported by strategic direction.

The competing firms are ranked one through six by the Review Committee, and this consensus is compared to the Qualification Audit average scores. They match. The president finally expresses an opinion. He concurs with the committee consensus and the Qualification Audit scores and indicates his preference. The Review Committee makes a decision.

May 11: Jan Jones makes a telephone call to the winning agency, congratulates the general manager, and asks him not to say anything until the other firms have been notified the next day by mail. She sends nicely worded consolation letters to the other firms.

The Agency

May 11: Bob Smith gets a telephone call from Jan Jones, expresses his pleasure, thanks his new client for the business, and arranges a start-up meeting. He swears the supervisor and account executive to secrecy until the next day and asks the office manager to lay on an office celebration for late the following afternoon.

May 12: Bob Smith gets a call in the morning from one of the other competing agency principals who congratulates him on the win. The principal has not received his letter but he has heard "on the street" that the Agency has won. Late in the afternoon, Agency staff members are called to a meeting where Bob announces that they have won a substantial new client. He congratulates the supervisor and the account executive and thanks everyone for their help. Champagne is poured. (The Agency did not win the second pitch that Bob was working on, but he figures that one out of two is better than none.)

The Other Agencies

May 12: The consolation letters arrive. In several cases, word of the defeat is passed to staff members. Two managers call Jan Jones to thank her for considering them and to ask what the Review Committee had based its decision on. "It helps us in the future if we know what the deciding factors were in cases where we didn't get the business," one manager says. The Company director of public relations is vague; she says, "The Agency seemed like it would be better able to meet our needs." (Her favorite did not win.)

The five losing agencies swallow their disappointment. One manager tells his staff members that they did a great job and he's proud of them. He says he wouldn't do anything different if he had it all to do over again.

All six agencies continue their eternal quest for new business.

ANOTHER ENDING

The Agency

May 11: Bob Smith knows the ABC Review Committee met yesterday to select an agency. He tries not to think about that while helping to solve a client problem and preparing for another new business pitch scheduled for the following Monday morning. He waits for the "good news" telephone call.

May 12: Before the mail arrives, an account executive tells Bob that she has heard from friends the night before that another agency has won the ABC business. A letter arrives from Jan Jones. Bob calls to congratulate the head of the winning firm.

Bob then calls Jan Jones to thank her for the opportunity to be considered and ask what the Review Committee had based its decision on. The ABC director of public relations is warm and friendly. She says it was a very close race and a tough decision but the committee felt that the winning firm had done a slightly better job of addressing the Company's needs. She invites Bob to stay in touch for possible future opportunities. (The Agency was her favorite.)

Bob asks the supervisor and account executive into his office and informs them of the loss. He congratulates them on their effort and says he wouldn't have done anything differently. In a memo, he informs the staff of the decision, comments on the great job done by the supervisor and account executive, thanks the secretary for her overtime assistance, and says he thinks the Agency has a good chance in the competition coming up the next Monday.

The five losing agencies swallow their disappointment. All six firms continue their eternal quest for new business.

FOOTNOTE

The two firms who made the best impressions during the first briefing meetings finished one and two in the competition. Well-balanced culture compatibility, expertise, enthusiasm, creativity, and strategic thinking, plus the Review Committee's "gut feeling," won the day.

It could have happened—in fact, it probably did happen—that way.

PROFILE 3: JOE BOYD

President, MCS Inc.
Bedminister, New Jersey

The toughest thing for a person starting out as a principal in a PR firm is
to realize that his or her days as a creative guru need to be over as soon as
possible. That should not be the sole
job of the principal. It is the responsibility of the agency principal to lead
the business. That means learning how
to be a good business person; how to
be a team leader; know not to go in
debt but when to sign a lease. You have to ask yourself what you
really want to do. If the answer is (do) great public relations,
(you probably shouldn't) open an agency. If you want to create a
company that does great public relations, that's when you might
be ready to become an agency principal.

Based on that credo, Joe Boyd, president of MCS Inc., grew his
specialty health care PR firm in 20 years from $75,000 fee income the
first year to more than $4 million currently, while focusing on the
business of his clients as well as on the practice of public relations.

MCS serves its clients by assigning a member of the firm's executive committee as the most senior AE on every client's business. That
way the client always has access to someone with at least 10 years'
experience, a "perk" generally offered by small firms but not always
by larger midsized firms such as MCS. Boyd says,

The best and most profitable lesson I learned was when I started
looking for the best way in which a problem could be solved—
instead of only looking for the best public relations tactic. Our
recommendations will center on the steps that can solve the
problem and that will likely involve a number of disciplines including public relations.

Chapter 4

Developing a Marketing Plan

If you rely for sustenance and growth only on current clients, refer-rals, and over-the-transom inquiries, sooner or later you will find that revenue has plateaued or begun to slide. Set a goal; spend at least 40 to 50 percent of your time actively seeking additional business.

Realistically, if your firm is small, client needs may restrict the amount of time that you can devote to new business development. However, it is vital that you make time available—as much as possi-ble, as regularly as possible—to plumb for growth opportunities.

Because of the cyclical nature of the agency business, the most im-portant—as well as the most difficult—time to pursue new business is when you are the busiest with current clients. Unfortunately, you may lift your head at the end of an intense client campaign or project only to realize that no more work will be coming from that client for some time or discover that other business has dried up while you were heavily involved with several clients.

As difficult as it may appear at the time, devoting disciplined, con-sistent, and substantial time to business development will pay huge dividends over both the short and long run. In fact, it could make the difference between your firm's success or failure.

To apply your limited time most productively, combine rifle shot and scatter gun approaches to new business solicitation. There is no need to go after or accept every piece of business that falls your way. Be selective. Decide the kind of business you want and take your best shot at it.

To provide direction and priorities, invest the time to develop a de-finitive, realistic marketing plan that outlines an ongoing promotional and solicitation program. Include the following steps in your firm's marketing plan.

doi:10.1300/5561_04

ASSESS AGENCY STRENGTHS
AND WEAKNESSES

Evaluate your firm objectively. Consider utilizing an outside consultant to add objectivity.

What are your strengths? Technology, media relations, crisis response management, investor relations, special events, experienced senior management back-up, business-to-business experience, consumer product marketing background, distinctive culture, low staff turnover?

Look at every element and aspect of your organization that could be of value to a client or that could help convince a prospect that you can do a better job than competitive firms in serving his or her needs. Write down the strengths of your firm.

Similarly, also in writing and brutally candidly, list the weaknesses, the holes, in your organization. Describe your limitations in detail. Again, you might want to ask a consultant to help you analyze your firm's fragility:

No senior back-up? Limited experience beyond one or two areas? High staff turnover? Shabby or cramped quarters? Inexperienced staff? Little or no experience serving major large-budget clients?

Don't ignore the warts. List every aspect of your agency that might possibly persuade a prospect that he would be better off awarding his business to another firm. Note the effect these weaknesses could have on your ability to acquire new clients. Do the weaknesses cancel any of your firm's strengths? Can the weaknesses be cured? How? How long will it take, and how much will it cost? Is it worth doing?

Develop a realistic plan, budget, and timetable to eliminate or ameliorate the weaknesses. And do it!

Business development efforts needn't be put off until all your firm's weakness are eliminated. Simply take the warts into consideration while preparing the remainder of your plan and in implementing your promotional campaign. (Walk around the stone wall until you're strong enough to knock it down.)

EVALUATE SERVICE POTENTIAL

What kind of services could you provide with your current staff that you are not providing now: special events, publications, promotion, employee communications? Make sure that you are fully aware of your staff's past experience. For example, would a staff member's experience preparing annual reports provide an opportunity to offer limited investor relations services to current or new clients? What kind of additional services could you provide by making some staff changes? Think about such possibilities when you hear about or interview good people.

EXAMINE MARKET POTENTIAL

Analyze your market or industry intensely and comprehensively to determine the hot service areas. It's one thing to offer additional services such as consumer marketing or investor relations. It's another to be sure that the need is there. Otherwise, you'll waste a lot of time and money.

Consider using a blind telephone survey of PR executives to garner information on the kinds of services that are valued by companies in your market, what services companies are currently buying from competing firms, and what they wish was available. In addition, use the survey to learn how the corporate PR community regards leading PR firms in your area, including your own.

How big is your market? In terms of miles and dollars? How far can you afford to travel to serve what size client? When expanding a Chicago firm's reach some years ago, I decided that every company with at least $50 million in sales and within one hour's flying time or three hours driving time was a potential client and belonged on my mailing list.

Today, the list would probably cut off at $100 million and two hours' flying time. (But not more driving time. It's too tiring and time wasteful.)

All of this depends, of course, on the size of the client's budget and how often he expects to see you in his office . . . and how badly you want the business.

We served a major Los Angeles consumer product client successfully from our Chicago office with no logistical problems and with satisfactory profitability. West Coast technology firms commonly and easily serve Midwest and East Coast clients. With the advent of fax machines, modems, and interactive computer software, distance is probably more a problem in a client's imagination than in reality.

The likelihood of a client needing to see you frequently on very short notice (minutes, rather than hours) should determine how far away you can afford to be.

The extent of your market potential lies primarily with your own personal choice, your agency specialties, and your prospects' willingness to be served long distance. Obviously, if you're located in Minneapolis, it will be more convenient and efficient to reach prospects in that city than in New Orleans. However, New Orleans is not out of reach. Be aware, though, that when you reach out beyond arm's grasp, you will then be competing with all the local firms *on their turf.*

Here are some other questions to ask when analyzing your market. Check *O'Dwyer's Directory of PR Firms* or *PR Week's* contact directory to find the companies in your market area that use counseling firms. Do the companies that make your mouth water currently use other PR firms? Which? How? Is your firm more or less competent?

CONSIDER THE PROFIT POTENTIAL

Many firms set minimum annual income or minimum project income that they will accept. ($60,000 minimum annual income per client is a good bogie. The larger your firm, the larger your minimum should be.) Income potential should be a prime factor when determining the viability of a prospect. However, an even more important factor when prioritizing prospects is the prospect's profit potential.

Some generalities apply:

1. Small business-to-business clients—in fact, most business-to-business clients—can be just as profitable percentagewise if not dollarwise as large consumer product clients—and often are easier to handle because of less complex demands.
2. However, small, unsophisticated companies, particularly start-up companies backed by venture capital, can demand almost as much of your time as a large company. They also may be reluctant to pay higher hourly rates and may nitpick invoices.
3. A client who requires a heavy investment of your most senior peoples' time will lean toward low or no profit unless you can convince the client to accept an hourly rate that returns full profit. (Because they would probably not be competitive if com-

puted realistically, many seniors' rates are not profitable. Junior rates, on the other hand, tend to be very profitable.)

Establish profit potential guidelines in your marketing plan. And consider the above generalities and your need for a consistent profit level when adding or subtracting companies from your mailing list or solicitation schedule.

ANALYZE COMPETITION

One of the most important aspects of your new business effort will be your understanding of the reality and reputation of other PR firms in your market.

Use that knowledge in competitive quests for new clients. This in no way suggests that you attack or criticize other firms. That tactic will sink your ship faster than almost anything else you can do wrong.

On the other hand, understanding the strengths and weaknesses of firms you may be competing against can help steer your presentation in a direction that will shine the best light on your firm.

Get to know your competition personally. Meet as many of your potential competitors as you can, given the number of firms and geographical spread of your market.

What are the principals like? Are they low key or high pressure? Are they casual or formal? How good are they? What are their professional backgrounds, strengths, and reputations? What kind of new business presentation do they normally give: informal, across-the-table, or heavy on glitz and audiovisual?

Participate in local chapters of the PRSA Counselors Academy or independent groups of agency principals. For example, in each of three cities where I assumed responsibility for faltering or nonexistent PR firms, one of my first moves was to organize an invitational group of local agency principals so that I could get to know my competition. Chow & Gab, a monthly luncheon group of about 40 PR firm principals that I founded in Chicago in 1983 with two other agency principals, was alive until recently. Similar groups exist elsewhere.

There are some obvious things to consider when analyzing your competition: Size. National, international, or network ties. Leadership. Senior strength. Service specialties or strengths. Size and type of clients.

There also are other more subtle pieces of information that will be helpful. What is the firm's reputation, not only among corporate public relations executives, but among senior corporate officers as well? (For example, in one Midwest city, a national firm's general manager had good contacts with corporate CEOs but was not generally well liked by corporate PR executives because he tended to go over their heads. Competing firms used that fact to make subtle points with prospects.)

Is the firm's leadership active in community service, in the social and cultural communities? (If a firm's leader or senior management is active in community cultural organizations—the opera, ballet, symphony orchestra—will that give his or her firm an advantage with a prospect who either also is active in the same organization or who would like to gain a prestigious community board seat?)

Is the competing firm growing, shrinking, or static? Is it going after smaller clients than formerly? What is the word on the street about the firm as a place to work? Does it have a number of long-term employees or heavy staff turnover? Why the latter? (You can gain valuable information about other firms during interviews with their employees or former employees. Is the firm highly structured or more collegial? Is client contact restricted to senior people or broadly encouraged? Why does the practitioner want to leave?)

Are there cultural differences between your firm and others that are worth emphasizing? In *Butch Cassidy and the Sundance Kid,* Robert Redford and Paul Newman are pursued by an unknown but seemingly indefatigable posse. As the duo tops a rise with the dust of the posse close behind, one of the pair asks plaintively, "Who are those guys?"

My upstart Chicago firm, seeking to position itself in a market jammed with well-known local and national outfits, used that line as our business development theme, symbolizing our "unknown but coming fast" culture. In four years, by emphasizing this kind of employee spirit combined with hustle, strategy-based creativity, and a targeted new business campaign, we became the tenth largest firm in the city.

DEVELOP A UNIQUE STRATEGIC POSITION

Now that you have assessed your firm's strengths and weaknesses, evaluated the potential for additional services, examined the size and peculiarities of your market, looked at income and profit potential, and analyzed competition, it is time for the most important part of your marketing plan.

Develop and communicate a unique strategic position that describes your firm succinctly and persuasively and takes into account what you know about your competition. Decide how you wish to be seen by clients, prospects, and the PR community. Set down the words that you will face up to and live by and that—if you do the job right—will drive your firm into prominence and profit.

What is your firm all about? What makes it different? What will prospects see that they will like particularly well about your firm? What kind of working philosophy do you live by? Here is one firm's strategic position (that I'm most familiar with because I wrote it and lived it):

> "Good Enough" is Not Good Enough. In today's business marathon, no corporation, institution, association or other organization can afford to settle for "adequate" when it comes to public relations service. *Exceptional has to be the least acceptable standard . . . without exception.* The public relations service you receive determines how you are viewed and judged by investors, customers, employees, suppliers, regulatory authorities . . . the worlds in which you work.
>
> Here's how we define exceptional: powerful resources; strategic planning strength; fresh, creative ideas; work ethic style; honest value; full range of services; worldwide services; and outstanding people.

The cover of the firm's brochure carried one word: "Exceptional."

That was a general strategic position. There are others, more market or specialty specific. With some elaboration, "The best health care firm in the area with a long list of well-known, long-tenure clients" could be one.

In Philadelphia, a market molded in the who-you-know, establishment "Main Line" image, my firm fought to be different and to be noticed. Our strategic position was largely internal: to create a charged atmosphere and motivate employees to excel. Rock the boat. Up the establishment. Be unique. Sometimes raucous.

Emphasize competence, creativity, and experience. (No practitioner had less than ten years' experience. That's not practical today, of course.) New employees conquered the toughest writing test in the city and their pride showed. We took our work very seriously but laughed a lot at ourselves.

In a loud and bustling ambiance with few private offices, we functioned with noisy enthusiasm. We hustled. Shouted messages—some crude, some funny, most team oriented—across the partition walls. Assigned women to technical accounts. Unthinkable then. Esprit soared. Staff turnover was unknown. So was client turnover because we produced results.

And in five years, from a stumbling four-man crew, we became the second largest in the city.

How will your firm be seen? Incorporate your vision in your market plan. And then tell the world about your firm. Promote your uniqueness: JSH&A, a consumer-oriented boutique in a Chicago suburb, regularly advertises its position as a "LIF™style public relations" firm and conducts consumer research to support its claim that "We look at how people really live." Kathy Schaeffer and Associates, another Chicago agency, conducts a continuing, highly creative direct mail program supporting its position as a "Smart, Passionate and Ingenious" firm.

DNA BRANDING FOR PR FIRMS

Ever think about creating a "DNA Brand" for your agency? Read on.

Writing in *PR Week*, columnist and editor Paul Holmes described "DNA Branding" for corporations. According to Paul,

> DNA Branding is the process of building a brand from the inside out; of starting with a clearly defined vision to create a distinct corporate culture; and then fashioning a brand that's an extension of that culture. Practitioners of DNA Branding understand that their brands are defined not just by what they say, or even by what they do, but by who they are. Their brand personality is rooted in the DNA of the organization.

According to Paul, "DNA Branding is hard work. It can't be achieved with a snappy slogan or a catchy jingle. DNA Branding begins with employees and is all about building relationships."

Consider this: Does or could your firm have its own DNA Brand? If you looked closely, what would you see? What would you like to see?

Paul points out that DNA Branding starts with a clearly defined vision and then uses that vision to create a distinct corporate culture. What is your vision for your agency? Does it include three components: your firm's purpose, business, and values? Is your vision clearly, distinctly, powerfully, and repeatedly stated? Or could it describe most any other agency if you simply substituted another name? Do your staff and clients recognize, believe, and, more importantly, respect it? Or have you even taken the trouble to think about an agency vision?

Do your workplace culture and client service reflect your vision? Does that vision call for a workplace environment that is, among other things, nonthreatening; that recognizes and rewards staff prowess; that provides individual growth opportunities? Does your vision engender feelings among clients of trust, respect for your firm's capabilities, ethics, and integrity, and a strong sense of personal chemistry?

Schenkein, a well-known, midsized Denver firm, has a powerful DNA Brand, possibly without even knowing it. The firm's mission statement is "To create a values-driven workplace dedicated to the growth of our people, where we partner with our clients to provide communication strategies that contribute to their growth and success."

The firm's "values" are posted prominently in the agency's lobby, on its Web site, and other places: "Enjoyment; Integrity; Quality; Creativity; Client Service; and Community Contribution." The firm says, "Our value-based culture provides an engaging work environment for employees as well as a commitment to client service."

A close personal look at the 30-plus-year-old agency over a number of years supports that claim: A comprehensive employee "coaching" program requires a heavy investment of executive time, puts staff training and motivation ahead of agency profits, and leads to low staff turnover; a preference for a relatively small number of really good size clients rather than taking anything and everything that comes over the transom; industry and peer recognition for creativity; client comments such as, "We like each other, understand each other, and are on the same page"; and a seamless seven-years-in-the-process management transition several years ago from the founder, Bob Schenkein, to new co-owners Leanna Clark and Christin Crampton Day. (Those are my personal observations, not the agency's published mantra.)

There are, of course, other agencies, maybe many of them, with a DNA Brand. I wonder how many have stopped to consider the power of their brand. Have you? As Paul Holmes said, "DNA Branding begins with employees and is all about building relationships." How recently have you applied that measuring stick to your firm? How well did you stack up?

HOW DOES YOUR FIRM STACK UP?

If you buy the idea that your agency's reputation largely determines whether you live or die, then it immediately follows that before you spend a lot of time developing a marketing plan, you ought to know what your firm's reputation is, whether people tend to wrinkle up their nose when they hear about you or whether you are universally or at least largely loved or only abided. (Does anyone out there care?) Chances are you may not be too clear on that subject because, as Harold Burson, founding chairman of Burson-Marsteller, said, "Many [agency] executives delude themselves about their reputations because they're too close to the subject." The first logical step would appear to be, as Burson recommended, to assess your firm's reputation; find out how people "feel" about you.

Start by choosing a group of people to survey: your local PRSA chapter; a local business organization or industry association; a group that you hope knows "something" about your firm. This doesn't need to be a large group; you're probably not looking for what the research gurus call "statistically significant" data. You just want to know where the bad smell is coming from or, hopefully, why so many people seem to be smiling at you.

Of course, if you can afford to invest several thousand dollars, you can always find a bona fide research firm to dig up statistically significant information about your firm. However, you'll probably learn enough to be helpful in a simple mail survey with anonymous responses. (You want answers to be plentiful and candid, so don't ask respondents to identify themselves. Emphasize that you're not going to solicit their business as a result of their feedback.)

I recommend that you include a stamped, self-addressed envelope. Don't ask for responses to be faxed or e-mailed back to you; respondents can be identified that way.

Exhibit 4.1 is a draft of a questionnaire that you could follow or amend and send to that group of people who ought to know or feel something about your firm. (At the same time, remember the ancient claim that a PR firm's reputation/image usually lags about two years behind reality.)

Measurement

So what will responses to this questionnaire tell you? (There may be other "yes/no" questions you'd like to ask.)

At a minimum, it will tell you what or whether people who are important to your firm know anything at all about you (or think they know you but may be wrong). It will point out areas that you need to

---

EXHIBIT 4.1. PR Firm Reputation Questionnaire

Dear Colleague:

We need your help. To help us plan for the future, we'd like to know what you think of [agency] in several different areas. In effect, we'd like to learn what our reputation is with other public relations professionals and in the [city] business community.

You can help us fulfill that need by candidly and anonymously answering the following questions. It will only take about ten minutes of your time. Please return the questionnaire in the enclosed stamped self-addressed envelope.

Because your response will be anonymous, there's no way we can solicit your business as a result of what you tell us. Thanks very much.

[Agency principal]

Agency Reputation Scan

Circle One: I am very aware / moderately aware / not aware of [agency name]. (If you're not aware of us at all, go no further. However, please return your questionnaire with "not aware" circled. That will tell us a lot.)

Circle One: I am very familiar / moderately familiar / not familiar with [agency name]. (You could be aware of our firm but not very familiar with it. That knowledge also will be helpful.)

Please check "Yes," No," or "No Opinion."

I think of [agency name] as

	YES	NO	NO OPINION
Innovative	—	—	—
Original	—	—	—
Creative	—	—	—
Credible	—	—	—
Honest	—	—	—
A good place to work	—	—	—
Having a quality staff	—	—	—
Having a stable staff	—	—	—
Having good management	—	—	—
Providing quality service	—	—	—
Being high cost	—	—	—
Being average cost	—	—	—
Being low cost	—	—	—
Providing good value for cost	—	—	—
Providing poor value for cost	—	—	—
Operating on a sound financial basis	—	—	—
Socially responsible	—	—	—
Active in professional organizations	—	—	—
Involved in civic organizations	—	—	—
Providing professional leadership	—	—	—
Providing business leadership	—	—	—
Having a good reputation	—	—	—

In essence I think of [agency] as: _____

---

work on, those that get a significant number of "no" or "no opinion" responses. It will tell you how well your street reputation matches the reality of your firm. It also will tell you whether you personally think your firm is better than the public/clients do.

Admittedly, all of this will be pretty subjective. But then, you're in a pretty subjective business. If you use the responses properly, by promoting the positives and fixing the negatives, the survey responses will be extremely valuable. (Or, as songwriter Johnny Mercer once said, "You got to accent the positive, eliminate the negative, and don't mess with Mr. In-Between.")

PROFILE 4: JOHN CHARLESTON AND LYLE ORWIG

Chairman and CEO, Charleston/Orwig
Hartland, Wisconsin

In 1992, after more than 10 years' experience as principals of successful Wisconsin
advertising and PR agencies in addition to
having publishing backgrounds, John Charleston and Lyle Orwig embarked on their entrepreneurial enterprise in more humble
surroundings—working from the basement
of Lyle's Wales, Wisconsin, home. After
generating almost $500,000 in fee income
the agency's first full year, revenue grew to

more than $7 million by 2004. (Note: John Charleston was an ad-
mired Milwaukee colleague.)

Service to the firm's first three clients set the pattern for today's operation—full-service business-to-business marketing communications
coupled with issues management. The duo started their firm as a PR
agency with the intention of building full-service capabilities as cash
flow permitted. Today, with a specialty in global food and agriculture
products and services, the firm serves such major corporations as
Pfizer Animal Health, Arm & Hammer, and Smithfield Foods. In addition, a separate division of the firm is national communications
consultant to Fortune 500 companies on public issues. The combination of full-service marketing communications and issues management under one roof is strong differentiation for the firm, according
to chairman Charleston.

Charleston admits one of the pair's early mistakes was being too
lenient with staff—a "mistaken sense that we were more parents than
employers." But Charleston also wonders, "Why we didn't start it
earlier. Why did we wait this long to have this much fun?"

Advice to new agency owners or those considering starting a firm:

Believe you can do it. Price your services where they belong;
never position yourself as a cheap alternative. Avoid trying to
make yourself look bigger by alliances. Prospects want it under
one roof. If you ain't got it yet, go after clients that fit you, but
keep building it out of cash flow as you go.

Chapter 5

Communicating to Prospects

Because your firm has existed for several years does not mean that it is well-known within the business community in general or among prospective clients specifically. If your firm is relatively young, you can assume that very few have heard of it. Most senior executives and many public relations directors tend to have only a vague knowledge of the counseling firm community. In fact, some companies know so little about the extent and variety of available firms that they turn to the Yellow Pages when seeking a counseling firm. (Buy at least a bold-face listing for your firm.)

The fortunate firms, those who have at least some degree of recognition and credibility, are the large national firms, long-tenure mid-sized firms, and smaller firms that invest the time and money to create effective self-marketing programs. To maintain or increase your firm's visibility and improve your potential for growth, it therefore behooves you to use every available avenue and to apply every affordable tool to communicate your firm's capabilities, culture, and achievements to a targeted group of prospects.

Marketing your firm should be easy. Right? All you need to do is apply the same kind of communication techniques in behalf of your firm that you recommend to your clients. No sweat, right? Wrong!

Unfortunately, the "Shoemaker's Children" syndrome frequently gets in the way of a firm's self-marketing efforts. There's always something that keeps you from communicating with prospects as often or as well as you should. Client demands, lack of cash, lack of objectivity (face it, it's tough to be objective and say nice things about yourself), or maybe you just don't know how to do it. Forget these excuses. Here is all you need to know to design and carry out an effective self-marketing program.

doi:10.1300/5561_05

BE VISIBLE

If you don't do anything else, make time to join groups where you can meet and talk to prospects. Your current clients may even be impressed when you attend a meeting of the local business association (where your client's CEO is president or is speaking).

If you are going after primarily local clients, Kiwanis, the Lions Club, and the Chamber of Commerce are good sources. Join national trade associations covering industries that you're interested in and attend their conferences and trade shows. Join the Public Relations Society of America (as well as its Counselors Academy), the International Association of Business Communicators, the local publicity club, and maybe the American Marketing Association.

Get involved in these groups; run for office, chair committees, lead programs, if that is your thing. (It never was mine. I knew it was a good idea, but I'm not a committee person, and I don't function well in most groups.)

A better idea, one that I was always more comfortable with, is pro bono (meaning no charge) work for worthy charitable, civic, and cultural organizations. In addition to being a good public service thing to do, the people you meet in these organizations are the same ones you'd probably meet at the Kiwanis or PRSA.

WRITE AND SPEAK

Use your writing, speaking, and public relations skills to find and take advantage of opportunities to appear before target prospect groups or write articles for publications reaching prospect audiences.

For instance, if you'd like to have a bank as a client, offer to speak before a bankers' group on a subject you're familiar with and that the bankers would find interesting and useful (how to increase the return on their PR budget). In the same light, offer to write an article for a bankers' trade publication (same subject). National, regional, and local business, marketing, and sales publications offer good article placement opportunities. Write an opinion piece for *PR Week, PR Quarterly,* or another industry publication. (And don't forget to reprint and merchandise your articles to prospects and clients.)

Most important, keep your articles and speeches 99 percent noncommercial. Concentrate on information or ideas that demonstrate how well you know the topic and the particular industry for which you're writing or speaking. Prospects will get the idea that they ought to talk to you without you beating them over the head about how great your firm is.

This is all so basic that I hesitate to even mention it. However, the fact is, not all that many PR firm principals take advantage of such opportunities unless they're approached by a group looking for a speaker or a client pressures them to help fulfill his or her program chairperson obligations. And few write as often as they should.

The truth also is that many PR firm principals are not the greatest speakers in the world and need their knees tied together when addressing a large group. Practice!

When you write an article or speak to a group, be sure to reprint the article or speech and merchandise it to your clients and prospects. Use "Third Party Credibility" in your behalf as well as your clients'.

In the same vein, publicize such agency events as new client wins, creative awards, significant anniversaries or milestones, personnel hires, acquisition or merger with other PR firms, or industry survey results. Send news releases to local business journals, newspaper business editors, and/or the advertising/PR columnist, if there is one, and to well-read national public relations publications such as *PR Week, The Holmes Report, PR News,* and *Jack O'Dwyer's Newsletter.* Get to know your local newspaper or business journal's advertising/PR columnist. Your growth story, awards, comments on business practices, or unique approach to client service may warrant an interview and column coverage.

TREAT EMPLOYEES AND APPLICANTS WELL

You may not think of human relations as a communications channel. However, your relations with current and prospective employees play an important role in the way your firm is viewed by prospects and others in the business community.

To a great extent, because of the multiple contacts that your employees have, the business community will tend to see your firm the same way that they do. If employees categorize your firm as a "sweat shop," whether this is fact or fiction, you may be sure that many others in the PR and business communities will be exposed to this pejorative comment. If your firm has excessive staff turnover, others will wonder why and may invent "reasons" that have no relation to the truth. In the same light, if your firm has a sudden run of client departures or budget cuts, requiring staff layoffs, the rumor mill will have you in bankruptcy almost before the ink dries on the first termination notice.

For these reasons—beyond the positive impact it will have on staff morale, employee productivity, and, in the end, your profitability—treat employees as if you were the originator of the Golden Rule. Remember that in the public relations community in particular, and in the business world in general, people—especially your competitors—are always ready to hear, believe, and pass on negative information about your firm. Don't give them that opportunity.

Prospective employees are another thing. Treat every person whom you interview or who asks for an interview as if he or she were about to become a prospect with a $500,000 budget. Even if you have no openings, take time to interview candidates. (This also will give you opportunities to learn more about your competitors and local corporations.) Treat every candidate with the same respect and courtesy that you would a prospective client. There are two reasons for this.

First, one-year-out-of-college, can't-spell-Mississippi job candidates have a way of suddenly gaining substantial experience and significant corporate credentials, not to mention large budgets. People have long memories about the way they were treated by a prospective employer. It makes good business sense to ensure that job candidates have only good memories of your firm.

Second, the way you treat candidates will affect your ability to attract the best possible staff members. Job candidates sense the way your firm is run by the way they are treated in a interview. It is hard enough to find good people. Why turn them off by treating them badly during the interview or refusing to even take their call requesting an "information" interview?

I would practically have laid my neck on a railroad track for Andy Anderson, then-president of Ketchum Public Relations in Pittsburgh, Pennsylvania, who said gently, "We'd like to persuade you to come to work for us." He wanted to *persuade* me to come to work for him? Who do I have to kill?

In later years, I often had job candidates come back for a second try or become a prospect after they were treated fairly and politely when either they didn't qualify or there was no opening. In one instance, a young woman said, "You told me I needed another year's experience. I have it. I'd like to talk to you again." She become one of our most competent account supervisors.

USE BUSINESS CONTACTS

There are several other groups of people who can help communicate a positive message about your firm to prospective clients. Some of these also can be good leads to companies that are actually looking for a PR firm. It is important that they all have a good opinion of your firm.

- *Trade publication space reps:* Although you may not have much direct contact with individuals who sell print advertising space, they are a great source of information about companies that may be disenchanted with their current PR firm or actively looking for a new one. It may pay to take a space rep to lunch once in a while.
- *Editors:* Companies often ask newspaper or trade publication editors for opinions about a specific PR firm or for recommendations of firms that the editor respects.
- *Vendors:* Printing salesmen, video news release (VNR) producers, photographers, graphic artists, and other vendors to the public relations industry also tend to have a good feel for companies that are looking for a PR firm and are often asked for their impression of specific firms.
- *Clients:* Many PR firm principals will tell you that they get most of their new business from client referrals. It's probably wishful thinking. However, clients who like what you do for them also talk to other prospective clients. Hopefully, they will not hesitate to recommend your services. There's nothing wrong with telling clients that you will appreciate business referrals.
- *Other agencies:* Agencies often learn of companies that are too small for them to handle, that conflict with other clients, or that, for some reason, they cannot accept or are not interested in. It is common, in such situations, for the original firm to either refer

the prospect to other specific firms or to tell other firms about the prospect. Stay friends with your competitors.

• *Mine social and civic activity:* Personal friends and contacts made in pro bono civic and cultural work can provide good leads to new business. These people should have a positive impression of your firm. Urge your employees to keep their ears open during social situations and their negative comments to themselves. A social hour before a business meeting, a cocktail party, your tablemates at an industry dinner, a fund-raiser, can all be good sources of new business leads. Keep your ears open and your mouth closed when riding in an elevator. More than one new business tip has come from listening to elevator conversation.

COMMUNICATE REGULARLY

Listen to the advice that you give clients. Communicate consistently to prospects. Ideally, they should hear from you at least every six to eight weeks. If you publish a newsletter, do it at least quarterly. Anything less and you might as well spend the money on a lottery ticket. (On second thought, you'll also probably have better luck at the lottery if you buy a ticket regularly.)

One of the goals of your communication program should be to establish memorability for your firm with prospects. And sell them on the benefits of public relations and on your ability to meet their PR needs. These are both good objectives. However, the real reason for communicating regularly is to hit prospects at the exact time that they are ready to or are thinking about hiring a new PR firm. In that light, marketing your firm has more than a little bit of scatter gun approach to it.

You should have a small list of prime targets whom you contact regularly and personally. However, most of your prospects will be little more than names on a mailing list. Qualified names, yes. But still little more than names about whom you can know little, especially their interest or need to retain or change PR firms. So you load a shotgun with your most powerful ammunition and you fire it regularly in the direction of people whom you have defined as prospects. If your message is strong and you shoot often enough and your luck is good, you will hit some targets. (Lesson for the day: this is why a hunter does not usually shoot a rifle at a flock of geese. And why he likes to take more than one shot at a flock.)

Make it easy for prospects to communicate with you. Be sure that your business address, e-mail address, Web site address, and telephone and fax numbers are on every printed piece in a type size large enough to be read easily. (Oh yeah, and be sure to put your name on communications. I've actually seen agency Web site addresses in which there's no personal contact listed.) Enclose a postage-paid return card with every communication. Ideally, your return card should give prospects some choices: Send more information; call me immediately about a specific subject; call me on a specific later date; send me a list of clients; keep me on your mailing list.

There's a reason for the latter. Of course, you're not going to remove prospects from your list just because they do not signal that they want to remain. However, when a prospect indicates that he wants to be kept on your mailing list, you can bet that, in most cases, you have hit a nerve and that somewhere, perhaps hidden in the back of his mind, the prospect has or will have a need for a PR firm.

Your immediate written response should be, "I'll be delighted to keep you on my mailing list. Even though you don't have a need right now, I'd like to come by and get acquainted and tell you a little bit about our firm. I'll call you for an appointment." (Despite the fact that the prospect has returned a card to you, he may not remember your firm's name. Therefore, it's better to reinforce the name to him in writing rather than try to reach him immediately by phone.)

Once in his or her office, you have a great opportunity to probe the prospect's needs. And to turn an unknown name into a client.

FOCUS YOUR MARKETING PROGRAM

Much of your marketing program may necessarily take a shotgun approach, aimed at reaching a broad, multifaceted audience. Therefore, your marketing materials should describe your firm's ability to serve varied markets and multiple client needs. On the other hand, you will want to be able to customize a package of promotional materials to appeal to a specific prospect.

Many firms satisfy this need by developing an attractive "kangaroo" folder that can be customized by inserting a general agency brochure plus material such as letters, reprints, photographs, and case histories tied to a prospect's specific interests.

Add to the need to customize material to match prospects' interests the need to fit within their culture as well. Examples: The public relations manager of a large Midwest manufacturer of marine engines chortled over the three-piece-suit-clad national agency representatives from Chicago who ventured to the manufacturer's Lake Michigan test facility. And who then managed to look uncomfortable, scared, silly—and somewhat seasick—with tie, coat tails, and hair whipping in the wind as they clutched the top of a boat's windshield on a high-speed run across the lake. A telephone would have explained the manufacturer's lack of a dress code. The agency didn't get the business.

In a similar incident, national agency representatives descended on an outdoor writers' national conference clad in suits and lugging stacks of an elaborate 24 page agency brochure for distribution to the group of relatively small outdoor product manufacturers attending the meeting. And were promptly labeled "Arrogant!" by the very people they were trying to impress.

Keep Dual Prospect Lists

There are two kinds of prospects: (1) those who are referred to you or come in "over the transom" because of your firm's reputation and (2) those you target and solicit. The first type is usually the easiest to convert to client status; the second is the most difficult and usually the most expensive to win, yet perhaps the most satisfying.

Your new business prospect list—a vital tool in your quest for new clients—should contain as many names as you can qualify within your target markets. Building and maintaining a new business prospect list is a boring, time-consuming pain in the neck, make no mistakes about that. Your list will be only as valuable as it is current. Strangely enough, the anticipated labor and time required to build and maintain an accurate list is probably one of the biggest reasons why some PR firms do not have an effective marketing program. The principal never gets around to seeing that an up-to-date list is assembled and maintained.

You have two choices in building a list; you can buy one from a list broker or assemble your own. Buying is faster, but you have no guarantee as to accuracy of the names on the list. Doing it yourself or assigning it to someone else (maybe an intern) is slower but probably more accurate and can be customized to reach exactly the audience that you are interested in.

I prefer the do-it-yourself approach, although I'm sure the modern, computerized approach is easier. In Chicago, I built and maintained two different lists based on the same corporations located in six Midwest states: one contained CEOs; the other listed marketing, sales, and public relations executives. Manufacturer, association, and Chamber of Commerce directories, *O'Dwyer's Directory of Corporate Executives,* and the "Red Book" of corporate advertising clients will give you information on which to base your lists. You may need to make telephone calls to update information.

Side note: Every time you use your list, ask the post office to not only forward the mail but also provide forwarding addresses so that you can update your list. It'll cost you $.70 for every changed address you get back, but it's worth it. About 5 to 10 percent of my list of more than 1,000 agency principals changes every time I use it.

Your list should actually have two parts: the largest portion will be those with whom you maintain regular indirect contact, largely through direct mail. This is the B list. The A list may contain no more than 10 or 20 names. These are your high-priority targets. The people on this list have either previously indicated a possible need for a PR firm or fit your definition of a prime prospect: a company or institution whose name you passionately want to see on your client list. This list should comprise only as many people as you can comfortably contact regularly and frequently, preferably at least monthly.

Contact these individuals in person, by phone, or by personal letter, initially to qualify them as potential clients. If, after several months, you sense that there is no possibility of converting a company to a client in the near future, move it to your B list and switch another B name to your A list.

Try to visit or otherwise personally reach out to each A individual at least once a month. Learn as much as possible about the company; invest in secondary or database research on the company and its industry. In addition to such accepted approaches as brief "get acquainted" meetings, lunches, breakfast, and after-work socializing, here are some other techniques that will help win a prospect's heart, and, most important, build memorability for your firm:

- If a prospect company hires a new out-of-town PR executive, welcome him or her to town; invite the new executive to accompany you to professional group meetings; invite the executive and spouse to dinner with you and your spouse or significant other.
- Congratulate individuals on promotions.
- Comment on industry events and/or trends; suggest ways to take advantage of opportunities or help solve industry problems.
- Forward articles about the prospect's industry that he may not have seen; comment on the articles.
- Respond to favorable publicity on the company or offer suggestions to help ameliorate negative publicity.
- Be interested in the prospect's company. Show it! Consistently!

Example: After 18 months of steady pursuit with only lukewarm response, Harley-Davidson Manufacturing Company, in Milwaukee, the last U.S. motorcycle manufacturer, became a major client on 48 hours' notice for a national public affairs campaign that eventually won the agency and client a PRSA Silver Anvil.

Use Direct Marketing

One of the best and yet most difficult ways to reach and interest prospective clients is though direct mail. "Best" because it offers an effective and relatively economical method of communicating with a large number of people using a shotgun approach. "Most difficult" because your mailing piece must compete for time and attention with the mass of other material that lands on your prospect's desk every day. Unless yours is extremely well done and aimed precisely at the prospect's interests, it will be ignored or consigned to the infamous "round file."

This volume is not intended to explore all the intricacies of direct mail. Your local library or bookstore undoubtedly has at least one good book discussing all the most potent tricks and tactics of direct mail. Direct mail vendors also can be very helpful.

Remember that, in order to be noticed and read, your direct mail must appeal to a reader's interests and needs. The piece must give the recipient some reason to read it other than the fact that it shows up on his or her desk.

Here are some direct mail tools that may prove useful:

- A letter accompanying a brochure or other mailing piece is reputed to increase the return over a no-letter mailing.
- Case histories that show your problem/solution approach to work you have done for clients can be very effective, particularly if they can be applied to a prospect's specific needs.
- Small brochures that fit in a #10 envelope are more practical and effective than a single large brochure because they require less reading time.
- Reprints of articles you've written, speeches you've given, or other favorable publicity about your firm should be reprinted (with the publication's permission if necessary) and distributed broadly to both current clients and prospects.
- Newsletters can be very effective if done properly. The most effective newsletters are published regularly and emphasize information that interests and benefits prospects. Their sole purpose should *not* be to pat the agency on the back. Unfortunately, many agency newsletters seem to be published primarily to aggrandize the agency's principal.

Employ Cold-Call Marketing

"Cold calling" makes the sweat pop out on many agency principals' foreheads. At its best, prospecting for new business opens up the potential for rejection. (No one likes to be rejected, whether by a lover or a business prospect.) Cold calling doubles, maybe triples, that potential. Few principals like it. Most are not very good at it. But many—this writer included—force themselves to do it.

Industry surveys would have you believe that most PR firms get their new business primarily through "referrals"; i.e., it falls over the transom or is referred by kindly clients. However, according to New York consultant Lee Levitt, principals of a number of the largest PR firms do not rely on referrals, but do cold telephoning regularly and personally.

PR firm principals like to say that they get most of their business from referrals, says Levitt, because it sounds good, implying that a firm that gets clients primarily through referrals must not have to seek them out. These principals may be concerned that people will think that a firm that uses cold marketing techniques is hard up for business or that it is (perish the thought!) "pushy."

Levitt claims that cold calling generally brings in better clients more economically than any other sales technique because it allows you to go after the clients you want to serve and can serve profitably now. Conversations start on your timetable at your convenience. You talk to prospects most likely to appreciate what you have to offer. And you establish the terms of the discussion at the outset.

Levitt supports my belief that many PR firm principals are not comfortable with the idea of "imposing" on an executive's time to sell him something he may not need or want (25 years of agency experience and lots of new business success never quite cured me of this phobia). But, says Levitt, many corporate executives have a sales mentality and react well to cold sales calls.

Levitt lists these keys to successful cold-call marketing:

- A strategy that targets an industry or field
- A reasonably good knowledge of that field/industry
- A carefully researched contact list
- A "gimmick" to grab the prospect's attention
- Relevant material to send interested prospects
- Knowledge of telephone-solicitation techniques
- A good telephone manner, feeling for people, and patience
- Commitment

Chances are, you will have to do some cold calling—you may even like it—and face that potential for rejection. Remember what I said earlier in this book: The successful agency principal must possess in massive quantities the capacity to bounce back; to pick himself up off the floor of defeat or despair one more time. And then do it again.

(A favorite line of Depression-era radio comic Herb Penner fits the cold-call trauma perfectly. Playing a sad-sack door-to-door salesman, Penner would intone, "You wouldn't want to buy a duck, would you, Mister?")

Sending a letter to a prospect several days before a call can take some of the onus off the task. At least it gave me a wedge into the conversation, assuming that my letter had been persuasive enough.

Use the Group Approach

PR firms often recommend that their clients sponsor a seminar as an effective, noncommercial means of reaching potential and current customers. You can use the same technique with good results in your own behalf.

Pick discussion subjects of broad interest and on which you or one of your senior staff members has in-depth knowledge and experience. A seminar could cover such topics as "New Regulations Affecting Initial Public Offerings"; "How to Introduce and Position a Commodity Product"; or "How to Satisfy Your CEOs' Demand for Measurable Return on PR Investment."

Invite a small group of editors and PR and/or marketing executives (clients as well as prospects) to attend a breakfast or late-afternoon discussion of the selected topic. Serve coffee and rolls or light refreshments.

Either give a short presentation yourself—not more than thirty minutes—or invite an outside expert to discuss the seminar's topic. For instance, if your budget is tight, you could invite a newspaper business editor, a client's vice president of marketing, or a local investment banker to meet with seminar participants. If budget is available, a nationally known expert will attract a larger attendance.

The seminar should be noncommercial, with no obvious plugs for your firm. Give each participant a package of material on your firm and let it go at that. Later, you will want to follow up with a phone call to each participant.

Have a Basic Capabilities Presentation Ready

Sooner or later, a prospect will call at 3:00 p.m. and ask to meet with you at 9:00 a.m. the next day. Or the prospect that you've been chasing for months will finally agree to see you or visit your firm. This could be your big opportunity. Don't get caught short in such situations.

To respond to prospect requests or for get-acquainted meetings that you schedule, you should have a brief—15 to 20 minutes—in-the-can capabilities presentation ready to deliver to prospects on short notice. The presentation should be casual but well scripted. It should describe your firm's strengths, unique strategic position, and results that you have obtained for clients. Although much of the presentation will be standard, you should be able to easily and quickly customize segments for specific prospects by changing elements such as case history examples.

Depending on your facilities and/or those of the prospect, you may want to incorporate PowerPoint slides, videotape, and/or computerized material in your presentation.

Use Web Site Marketing

There are a number of books available on Web site design and marketing plus an equal number of consultants eager to design your Web site and/or tell you how to use it effectively. So I need not dwell extensively on that subject.

However, a couple things I've learned from talking to agency principals:

- Many principals aren't all that satisfied with their firm's Web site and the results it produces.
- On the other hand, principals have come to recognize that more and more prospects look at their firm's Web site, perhaps even before they talk to the agency. As one principal told me, "Capabilities brochures are going the way of the dodo bird, replaced by agency Web sites." Does that say that your Web site better be good enough to attract prospects (and peripherally employees) like flies at a Sunday school picnic?

I look at a lot of agency Web sites, maybe more than you do. Allowing that I'm an amateur at this, here are some of the things I've noticed about agency Web sites that may turn off potential visitors:

- They're sometimes hard or impossible to find via Google or one of the other search engines.
- When you do find one you're looking for, it may take too long to download or force you to wait endlessly while some complicated animation unwinds.
- When you do find the agency's home page, it's often hard to figure out what makes the agency different from its competitors. Like capabilities brochures in the bygone years, Web sites are beginning to sound a lot alike.
- Finding the name of a human contact can often be frustrating. If you're a prospect, I don't think you're going to look favorably at a suggestion that you submit your name in the blind as an e-mail

message and hope you'll get a warm human response. Web sites need to act like there are real people running them.

Be a Better Speaker

I can see her now; she was about 30, attractive, a skilled writer, a good account supervisor, but scared to death. Sally (not her real name) was about to be part of her first stand-up new business presentation. We were probably cruel; we kidded her about needing Velcro strips on her knees to stop them from shaking and distracting the prospect. She laughed, but her nervousness showed.

Even many experienced actors say they get "stage fright" when they're about to face an audience. On the other hand, the same actors will tell you that if your engine's not racing at least a little when you're about to face an audience, your performance will come off as quite a bit less than "Tony" quality.

Many, if not most, agency principals have enough "ham" in them to handle a live presentation without embarrassing themselves. A speech major in college, because I couldn't hack the second year of a foreign language required of a journalism major, I waded through subjects like voice and diction, public speaking, and (ugh!) "acting." That training has served me well. I'm still nervous but not panicky to speak before any group, large or small.

But what about you? Do you come across polished in prospect or client presentations? Chances are you're better than the other people from your staff whom you might involve in a presentation. Client meetings aren't bad; at least the audience is known and most times friendly. Except, of course, when you're pitching to keep the account and things haven't been going well.

However, new business presentations are something else. You're trying to be better than your competition and win the business. The people who work for you may be scared witless, especially if it's their first new business pitch. Read on; help is on the way.

Here, excerpted from *Guidelines for Successful Presentations* by Charlie Hawkins, are a series of tips that should help make you a better presenter and, for sure, will ease the strain on the people backing you up in presentations. Charlie, who is the Sedona Round Table facilitator, is an experienced presentation trainer and author of *First*

Aid for Meetings. He teaches presentation skills to corporate executives and facilitates corporate and nonprofit meetings.

Learning effective presentation skills is similar to learning how to improve your golf game if you've played for years but never had a lesson. At first your game falls apart, then as you internalize the new skills, it slowly comes back, stronger than ever.

Your success [in a presentation] is often directly proportional to the time you spend analyzing your audience, preparing content and practicing delivery skills. On the other hand, your presentation is probably NOT the most important event in the day of every audience member. The average attention span for adults is measured in seconds. Audiences expect boring presentations because most of them are. You must connect immediately and give audience members reasons for listening or you will lose them.

The way you stand provides a foundation for your presentation. It sends the right signals by showing the audience that you are "grounded," confident and in control. Stand squared away to the audience. You should be able to see every audience member and vice versa. Put your feet shoulder width apart, toes straight ahead. Balance your weight evenly on both feet with weight distributed slightly more on the balls of your feet. Be careful not to let your shoulders droop. Start with your arms relaxed at your side; this will make them accessible for gestures which add interest and impact. Lean into the audience slightly.

Slow your eye movement down to connect one-on-one with audience members. Focus on one person at a time; make contact before you begin speaking.

If your body language is not consistent with your content, the audience may not believe you. What you say is important, but how it's said makes the difference. Your facial expression tells the audience how you really feel about your subject. Gestures make an essential contribution to the spoken message. Your body language can communicate confidence and commitment . . . or the opposite. "Nervous" energy will distract your audience.

How you express yourself is at least as important as the actual words you use. Vocal factors that you can control include the following: *Pitch*—Generally your pitch should be varied, going up and down to create interest; *Pace*—Your audience needs time to take in what you're saying; *Inflection*—Being flat at the end of a sentence is regarded as authoritative; Going up at the end of sentences sounds as if you are seeking approval or in the extreme can be annoying; Pitching down at the end of sentences is generally preferred. Listen to network news anchors; *Resonance*—Lower is better; *Volume*—Err on the high side. You're probably not as loud as you think.

Many presentations really come to life when the questions begin. (Make sure you allow time for questions during that critical new business pitch.) There are several options for how and when to handle questions: (1) Take questions as you go, anytime during the presentation. This keeps a more informal tone and involves the audience throughout. It also may be distracting to you, especially if you might answer most of the questions during the presentation; (2) Hold questions until the end. This is fine if your presentation is 15 minutes or less. Going much longer risks losing your audience.

Times such as after lunch, Monday morning, and Friday afternoon are particularly challenging. Shorten your presentation and get the audience involved as soon as possible.

About Sally: She soon found her way to the corporate world, where presentations were not as daunting and there were no new business pitches.

Communicating regularly to prospects is half the job of winning new business. The other half consists of an array of sometimes mystical truths, techniques, and tactics, all aimed at influencing prospects to pick your firm above all others.

PROFILE 5: HERBERT CORBIN

Managing Partner, KCSA Public Relations
New York, New York

Four years with a national PR firm led
Corbin to a strong belief that typical PR
firms were structured wrong. According to
Corbin,

> We're in a service business; all we
> have to sell is our time. If you tell a
> client that senior people are going to
> be accountable for his work, you better
> have those people around. The per-
> son can't be here one day and gone the next.

When Corbin founded the firm in 1969, he followed this philosophy, developing a horizontal management structure in which senior
partners—now nine of them—are responsible for the management
and implementation of each account, much like a law firm operates.
The partners relate directly to each client and manage the day-to-day
work of supervisors and other practitioners.

Corbin also believes that every client requires at least 40 hours per
month to produce results. Fees are set to cover at least this minimum
number of hours. To avoid any surprises, the firm projects the required number of hours at the beginning of each month and how they
will be utilized. Once the client signs off, the work is performed, and
at the end of the month the computer prints out the number of hours
utilized.

To prevent confusion, and to make it feasible for the most senior
executives to be "hands on," the firm uses a single average or blended
billing rate.

"With this system, we can assign senior people to each client at affordable costs and sustain good relationships," Corbin says.

The system works. KCSA has grown from $100,000 income to
more than $7 million and is rated one of the best-managed midsized
firms in the country.

Chapter 6

New Business Rules

During 25 years hustling business for three PR agencies, I learned two very important rules:

1. Never work in the dark.
2. Never put your prospect to sleep.

If you follow these two rules, you will consistently win more than your share of new business—because many other firms do not adhere to the same rules.

CROFT RULE NUMBER ONE:
NEVER WORK IN THE DARK

In the dim, dark days before computers, this writer was a public relations vice president for a national advertising and public relations firm (an agency, incidentally, that fully appreciated the worth and profit potential of public relations and the power of a combined advertising and PR campaign). On one memorable occasion, I was scheduled to make a brief pitch in behalf of PR as part of a major presentation to a large advertising prospect who had indicated no interest in public relations.

I don't recall the prospect's name. However, I vividly recall fretting nervously outside the conference room door as my appointed time approached. The agency president was leading the presentation, and I wanted to make a good impression. Finally, the door opened and a hand waved me in.

Inside, the room was totally black, with only a dim glow lighting the podium. I laid my script on the podium, tried to see faces in the

doi:10.1300/5561_06

71

dark, and began my pitch. And was suddenly stricken with dismay! *What the heck am I doing here?* I thought. *I don't know anything about these people; they don't know anything about me or what I'm talking about and could care less. I am wasting their time and mine with this bland plea in behalf of public relations. This is dumb! I am not going to do this anymore. I will never work in the dark again.*

And I never did. From then on, I refused to present to a totally dark room. More important, I always made sure that I learned enough about the prospect to make my comments pertinent to his business. And when I began running my own PR agency show, "Never Work in the Dark" became a new business development credo.

Moral: Always take the time to learn the prospect's business, markets, and industry—so that you can look smarter and more interested in the prospect than your competition. And so that you can do a really top notch job of extolling the rewards of a public relations investment. This is especially necessary when you are talking to someone who thinks primarily in terms of advertising, either paid or "free."

CROFT RULE NUMBER TWO:
NEVER PUT YOUR PROSPECT TO SLEEP

As the head of a growing Philadelphia public relations operation, I traveled to the Midwest to pitch the owner of an automotive products company. By this time, I had about 10 years' experience in the agency business and was pretty impressed with myself, particularly my ability to convert prospects to clients.

I was ushered into the office of the company president, a gray-haired gentleman wearing a number of summers. (In those days, in the callowness of youth, people always looked older to me than they probably were.) That we were in the president's *office* was the first surprise. I had assumed that we would meet in a conference room. But here we were in his office, where he sat behind a huge desk festooned with layers of paper.

I looked around the office for the easel on which I could stand the carefully prepared flip charts that I carried in a "pizza case." Second assumption gone wrong. No easel. (In those days, I also didn't know enough to make sure that the accessories I was going to need in a presentation were available at the prospect's location.)

So, improvising, I balanced the flip charts across the arms of a large straight chair in front of the president's desk and launched into my pitch. (Of course, that meant I had to hold the flip charts with one hand while I turned pages with the other. Awkward!) The president continued to casually thumb through the rat's nest on his desk. With hardly an eye skewed in my direction. Not too encouraging.

Even less encouraging was the moment when I realized that the reason he had stopped rearranging papers on his desk was not because he had become fascinated with my golden offering, but because he had fallen asleep. Head nodding on his chest. There was nothing to do but fold my tent and creep silently out of the room. (A lot of years later, and now a consultant to PR firms, the president of an East Coast agency also fall sleep during our meeting. But at least this one wasn't bored; she suffered from narcolepsy.)

Moral: Always aim your proposal and presentation directly at the prospect's interests and needs rather than spending excessive time discussing your firm's capabilities and conquests. Talk in terms of benefits to the prospect rather than extolling the virtues of your firm or the services you are trying to sell. Do not put your prospect to sleep by dwelling on things that he or she is not interested in. (Try not to present after lunch or in the middle of the afternoon. That's nap time.)

DESIGNING A NEW BUSINESS CAMPAIGN

I also learned that to be successful in soliciting new business, you should do the following.

Commit to a Consistent and Substantial Investment of Time in the Quest for New Business

Time is generally in short supply in most agency principal's lives. However, time is a vital element in every successful new business campaign. You should devote a good chunk of time regularly—40 to 50 percent—to planning the campaign; compiling and maintaining the prospect list; writing or supervising letters, literature, and other mailers; making cold calls; making warm calls; preparing proposals and presentations.

If you remember only one thing about new business development, remember that the most important time to press for new business is when you are the busiest with current client work. Bringing in a new client usually takes much longer than you expect or would like. To avoid the cash flow gap that can occur when work dries up from one or more clients, you need to press continually for additional business, either from a new client or from new areas within current clients.

Conduct a Focused, Organized, and Budgeted Self-Marketing Campaign

One of the biggest mistakes made by PR firms is failure to conduct an effective and ongoing self-marketing and new business campaign. The "Shoemakers' Children" syndrome at work again.

When a firm comes up short in the cash flow department, the principal may decide that the answer is to attract some new clients. (By this time, however, it may already be too late to solve the cash flow problem comfortably.)

Naturally, to attract new clients, you need an agency brochure, literature, case histories, or article reprints. However, just producing the brochure can take months, not to mention the time necessary to develop the mailing list that the piece will be sent to. Then the firm gets busy with client work again. Cash is flowing.

Everybody forgets about the self-marketing campaign. No one calls anyone on the firm's prospect list; no one pays any attention to the postage-paid cards that possible prospects have sent in (assuming that you remembered to include such a card with each mailing); no one spends any time planning the next promotional mailing.

Another mistake is the failure to adopt and adhere to a self-marketing budget. Between 1 and 2 percent of projected annual income is a realistic figure for new business expenses. However, if your firm is young and in a growth mode, you may want to budget 3 or 4 percent of income. Plan your self-marketing budget—from both time and out-of-pocket standpoints—the same way you would a client's budget.

Do not leave your self-marketing program to chance, something you do when you have nothing better to do. If you do not conduct a consistent self-marketing campaign, you may very well end up with nothing else to do. And then it will be much too late.

Act Smarter Than Your Competitors

The truth is that, on the surface, public relations firms seem pretty much alike to many corporate PR executives. Agency offices tend to look alike: the same cluttered desks, the same pile of press kits in the corner of the conference room, the same stains on the coffee room counter, the same people huddled over glowing computer monitors.

PR firms even tend to say the same things to prospective clients. They promise day-to-day service by the principal; they say they are big enough to provide a wide range of services but small enough to care about each client; they say that they are creative and that "we're ready to go to work for you tomorrow."

What they need to say is, "Here is what we have learned about you. Here are the problems you told us about and some others that we see on your horizon. Here is how we recommend that you solve your problems and take advantage of your opportunities."

Want to look smarter than your competition? Want prospects to pay more attention to you than to your competitors? Couch everything that you say and do in terms of your prospects' needs. It's that simple.

SELF-MARKETING CAMPAIGN ELEMENTS

Your firm's self-marketing and new business campaign should contain equal measures of the following:

Research: Remember, *never work in the dark*. That advice—in effect, get to know your prospects—applies whether you are attempting to break into a lucrative new industry or are pitching an individual company.

Planning: Organize your thinking. Plan your overall campaign as well as each individual presentation and proposal. Leave nothing to chance, especially remembering to take extra extension cords when you're pitching in the prospect's conference room.

Strategy: Strategy-based creative ideas win the day every time. Unsupported "Big Ideas" get little applause. PR firms that are strong in strategy win; firms that are only function-strong lose . . . sooner or later.

Creativity: Strategy-based creative ideas win the day every time. Unsupported "Big Ideas" get little applause. PR firms that are strong in creative strategy win; firms that are not strong in creative strategy lose . . . sooner or later.

Positioning: How do prospects and clients see your firm? How do you want to be seen? As a generalist? As a niche market player? How are you different, really different, from other firms? Define your firm's strategic position in 25 words.

Intensity: New business solicitation is not something to be taken lightly or approached haphazardly. It requires emotion, purpose, and seriousness. Impress the prospect with your integrity, character, and intelligence. Demonstrate that you are interested in the long haul, not in the greatest profit in the shortest possible time.

Commitment: Keep at it. Fight back against disappointment. Learn to live with rejection. Dedicate yourself to success. Do not accept less than your best effort. Encourage others to emulate your commitment.

Focus: Decide what you want and go after it. Brush aside easy pickings that could pose profit problems. Waste little time trying to teach public relations to the unwashed. Seek clients that offer fun, profitability, and professional satisfaction.

Remember Your Web Site: Remember, chances are good that that bright new prospect will have critiqued your credentials as displayed on your Web site, before even deciding to talk to you. Or deciding not to talk to you. Are you satisfied with your firm's Web site? Should you take another look at it, and, while you're at it, look at a half dozen competitors' Web sites? Maybe you should make some changes in yours or, at least, bring it up date.

PROFILE 6: ROGER FISCHER

President, FischerHealth
Los Angeles, California

FischerHealth is a glowing example of an agency taking advantage of the times. The firm was founded in 1983 as Pollare/ Fischer Communications (Partner Frank Pollare left the agency business in 1992), changed to Fischer & Partners in 1992, and reformed as FischerHealth in 1994. According to Fischer,

> In the 1980s, we built a midsized independent firm that was clearly a generalist. The 1980s rewarded midsized generalist firms. However, the 1990s demanded increased specialization, particularly from midsized firms. To succeed against these new demands, in 1994, we decided to specialize in the health care industry, which we'd been serving since 1983, including medical devices, diagnostics, health services, and health information technology. We now offer a broader array of communication services, including integrated marketing, to narrower segments of the marketplace.

Annual agency income has grown from $150,000 to about $7 million while serving such major clients as Guidant, McKesson, Humana, and Johnson & Johnson. Average revenue per client is $450,000. Fischer notes,

> Our early success was probably attributable more to the boom years than a brilliant strategic plan. However, we did learn that you ignore the "business of the business" at your peril. Succeeding in business is a matter of doing something better than anyone else.

Complying with that edict and maintaining a single-minded focus on the health care industry have evolved the firm from a boutique to a strong niche firm and since late 2003 to a wholly owned subsidiary of Porter Novelli, part of the Omnicom group.

Chapter 7

New Business Secrets

The most important secret about winning new business is hardly a secret at all. Unless you prefer to remain small, so that you can be heavily involved in client service, prospecting for and winning new business must be one of your most important, continuing tasks.

However, even small firms must be able to gain new business. It's no secret that the agency business tends to be highly cyclical and unpredictable. Clients depart or reduce budgets with little warning and for reasons that cannot be controlled or even explained at times.

On the other hand, there are some secrets to gaining new business that are not so well known or practiced. For example: how to win business against the big PR firms if yours is a small one; how to cold call prospects successfully; which prospects to pursue and which to walk away from; the kind of questions you should ask prospects; and the kind of mistakes that prospects make during an agency search (so that you can watch for them and turn them to your advantage).

TEN WAYS TO BUILD BUSINESS

Former nationally known "consultant to consultants" Howard Shenson, in his "101 Proven Strategies for Building a Successful Practice," recommended the following:

1. Add sales letter impact with a hand-written P.S.;
2. Don't hesitate to charge for problem diagnosis and needs analysis;
3. Spend half a day, at least twice a year, walking around the reference room of a major university library. You will learn about

doi:10.1300/5561_07

interesting marketing opportunities and new services that you could offer;

4. Devote half a day each month and call people who could be prospects for your services or good sources for referrals whom you haven't talked to in the last six months;

5. If you have developed a proposal for new business that fails, identify others who would benefit from such services or ideas and recycle your proposal;

6. In direct mail campaigns, include a (postage-paid) response card to increase response. (On your postage-paid response card, include a "Keep me on your mailing list," check-off option. Prospects who indicate such a desire usually have a nascent PR need. This gives you an opportunity to get a head start on competition by arranging an introductory meeting to ". . . discuss your possible future needs and our capabilities.")

7. Multiple page sales letters usually outpull single page letters. Interested prospects will read a great deal and the extra copy increases response.

8. Increase your credibility by recommending that your services not be used for certain needs which the client or prospect may have, but which can be met internally.

9. When meeting with prospects, be sure to answer the five questions that they need to have answered, but frequently fail to ask: How will I profit from your advice/services? Why will I profit from working with you? How can you demonstrate that I will profit? To what extent will I profit from your advice/ services? When will these profits/benefits be realized?

10. Don't beg for the business. No one wants to do business with a firm they think is needy or hungry. When setting a meeting time with a client or prospect, don't say, "Any time next week would be fine." You give the impression that you have nothing to do. Instead, provide several time/date choices.

HOW DAVID CAN BEAT GOLIATH

Small firms can win big business against the Goliaths by following the giants' example, suggests Ward White, former colleague, former president of Golin Harris International-East, and retired vice president, corporate communications, of Northwestern Mutual Insurance,

Milwaukee, Wisconsin (and a top-notch new business proposal writer to boot).

In a speech to the Public Relations Society of America's Counselors Academy Spring Conference, White recommended the following:

1. Recognize that the giants use sound strategies in their new business efforts. Big firms have good, smart people who are good strategists. They respond to what the customer wants.
2. Recognize that it's a changing world. No practitioner can keep doing the same old tricks. There are new strategies . . . old strategies with new tricks . . . and they are used because they work.
3. The expert is the guy from out of town. Goliath may bring bodies from each of the prospect's markets or people who have worked in his business. You can combat this by making sure you get very smart about the prospect's company, industry and markets.
4. Nobody wants to hire a generalist. Clients want to hire a specialist, someone who can speak their secret language, someone who knows their markets even better than they do and who can teach them new things.
5. You can't fake it anymore. Today's market demands legitimate specialization and genuine expertise, either geographic or industry specific. If you don't have the in-depth experience, you have to go out and get it . . . any way you can . . . through alliances, subcontracts, contingency hires.
6. Become a specialist . . . in many areas. In truth, you are a specialist in each of the areas you've worked. Go modular in your brochure and presentations. A multipurpose, one-size-fits-all capabilities brochure . . . because it lists all your specialties . . . is not credible. Your general brochure can be very general: what you believe in, your technology, your commitment to service, your systems. However, also produce companion pieces, with the same look, on each of your specialties. Talk only about relevant clients. Resist the temptation to showcase every talent. Customize videos and PowerPoint presentations.
7. Research sells. It's extremely powerful to fascinate the prospect with something new. There are lots of ways to gather information: survey trade editors, the metro press, consultants, ana-

lysts, customers, and especially use Internet search engines like Google. Read annual reports, security analyst research reports, sales literature. Clients want a firm that not only understands their business but also knows their customers.

8. Strategy sells; PR tactics don't. Prospects are not interested in how you're going to get the job done; they're interested that you understand the job that needs to be done.

9. Don't be tempted to over-promise. (Even though others may.) Emphasize that your style is to under-promise and over-deliver.

10. Don't be worried about a lack of international offices. Almost nobody ever uses them. Arrange to put dots on a map through a network or loose affiliation and concentrate on your home market or specialty market niche.

11. Emphasize details such as proofreading. If you make a mistake, don't call attention to it.

12. Emphasize thoroughness and reliability.

13. Keep in touch with lost prospects. When the honeymoon is over, in three to six months, you may be in a good position to pick up the once-lost business.

14. Don't shoot yourself in the foot. Don't take unnecessary chances. Forget that really-off-the-wall creative brainstorm. Stick with sound fundamentals, especially if you're the favorite.

15. Business people can't read. Make things clear and simple. Use bullet-dot phrases. Elliptical sentences. Pare it down to the bone. Eliminate words. Explain all you want orally . . . just don't put it in the written pitch.

16. No Chinese menus. Be very specific on proposed program budget costs.

17. K.I.S.S. (Keep It Simple, Stupid.) Talk a lot about your research. But use discipline on objectives and strategies; only three or four of each. Keep recommendations simple. Leave out the details.

Summary: Think like a prospect; get inside the prospect's head. Put the prospect's interests first. Live his or her problems. Bring to bear whatever resources are needed, inside or outside your firm. Present a solution and you have a client.

If you take White's advice, you are sure to beat Goliath every time. Well, almost every time.

SEVEN SECRETS TO SELL SERVICE

Jim Lukaszewski, chairman, The Lukaszewski Group, White Plains, New York, recommends the following:

1. Structure and update. Ask "Has anything changed since we last spoke?" Often, there are critical changes between the time you receive the proposal request and first talk to the prospect and the presentation itself. Being first to present puts you at a disadvantage because each succeeding firm has more information on which to base their presentation as the prospect more clearly perceives his or her real needs.
2. Recommend ideas, concepts, goals and tactics. Deal as quickly as possible with the ways in which your firm would handle the assignment. Agencies often waste prospects' time with non-pertinent information, such as administrative procedures and current clients, because either they are afraid of having their ideas stolen or they don't have any substantive ideas and are hopeful that one or two will surface from the prospect during the presentation.
3. Organize your proposal with your prospect's goals in mind. Address first your prospect's most critical need. Agencies often spend too much time talking about rudimentary tactics such as news releases, media contact, etc. If your ideas about how the prospect should handle his most important issue are appropriate, the technical details will take care of themselves.
4. Leverage off the prospect's existing experience and resources. Recognize how much energy and talent the prospect can provide by clarifying the most valuable augmenting services that you will provide. Prospects are usually more interested in the ideas, concepts and criticism that they cannot generate internally than having you take over their entire communications effort.
5. Reveal key parts of your research early in the presentation. Share your strategy. Don't hold a good idea until the end of the presentation or be afraid to share it. Presentations are won on the

basis of chemistry between individuals and the ideas shared. Ask for the prospect's reaction to your approach.

6. Sell your unique capability to do this job. Too often, agencies spend all their time talking about their ability to do many things. The prospect cares only about how you can bring credible help to the problem at hand.

7. Focus on closing the sale. Go for the "Magic Two Minutes," the time in every selling situation when the time is right to close the sale. Three tips to move to the Magic Two Minutes: (1) Be enthusiastic about doing the work; (2) Talk in terms of positive, specific, meaningful project outcomes; and (3) Ask for the order by asking the prospect to hire you.

QUESTIONS TO ASK PROSPECTS

Here (from Howard Shenson's *Shenson on Consulting—Success Strategies from the Consultant's Consultant*) are some questions you may want to ask during your first meeting with a prospect. They will help get to the heart of his or her needs. (Remember, most new business is won . . . or lost . . . during your first meeting with the prospect.)

1. What is the major problem your organization faces?
2. What problems do you face that are shared by the rest of the industry or similar organizations?
3. What problems confront your organization that are unique to this geographic area?
4. Has inadequate planning contributed to the problems facing your organization? How?
5. Have government regulations affected the profitability of your organization? How?
6. How does your organization rank in the industry in terms of salary, benefits, employee perks?
7. If your organization is family owned, to what extent does this ownership affect promotions and employee morale?
8. What kind of staff turnover do you have? Is this trend up or down from previous years?
9. Have you made any changes in personnel policy based on your assessments of employee satisfaction and productivity?

10. How long have your key management and technical people been with your organization?
11. How far in advance do you make specific decisions about expansion?
12. What has been your most disappointing area of growth over the past two years?
13. In what ways do you ensure that expenditures on training will produce the desired results?
14. How do communications work within your organization?
15. How do you identify communication breakdowns in the organization?
16. Who reports to whom in your organization?
17. What is the biggest time bomb in your organization? What steps have been taken, or do you plan to take, to deal with this problem?
18. What impact do you see company problems having on management and staff?
19. What new products or services do you see as vital within the next ten years for your organization to maintain or increase its growth?

(Unlike the tactics used by trial attorneys,) "Don't ask questions for which you don't already have answers," Shenson said. "Don't waste the prospect's time. If you can't think of something new, creative, and interesting to ask, you probably shouldn't be talking to the prospect in the first place."

The prospect also will likely ask you a series of questions. In addition, Shenson suggested, prospects may have other questions on their minds . . . that they may not ask. However, Shenson recommended that you win points by answering such questions as these before or whether they're asked:

1. Do I need this service?
2. Do I really want this service?
3. Can I really afford this service?
4. Will I make use of the knowledge I gain? How?
5. Am I being given a good deal?
6. Should I check out the competition?
7. Could I get this service for less?

8. Is this firm professional, honest, knowledgeable and reliable?
9. Should I decide now or later?
10. What will my colleagues think?
11. What problems may result if I don't act now?

THE KILLER QUESTIONS THAT PROSPECTS ASK

You're trying to win the big one: an RFP shoot-out against four or five other agencies for a major piece of business (in which you had to pull out all stops just to make the short list); or an exclusive audience with the CEO of a desirable prospect you've been courting for a long time.

You rehearsed your pitch well and delivered it with gusto. Now it's time for questions. And the prospect hits you with a meat ax, the very questions you hoped you wouldn't hear.

Jim Lukaszewski, chairman, The Lukaszewski Group, White Plains, NY, suggests that there are seven killer questions that you should anticipate and be ready for. Even head off.

"Killer questions don't surprise you," said Lukaszewski.

> They irritate you. When you hear them you get a clung—an adrenaline shot that rips through your body and melts your guts like cream cheese down into your shoes. What's the answer? Be ready, perhaps even bring up these questions yourself and answer them to save the prospect the potential embarrassment of having to ask them, hurt your feelings or seem impolite. Clients have a right to the answers; you have the obligation to be prepared.

Lukaszewski's Seven Killer Questions:

1. *Have you ever done this before?* Prospective clients assume that you would not have allowed yourself ethically to be in the presentation without disclosing this up front. The prospect has a right to know this and to deliberately have you make a presentation knowing you don't have the experience or background for the work.

2. *Who else have you done it for?* Logically, if your answer to #1 is "Yes," the prospect is going to want to know who, how, when

and, most importantly, the results. This is the time when agencies like to waffle and say something like, "Well . . . not exactly, but we worked for XYZ Corporation doing something somewhat similar." Obviously, this answer is not a prospect confidence builder. (Try to present) relevant timely examples. If you don't have any relevant examples, develop scenarios you can achieve.

3. *What if it doesn't work?* So what? This is a problem if you only have one idea. This is like the fear of being asked a question about a narrow idea that the prospect may already have rejected. The answer is to always have a "Plan B," even a "Plan C" or "Plan D." Be prepared for the unanticipated consequence of an unsuccessful effort. And you'll be able to better talk about that in the presentation.

4. *Why should we select you?* Some years ago, Ted Kennedy, running for president, was asked by a national news anchor why he was running. Kennedy said it was a very interesting question, but he really hadn't thought about it. This is one of those kind of questions. Why do you want this particular work? There must be some unique reasons why your agency is particularly appropriate for the work you're pitching. What are the two or three most important reasons, from the prospect's perspective, that they ought to hire you? Hint: Prospects like to hear specific experience; unusually direct experience; creative approaches; and clear and direct solutions.

5. *Why should we hire you rather than XYZ agency?* It isn't necessary to know your competition thoroughly. (Side note: I happen to disagree strongly with Jim on this point, but that's another story.) However, you ought to look around your marketplace and, perhaps, pick a very large agency, a medium size agency, and a very small agency and determine why you should be hired instead of them. There is no reason to be unprepared to respond to this kind of comparative question. Your answer should reflect the insight, perception, and doability the prospect is looking for. If you can't answer the question, you may not have the other skills the prospect needs either. Warning: Stick to the positives. Prospects are reluctant to purchase on negative sales points. If you cut apart another agency's talents, capabilities, or track rec-

ord, it's likely that neither you nor the other agency will win. Clients want creativity without conflict.

6. *What are your weaknesses?* Prospects ask this question because they've been burned. They are used to having agencies say they can do just about anything. Surely, your firm does not do everything. It may be an important credibility builder to talk (briefly and unapologetically) about the two or three things that your agency does not do well. Caution: Clients will clearly and very directly remember what you do not do once you have told them. Although disclaiming certain skills and abilities will build your credibility, it also may foreclose you from ever doing that kind of work for the client . . . unless you can re-educate him or her once you've achieved these new capabilities. The secret is to have consultants or other firms on tap to handle areas in which you're weak.

7. *Will you teach our people what you know?* (Author's note: In twenty-five years in the agency business, I never heard this one. Evidently Lukaszewski has.) Your answer should always be an absolute and enthusiastic "Yes." Never be threatened by teaching your clients what you know. Clients hire agencies because agencies have unique skills that most corporate and other organizations simply are never able to capture or build. If you can teach a client what you know and they can turn around and do it . . . you don't deserve to continue the relationship unless you find another way to build value into your services beyond the level at which the client was able to take over.

TEN WAYS TO RUIN A NEW BUSINESS PRESENTATION

Unfortunately, no matter how good your initial chemistry with the prospect was, no matter how thorough your research was, no matter how well written your "leave" document is . . . a clumsy oral presentation can sink you and lose the business.

Here, based on experience and talks with firm principals and corporate PR executives, are ten ways that you can lose the business during the final presentation.

1. *Be arrogant:* One of the two biggest mistakes you can make is to alienate prospects by "preaching" to them or insulting them

by implying that their PR program is not effective or that their PR director has not been doing his or her job effectively. You also can turn off the prospect by putting down his current PR firm or your competition.

2. *Be uninformed:* This is the second biggest mistake: Misread, ignore, or never learn what the prospect expects from the presentation; what type of presentation he/she/committee would be most comfortable with; what kind of pitch would best match the prospect's corporate culture. Do a "dog and pony" show when a casual across-the-table dialogue would have been more suitable. Or play it ultracasual when the prospect would have been impressed by more "glitz." Use too few/too many or too elaborate visuals. Fail to consider the type of presentations competing firms will make.

3. *Be ignorant:* Tell offensive, racist, chauvinistic jokes. Use profanity. Ignore the "little people" on the prospect committee. Talk only to the most senior person . . . who may approve the agency choice, but not make the initial selection. Avoid learning the titles and job responsibilities of all review committee members.

4. *Be windy:* Do all the talking. (One agency head recommends that firms spend 30 percent of the time talking and 70 percent listening.) Try to cover too much in the time allotted. Forget about limiting your presentation to what the prospect really wants to hear. Don't leave time for prospect questions. Go over the time deadline.

5. *Be expensive:* Confirm what the prospect has heard or believes: "PR firms are expensive." Scare him or her by talking about all the big budget clients you have. Be too "showy"; use elaborate visuals or creative effects that look like they cost a lot of money. Recommend primarily big, obviously expensive projects.

6. *Be superfluous:* Bring too many people into the presentation. Include staff members who have no role in the presentation. Let one agency executive dominate the discussion. Don't involve practitioners who will actually serve the prospect's business.

7. *Be phony:* Try to make the prospect believe that your firm or people are something that they are not. Don't stay within your

own comfort range; maybe you can convince the prospect that you are what he's looking for—even if you're not sure what that is. Sell too hard. Appear desperate for the business. Forget human relations values and caveats. Don't worry about chemistry; who knows what that is, anyway? If all else fails, offer the prospect a kickback; theater, football, or baseball tickets are always nice.

8. *Be invisible:* Forget that the prospect may have sat through three to six other presentations (perhaps back-to-back). Don't worry about building something creative and unique into your presentation that will distinguish your firm from all the others in the competition. Also forget about being enthusiastic; don't show interest and desire to be involved with the prospect. When you say "we," make sure the prospect understands that you mean only the agency—not the agency and the prospect/client. Drone your way through a boring, canned presentation without lifting your eyes from the script. Don't try to present either first or last, rather than in the middle of a series of competitive presentations. After lunch is a great time to make a presentation, right? And, by all means, never follow up your presentation with a thank-you note or a broader answer to one of the prospect's questions.

9. *Be noncompetitive:* Don't worry about competing firms. Ride on your reputation; no need for a 150 percent effort in the presentation. This one is locked up; you're the biggest firm in town or the prospect's PR director formerly worked for your firm or is a good friend. (Side note: Many firms would rather lose the business than have a former employee as a client.)

10. *Be disorganized:* Don't visit the presentation site in advance to check out ambiance, size, acoustics, seating arrangement. Don't set up or rearrange the presentation room (if in the prospect's quarters) for good eye and personal contact between the prospect and agency people. Arrive at the last minute so there's little time or opportunity to set up your equipment or make room changes. Don't make sure needed audiovisual equipment will be available. Forget to bring extension cords, electric plugs, masking tape, marking pens, flip charts and easels, name tent cards, and other equipment. Don't bother checking whether your prospect has a PowerPoint projector you can use (or bring

your own). Do not rehearse your presentation. Forget about making sure that people know exactly what they are supposed to do and are comfortable with their assignment. Don't coach neophyte presenters or give them plenty of time to rehearse. Don't "role-play" answers to questions the prospect may ask or decide who will answer questions. Don't ask uninvolved agency people to critique your rehearsal; ignore their comments, if you do. Don't arrange for the presentation to be in your quarters or invite the prospect for a get-acquainted visit. If the presentation is on your turf, don't give the prospect an agency tour to provide a feel for your agency atmosphere and facilities. All agencies look alike, right? Don't clean up messy offices or make sure there aren't too many unoccupied, obviously unused offices. All agencies have cluttered halls and stacks of press kits piled in the corner of the conference room, don't they? When the prospect accepts your invitation to lunch in your conference room before the presentation, make sure that he's the only one who eats. (A corporate PR executive described his discomfort when a major firm pulled this one on him.) Don't place a welcoming sign in your reception area or prepare any prominent visuals or displays that relate to the prospect or his business.

Making one of these mistakes may not kill you. Two mistakes and you still might squeak through. (Maybe the prospect's PR director really is your best friend or cousin.)

But why take chances? Reverse the polarity of these ten ways to ruin a good presentation—and the big ones won't get away.

MISTAKES THAT PROSPECTS MAKE

Here are 11 common mistakes that prospects make during an agency search. By subtly alerting prospects to these potential mistakes, you will help ensure that they pick the right firm. Hopefully, it will be yours.

1. Does not meet personally with firms; will not permit firms to speak to company executives beyond the PR director.

2. Does not provide realistic budget parameters; describes bigger budget than available.
3. Is not candid/comprehensive about the company background/ reputation/problems/opportunities.
4. Searches for free ideas, not an agency (maybe never picks a firm).
5. Seeks competitive pitches when a new firm has already been selected . . . but not announced.
6. Does not define/provide PR/corporate objectives.
7. Does not define type of presentation expected.
8. Demands extensive, free, speculative recommendations.
9. Will not disclose names of competing firms.
10. Interviews too many firms.
11. Does not understand the difference between advertising and PR and what each can/cannot accomplish.

THINGS I'VE LEARNED ABOUT SUCCESSFUL AGENCY PITCHES: TOM HARRIS'S SECRETS

In his current role as a consultant, Tom Harris, author of three books, former university professor, and Golin Harris International vice chairman, helps corporations find new PR firms (see Chapter 3, "Anatomy of an Agency Search"). Here are a few of the things that Tom says he's learned about successful agency pitches:

- Speak up, sister. These guys pay big bucks to management consultants to tell them what to do. Don't come off like an order taker.
- Talk about their business, not yours. Draw them out. Energize them. A few credentials go a long way.
- Do lots of homework. The other guys will. Talk to analysts and the media.
- Surf the Net. Find out what they're chatting about. There aren't many secrets anymore.
- Give them your best shot. Those that go beyond what's asked for are rewarded.
- If the client has a problem, don't duck it. Tell them how you would fix it. If you don't think you can or don't want to, pull out and give somebody else a chance.

- Don't play bait and switch account teams. Stick with your team unless the client tells you it's time for a change.
- In the client's eyes, all 25-year-old account executives are created equal. Field a team with a few grown-ups.
- Your best people may not be your best salesmen. Find a way to get the client to know your people one on one.
- There's a thin line between self-assurance and arrogance. Nobody loves a know-it-all.
- Likewise, there is a thin line between friendliness and obsequiousness.
- Clients have short memories. Don't assume they absorbed your every word and will recall what you said the last time.
- Don't save your big idea. It's a risky gambit. If you've got it, flaunt it. You may never get another chance.
- Don't reveal a laundry list of every tactic you ever thought of. It shows a lack of discipline. Strategy sells.
- But don't be so strategic that they will wonder if you can execute.
- Don't get too cute. Your suitability to be a serious business partner may be at risk.
- Technology proves Murphy's Law once and for all. If you represent yourself as technically savvy, don't make your presentation a learning experience.
- Don't turn your back on clients or they may turn their back on you.
- Don't stand in the way of the projector. Unless you have always wanted to be in pictures.
- Don't waste their time. They've got better things to do than dish the dirt over coffee and see every nook and cranny in your office.
- Stay in touch. Ask good questions. Show them you want the business more than the other guys.
- But be aware that too much follow-up can drive them crazy.
- Beware of overstuffed selection committees. One dissenter can cause mischief big time.
- Attention must be paid to everyone down the line. Someone who feels ignored now can make life miserable later.
- Beware purchasing agents. You are not selling parts.

- Think twice about giving them little mementoes. Know the difference between a chotchke and a gift. If you can buy their vote with a gift, somebody else will come along with a better gift.
- Don't take the account if your employees have a good reason to object to working on it. Good men and women nowadays are hard to find.
- Don't knock your competitors. They are there because the client wanted them to be.
- Field a diverse team. Nobody does business with white men only anymore.
- All conflicts are in the eye of the client. Fess up up front. If they can't get past it, pack up and go home and wish them well.
- Many clients don't know diddly squat about public relations. If you engage them with insights about *their* business, they will believe you know *your* business.
- CEOs listen to fellow CEOs. You are in good company if you can get a member of the club to give you a thumbs up.
- Assure them a return on their investment but don't promise the moon unless your name is Armstrong.
- Be gracious in victory or defeat. Tomorrow is another day. They may see the error of their ways and hire you after all.
- Bigger isn't always better. Clients want a firm that fits, whether the size is small, medium, or large.

TEN REASONS WHY PR SHOULD BE PART OF EVERY MARCOM PROGRAM

Here are 10 specific reasons why public relations should be part of every corporate marketing communications program. Use them in selling business to reluctant or unsophisticated prospects.

1. *Credibility:* Editors' or broadcasters' implied third-party endorsement of your product or service attaches high credibility to the published, broadcast, or telecast information.
2. *Targeted messages:* Public relations can efficiently and economically reach a number of special interest target audiences. It can reach secondary markets or support secondary products that do not justify significant advertising support.

3. *Increased impact:* Research shows that six readings of an ad are required to generate the same impact that is gained from one reading of editorial material.
4. *Cost-efficiency:* Public relations is often more cost-efficient than advertising on the basis of cost-per-thousand audience reach.
5. *Comprehensive story:* A typical article or news release can effectively communicate a number of message points. Advertising generally works best when only one message is delivered.
6. *Generation of inquiries:* Public relations generates more highly qualified inquiries and sales leads.
7. *New market development:* Because of public relations' cost- and targeting-efficiency, it can be used effectively to determine the viability of a new market as well as help develop new markets.
8. *Marketing synergism:* Public relations can be used to both complement and supplement advertising. When used with advertising, it can double the awareness of advertising or promotional messages.
9. *Reprints:* Distribution of reprints of published material can double the readership and impact of the message and provide excellent sales "leave" pieces.
10. *Image enhancement:* Public relations can enlarge a company's or product's image, communicate a new image, and serve many other corporate purposes.

BENEFITS PROVIDED BY A PR FIRM OVER INTERNAL STAFF

Every now and then, an unsophisticated prospect or client asks an agency principal, "Why should I hire an agency when I can hire someone internally for less money?" Here are some answers to that eternal question that could help you win or keep the business.

Research by Edelman Public Relations and Northwestern University's Integrated Marketing Communications Department confirms that

- Sharing all or parts of a company's communication function with external communications firms has a measurable impact on the consistency and quality of communication messages.
- Companies that do not use outside agency resources report significantly lower effectiveness scores than companies that do use external communications agencies.

Here are additional reasons for using a public relations firm instead of building internal staff:

- *Objectivity:* If you could list only one reason, it should be what consultant Tom Harris in his book *Choosing and Working With Your Public Relations Firm* calls "one of the principal benefits of employing outside public relations counsel: the objectivity they bring to client problems."
- *Varied experience:* Harris also points out that "One of the principal attractions of the public relations firm is its broad-based experience with a variety of clients. The PR firm brings its clients not only technical skills but collected experience solving similar problems for other clients." Few companies can afford to match the breadth of experience and skills available from even the most modest-sized PR firms. Nor would they want to simply because they would have only infrequent need for many of the PR firm's specialized skills.
- *Flexibility:* Add to this the agency's ability to commit additional staff quickly to handle crisis situations or other peak work loads.
- *Independence:* As a Gable Group white paper said,

Agencies typically provide superior speed, mobility and creativity. Agencies offer an "independent" and fresher viewpoint without internal political considerations found in most companies. Outside consultants tend to be more aggressive, proactive and preemptive in recommending strategies for dealing with changing situations.

- *Cost:* One of the biggest fallacies is the "I can do it cheaper inside" argument. To the internal person's salary must be added all the related costs for benefits and overhead, often matching salary costs. Client or prospect executives may disregard this factor because, while they may be charged with an internal PR practitioner's salary, larger, more ambiguous costs for benefits, office space, equipment, and other overhead items may be hidden in a broader corporate budget.

- *Accountability:* As I used to tell clients when I was honchoing a PR firm, "Your hand is on the faucet handle. If we don't perform the way we promise or you expect, it's fairly easy for you to shut off the faucet. It's not as easy to do that with inside staff to which you're committed."

- *On the other hand:* Almost every experienced PR firm principal knows that the absolutely best combination of resources that produces the best results, most efficiently, is a strong, knowledgeable inside PR executive working in concert with—not in competition with—a strong counseling firm.

TWENTY-FIVE REASONS
TO WALK AWAY FROM A PROSPECT

But wait, maybe you don't want or need every potential new piece of business that looms into view. Here are 25 reasons to walk away from a prospect, prepared by Cathy Ackerman, president, Ackermann Public Relations, Knoxville, Tennessee, for her staff:

1. We give them a good proposal with a fairly priced budget and they want to decrease the budget without decreasing the scope of work.
2. They balk at any of our terms spelled out in "The Business Side of Our Relationship."
3. They will not agree to advance payment.
4. They want to see the actual finished product before paying anything.
5. They only want to pay for results, not for our time in trying to achieve those results.
6. They ask for special payment terms extending beyond our usual policy in this regard.
7. They want us to produce spec work before deciding to hire us.
8. They want to "test us" before committing to a business relationship and that "test" involves what we do for a living and normally charge for.

9. They want us to take shares in their company in lieu of cash for our fees.
10. They refuse or procrastinate about signing a letter of agreement.
11. They try to pit us against competing agencies in order to obtain special concessions.
12. They are under-capitalized.
13. They have no business plan and/or cannot articulate their business goals or company vision.
14. They are unclear relative to their expectations of us.
15. They have trouble making decisions.
16. They are overly bureaucratic and/or involve committees in every decision.
17. They cannot or will not meet deadlines or respond to us in a timely way.
18. They do not return our phone calls within a reasonable time.
19. They are rude or exhibit abusive behavior with others in their office in addition to us.
20. They think they know it all and will not listen.
21. They have no or inadequate commitment to public relations as an important part of their business.
22. Their reputation is questionable or negative with customers, vendors, and/or other service providers.
23. They have had several different PR firms within a relatively short time period.
24. Their associates do not seem to respect or like them.
25. The atmosphere in their office is overly strained or negative.

Run, do not walk, away from any of these prospects. No one needs business that badly!

WHAT ABOUT THOSE CLIENTS YOU CAN'T STAND— DO YOU NEED THEM?

Hopefully, the time will come—sooner rather than later—when you can get really fussy about the kind of clients you keep. Growing agencies often find themselves trying to serve a hodgepodge of clients. Do you have any of these on your client roster?

- Small, picky people who don't show up well on your bottom line and are never going to get any bigger or better.
- Clients who demand too much of your time and that of your senior people, but scream at your hourly rates.
- Clients who are demanding but who have too many other things on their plate and seldom have time to dig up the information or provide the guidance you need or push through approvals—or sometimes even can't be bothered to talk to you or return your phone calls.
- Clients who wouldn't accept a new idea if you offered to give it away and who are just plain boring to work for.
- Clients whose products or services are 10 years behind the times, who haven't done anything newsworthy in decades, and don't have anything interesting to say, but whose CEO keeps beefing because his company wasn't included in the most recent industry roundup.
- Companies whose idea of prompt payment is ninety days.

You also know the clients I didn't include: those who constantly insult or demean your account staff; who nitpick every invoice and hold up the entire invoice when they have a small question; who "lose" your invoice on their desk until their company's check-writing date is long past; who regularly ask for more than they're paying for. You get the idea. I'm sure you have a favorite or two.

What would happen if you resigned that pain in the butt client? Or the ones who are too small to meet your current minimum income requirement? Check your cash flow and financial projections. Can you withstand the loss of whatever income they're generating without counting on replacing it quickly? Would that give you the time and staff to find a couple new clients who would not only be interesting to work with, but who would be nicely profitable? Will your staff stand outside your office and cheer? If the answer to these questions is "yes," do it.

PROFILE 7: MICHELLE FLOWERS

President, Flowers Communications Group
Chicago, Illinois

Parlaying 10 years of both general and ethnic agency experience with a masters degree in advertising and a strong background in the black consumer market, Michelle Flowers founded her African-American PR agency in 1991.

The firm has grown from two employees and three clients in the cosmetics, packaged goods, and automotive industries to 21 employees providing award-winning integrated marketing programs to such national corporations as Lawry's Foods, Miller Brewing, and Luster Products.

The agency emphasizes campaigns designed to "reach and respect" the African-American consumer market, providing clients with what Michelle calls "ROI—relationship, ownership, and impact." Signature programs include "Know Your Money" (National Urban League), focusing on economic empowerment in the black community; "Black Heritage Bowl" (Lawry's), an educational Black History Month program; "Write to Achieve" (McDonald's), a literacy campaign designed to improve writing and reading skills; and "Urban Entrepreneurs Program" (Miller Brewing), aimed at inspiring and supporting young black business owners.

While creativity and client service were always her strong points, Michelle concedes that, like many agency owners, she initially didn't devote as much attention to the fiscal side of her agency as she should have. However, that all changed when the agency installed time and billing software and other needed administrative and operating procedures.

Michelle advises new agency principals to

> Create a clear vision for your agency; specialize in a niche that sets you apart from other firms; build a strong senior management team; pursue new business continually, especially when

you don't have to; and concentrate on your firm's fiscal infrastructure, including systems to ensure account profitability.

Michelle Flowers has not only crashed through the feminine "glass ceiling" but also sets a prime example for other African-American business owners.

Chapter 8

New Business Singular Truths

While competing for and winning—or losing—new clients, you will recognize a few singular truths. These truths should provide the critical core of your new business development campaign.

TRUTH NUMBER 1: THE FIRST ENCOUNTER WITH A PROSPECT IS CRITICAL

Chances are you already know that first impressions are very important. When it comes to new business solicitation, the first impression—your very first meeting with a prospect—is so important that it can make the difference between whether you win or lose a piece of new business.

The impression that you make in your first meeting with a prospect can overcome the organized frenzy of a series of formal presentations after which prospects may have trouble remembering the difference between competing agencies. In many instances, the first meeting will determine whether you make the "short list" and are invited into the final presentation round.

The first meeting or prospect briefing is an opportunity for you to dig into the prospect's background and needs and establish direction for your formal presentation. It also is an opportunity for the prospect to preview your firm's experience, eagerness, and intuitiveness in an unfettered, unstructured atmosphere.

Here's an example from real life.

I was retained by a well-known national corporation to assist in the selection of a new public relations firm. Six PR agencies were invited to receive separate briefings from a corporate committee that included senior executives. One of the firms, actually the PR depart-

doi:10.1300/5561_08

ment of the company's advertising agency, declined the briefing on the basis that they already knew enough about the company. Said they didn't need to waste the company's time. (Too bad! The firm bombed its presentation.)

The other five firms spent at least an hour each (some more) with the prospect's committee. I soon became aware that the committee was very impressed with the representatives of a national firm. Two senior officers of the firm had come into the briefing meeting well prepared. They had obviously researched the company and had even visited one of the company's retail outlets. They asked intelligent questions and made pertinent comments and suggestions.

On the morning of the first presentation—with six scheduled over two days—the committee assembled early to review the agency screening procedure. As they left to visit the first agency, the CEO moaned, "Why are we going through this? We know who we're going to pick."

And they did. The firm whose representatives had come into the first meeting smart enough about the company to ask intelligent questions won the business.

I saw this pattern many times over a period of years as I helped firms conduct agency searches. In the middle of the search process, a PR director would say, "We really like XYZ Agency." And, generally, that would be the firm that they chose.

Okay, so I'll repeat myself. Don't waste your time and that of your prospect—don't insult your prospect—by going into the first meeting unprepared. Run a database check. Talk to a couple of editors. Read a trade publication or two. Visit a trade show. Use the product. Invest enough time to learn the prospect's business so you can look smarter—can be smarter—than your competitors.

TRUTH NUMBER 2: A PROSPECT'S AGENDA MAY NOT BE AS IT SEEMS

Often, the prospect's needs, as he or she expresses them, may seem relatively uncomplicated and unsophisticated, centered largely on publicity and "big ideas."

However, be careful. Lurking behind such simplistic goals often is an unrecognized but nascent need for trend tracking, problem anticipation, strategic thinking, corporate or marketing positioning, and professional direction.

Depending on the sophistication of the prospect, he may not even be aware of the breadth of services he can receive from your firm. Probing the client's problems and opportunities during an initial meeting could lead to a broader—and more profitable—program than initially envisioned.

TRUTH NUMBER 3: THE IMPORTANCE OF CULTURE COMPATIBILITY CANNOT BE OVERESTIMATED

Culture compatibility, comfort fit, or "chemistry" between agency and prospect is often hard to discern or define and frequently relies on gut feelings. However, it can be the deciding factor in an agency search and one of the most important elements in a productive ongoing agency-client relationship.

Corporate or agency culture wears many cloaks; it can be billed as historical heritage—inherited interests, instincts, and ethos—personality profile, or, as one dictionary sees it, "The sum total of ways of living built up by a group of human beings and transmitted from one generation to another."

However defined, culture is the essence of corporate and agency flavor, drive, and direction. It is a given, established and nurtured over a lengthy period of time, and not subject to transient variations to fit individual situations.

A lack of culture compatibility between agency and prospect should not be judged as "good" or "bad," but only in terms of "viva la difference." Where culture compatibility does not exist in one instance, it will flourish in another.

Not all clients and agencies were meant to live happily ever after. Recognizing the potential for such compatibility at an early stage is one of the prime virtues and hoped-for outcomes of your first exploratory meeting with a prospect.

TRUTH NUMBER 4: THE PROSPECTS' PRIORITIES ARE SELDOM THE SAME AS YOURS

You're squirming, impatient, apprehensive. At the end of your pitch last week to a gargantuan prospect, the PR director promised to make an agency selection by the end of this week. It's Friday, but you haven't heard anything yet. You're convinced that you lost. The atmosphere tends to be gloomy, and you spend the weekend sulking and barking at your wife, husband, children, or dog.

Not to fret. Prospects' priorities are seldom the same as yours. They'll get around to it when they get around to it.

I have seen instances where the agency pitched last of six firms, left to return to its office, and was called back in and awarded the business on the spot. I have seen other instances where a promised quick decision stretched out to several months and sometimes to never.

Agencies often ask, "When do you expect to make your decision?" It's probably a useless question. Circumstances or events that you know nothing about—because you're not yet privy to the company's secrets—can delay agency selection decisions for a lot longer than you'd like.

A couple of generalities: Consumer product companies usually make decisions quicker than industrial companies. However, industrial companies that may take forever to decide to hire a PR firm will usually take equally as long to decide to fire one. The same may not be true of consumer product companies.

Selecting a new PR agency may not be a high priority of the prospect compared to other company problems. And you can't make it happen any faster even if the cold wind is blowing at your door and your cash flow chart is bleeding.

Your best bet is to make your presentation, follow up with a brief thank-you letter, and then pretend the presentation never happened. Go about your business. This way, you'll be pleasantly surprised when the prospect calls with the good news that you won. And if you didn't win, well, there's always that great prospect you're pitching next week.

TRUTH NUMBER 5: YOU MUST BE ABLE TO ACCEPT AND BOUNCE BACK FROM REJECTION

An agency colleague once asked me after we'd lost a new business pitch, "How can you get up off the floor so often?" (He later left for a less stressful corporate job.) I thought, *Why not? I don't like it down there. There are splinters, and the dirt gets under my fingernails. Be-*

sides, I'm having fun. I can't help it if the prospect is not perceptive or wise enough to chose us.

The truth is, every salesperson, someone who sells a product or service, must learn to accept and live with rejection. And not take it personally. As the principal of your agency, that's what you are, a "salesman" (or saleswoman). If you don't get up off the floor after being knocked down, the only sounds you will hear are the footsteps of your competitors running over you and the bank knocking on your door.

You must get up and wage the battle. Again. And again and again. That is the only answer.

TRUTH NUMBER 6: BE PATIENT— WINNING NEW CLIENTS TAKES TIME

Why Agencies Win or Lose New Business

In a survey of agency principals, chemistry, good fit, and industry experience were almost unanimously listed as reasons why agencies win or lose new business. Other reasons for winning business listed by survey respondents included the following:

- "We do our homework. We are perceived as genuine down-to-earth people who care about and invest a lot of passion and energy in our clients' success."
- "We are viewed as 'superb' at both strategy and execution."
- "Personal reputation and recognized expertise in certain areas."
- "Prestige of existing clients."
- "Good value."
- "Straightforward plan."
- "We make a point of being in the right place at the right time. That usually means being there first. We do a lot of homework on prospects. Our pitches are more strategic than cosmetic."
- "Listening to the prospect."
- "Breadth of services."
- "Aggressive attitude and quality presentations."
- "Assurance of quality and quantity of work at better prices."

In addition to a lack of chemistry, firm principals said they do not win business because of these reasons:

- "Clients who value one activity above all else might choose a firm that is good at that thing."
- "Small size."
- "Price."
- "The prospect doesn't realize that the agency is a business that needs to make money."
- "Preordained outcome."
- "No budget after all."
- "Lack of experience (in a specific industry)."
- "The prospect doesn't understand or accept (the value) of our comprehensive services when we're pitching against a narrow specialist."
- "Location."
- "Client goes with a 'safe,' better-known agency."
- "Unable to convince prospect of benefits."
- "Larger agency strongly recommended by prestigious friend of CEO or board member."
- "Prospect doesn't understand PR or our strengths."

One very strong reason firms fail to win new clients—a reason that companies seldom mention—is the firms' emphasis on functional recommendations—tactics and techniques—rather than on solid strategies supporting the prospects' corporate or marketing objectives. Good "chemistry" depends heavily on strategically strong thinking that will help prospects meet their goals.

That says it all. Good luck.

PROFILE 8: TOM GABLE

CEO, Gable-Cook-Schmid PR
San Diego, California

After ten years as a business editor, Tom Gable changed careers in 1976 so that he could stay in San Diego instead of being transferred to the East Coast. Gable believed that a market existed for a PR firm based on his experience on the receiving end. He felt that most public relations services were being provided by semiretired advertising executives. It turns out he was right.

From first year's revenue of $45,000, his first firm, The Gable Group, grew to 30 employees, income of $3.1 million, and a reputation as one of the best-managed and most progressive medium-sized PR firms in the country. (Tom's *Client Service Manual* is so good that other firms buy it from PRSA.)

To be successful, Gable says principals' firms must do the following:

Hire the best available talent, even if they cost more than you want to pay; be closely attuned to market and client needs; and be prepared to reinvent yourself every few years so the firm can continue to deliver consistent quality, creativity and performance.

This philosophy worked even when the dot-com meltdown in 2001 caused Gable to change from a traditional agency model with high overhead to a smaller virtual agency where the partners (Gable, Rick Cook, and Jon Schmid) directly manage every account. The change worked. In just three years, billing went over $1 million and GCS boasted major clients, including Pfizer for media relations in California and the San Diego County Regional Airport Authority.

If he was starting another firm today, Gable says he would use the virtual model or an adaptation, investing more in talent and technology than in trappings. He also would have everyone in the firm more targeted in their networking and new business efforts.

Gable advises principals to

Establish a vision for where you want the firm to be in two or three years; deliver results better and faster than anyone in the region through interactive team efforts to get there; keep ahead of the technology curve; and focus on measurable results.

PART III:
MANAGING YOUR FIRM FOR PROFIT

Chapter 9

Serving the Client

Way back in the first chapter of this nonfiction epic, in case you've forgotten, "account management"—one of the most loosely used terms in the counseling industry lexicon—was defined as "Bringing the agency's management, professional and creative services to bear against a client's problems and opportunities so that we serve the client with maximum effectiveness while also generating maximum income and profit for the agency."

It's pretty simple; to achieve the second objective, you must practice the first with the utmost efficiency, efficacy, and effectiveness. The two precepts are inexorably entwined; accomplishing one without the other is highly unlikely. (Well, I guess you could serve clients pretty well without making a profit. But that would do bad things to your retirement plans.)

Since most of the last half of this tome is devoted to helping you make a profit, it seems more than appropriate to spend a bit of time on serving clients.

WHAT DO CLIENTS WANT?

First, what do clients really want in the way of service from their agency?

According to consultant Mitch Kozikowski, in his *Client Service with an Attitude,*

- First and above all, they want Solutions to their business problems;
- Next, they want great Decisions. They want information and input that allows them to take the best course of action;

doi:10.1300/5561_09

- Communications as such means little to top management. They want some demonstrable Added Value from their communications;
- They need to communicate One Face to Stakeholders. They want and need consistency in their dealings with their publics;
- They want to Build Relationships with every constituency of their organization. They're wise to the waste and folly of programs that just provide temporary cosmetic benefits with no lasting value.

The following, then, become the key issues for PR firms, according to Kozikowski:

- Our clients don't want what we're selling;
- This has become a transactional-based craft; fewer fees, more projects;
- Management wants PR to join their team. Clients view the PR firm's work as part of an overall business plan. You should too;
- Tactics; YUK! What's the strategy? Less PR jargon and more about the business purpose of your recommendations;
- Everyone's getting into our field (and there are more one-person, senior-level shops doing a good, cost effective job for clients, making a living at it and taking business away from multi-person agencies);
- In less than a generation, technology has changed the rules about how we conduct and manage public relations;
- Communications has become direct and interactive; and
- Geography has become less important than expertise to the clients of our craft.

"It is, therefore, time," said Kozikowski, "to stop whining about the lack of understanding of what we do, lack of respect, blah, blah, blah, and move forward to refine our services to match what clients want and need."

PROVIDING OUTSTANDING CLIENT SERVICE

How do you define "outstanding client service"? What kind of goals should you—or will you—set for your staff? If you provide anything less than outstanding client service, you might as well shutter your shop and head for the poorhouse, because you will be sunk in the wake of all the other agencies that do provide outstanding client service.

Here are the characteristics of "outstanding client service" as defined by a group of agency principals meeting in Sedona, Arizona. They said that to provide outstanding client service, you must do the following:

- Provide strategically based solutions;
- Respond quickly with enthusiasm, energy, and creativity;
- Stay out in front; offer ideas and solutions before your client thinks of them;
- Provide relentless attention to detail;
- Become part of your client's team, including participating in strategic planning;
- Add unexpected value;
- Help your clients manage their marketing dollars wisely;
- Dare to be different;
- Commit to your client's success; understand what success means to the client;
- Provide expertise your client doesn't have or can't afford inhouse;
- Offer objectivity; ask tough questions;
- Listen, even to what is not said;
- Allow no surprises;
- Make your client a hero;
- Engage in proactive research; do your homework and provide your client with information about emerging issues;
- Serve as an "early warning system" regarding business opportunities and threats;
- Demonstrate a total can-do attitude;
- Deliver more than expected; and
- Think outside the box.

You might want to use this list as the basis for a staff meeting or as a memo to your staff. Less experienced staff members, in particular, should be reminded regularly that "outstanding client service" demands more from them than simply performing their day-to-day routine duties such as writing a news release or article or preparing a mailing list.

Every staff member needs to understand that your firm's success and, in turn, their own professional and financial success depends on how well the firm delivers outstanding client service. Consider establishing adherence to these principles as an annual goal and then measure on a regular basis—monthly, quarterly, semiannually, annually—how well you and your staff actually apply the principles. You also might want to establish these principles, and any others you'd like to add, as the basis for a staff reward or performance review system. For example, on a 1 to 10 basis (10 being the best), how well did (employee) "provide relentless attention to detail" in the past three months? Where was he or she weak? Where was the overall firm weak?

Simply saying that these are your firm's client service principles isn't enough. You need to measure how well you consistently follow the principles. And then correct areas where you don't measure up.

CLIENT SERVICE AUDITS PROVIDE
A RECORD OF ACHIEVEMENT

By its very nature, the agency business is a cyclical, pressure-laden, deadline-ridden, "What'd-you-do-for-me-today?" way of making a living. Anything you can do to smooth out the cyclical nature, lessen the pressure, and soften the deadlines will be a blessing.

Management information and systems often are the keys to making your life more livable and, not so incidentally, ensuring that your employees are as happy and loyal as possible and that your firm's bottom line is well in the black. You need software that accurately tracks employees' billable time; you need an hourly rate system that generates a specific profit on each employee (surely you're not still using that old three or three and one-half times salary cost system); you need annual performance reviews for employees; you need to know precisely how profitable each client is; and you ought to have a system to benchmark whether you're consistently doing the best possible job for your clients and generating the highest possible profit for your firm.

It therefore would be helpful to systematically document client service objectives and promises and agency profit goals. This way, if you have to suddenly replace a senior manager either by promoting from inside or hiring from the outside, you'll have a briefing document ready to familiarize the new account manager with client service needs and agency objectives.

The client service audit shown in Exhibit 9.1 (developed in conjunction with New York CPA Richard Goldstein), when used consistently and candidly, will

- provide a disciplined, systematic way to record basic client service objectives and agency goals for a new client or new client project;
- record whether client and agency objectives and goals were achieved and note the reason for failure; and
- estimate the future income/profit potential of the client relationship.

EXHIBIT 9.1. Client Service Audit

Instructions: A client service audit (CSA) must be completed in two parts for all (agency) clients. Part I must be completed at the start/change of a client relationship or at the start of a client project. Part II must be completed annually or at the end of a client relationship or project. The CSA is to be completed by the individual responsible for management/supervision of client service and reviewed by a senior agency officer.

Part I

Client _____

CSA completed by _____ Date _____

CSA reviewed by _____ Date _____

1. Client/project start date _____
   A. Length of contract/project _____
2. Client's business _____
   A. Business objectives (list on separate page)
   B. Communication objectives (list on separate page)
   C. Target audience/s _____

3. Client contact and title _____
4. Why were we selected over competition, if known? _____
5. Services we will provide or attach client plan: _____
6. Do we have the necessary resources to meet client needs?
   ____ Yes ____ No
   A. If no, describe additional full-time resources needed: _____
   B. Number of hours required monthly to serve client by
      Account manager ____   Account supervisor ____
      Account executive ____   Account coordinator ____
7. Project fee/budget; monthly/annual fee/budget? _____
   _____
8. Project/program/annual profit percentage goal? _____

Part II

Date completed _____
CSA completed by _____
CSA reviewed by _____
1. Did we meet communications objectives? ____ Yes ____ No
   A. If no, why not? _____
2. Did we meet business objectives? ____ Yes ____ No
   A. If no, why not? _____
3. Did we generate "Value Added" results? If yes, describe. _____
   _____
4. What additional services can we provide the client? _____
   _____
5. Final/annual profit percentage? _____
6. If below expected profit goal, why?
   _____
7. If ongoing fee, does fee need to be increased?
   ____ Yes ____ No
   A. If yes, explain. _____
8. Client potential (circle one):
   A. Terminating
   B. Decreasing
   C. Level
   D. Growing
   E. Unlimited

9. Client attitude toward agency (circle one):
   A. Hostile
   B. Lukewarm
   C. Polite/businesslike
   D. Friendly; refers other business
10. Should we continue to serve this client?
    ____ Yes ____ No
    A. If no, explain. _____

11. Will we need additional capabilities to do that?
    Explain _____
12. How should we have changed the original CSA?
    Explain. _____

MEASURING CLIENT SATISFACTION

One thing that you ought to be constantly concerned about is whether your clients are satisfied with your agency's service.

Probably the best way to keep track of whether your clients are satisfied with the job you're doing is to ask them. Don't regard "no news as good news." If you don't hear from your client, it probably means things are happening that aren't in your best interests. Schedule regular "How are we doing?" meetings. Be sure to meet at least annually with client CEOs if you don't see them regularly otherwise.

In case you've forgotten, here's what clients like and hate, according to The Gable Group's "Client Service Manual."

They Like	They Hate
1. Integrity	1. Bait and switch; disappearing senior managers
2. Candor	2. Overpromising
3. Professionalism, experience	3. Few results; many excuses
4. Knowledge of client, industry	4. Lack of client knowledge
5. Strategic thinking	5. Order taking versus counseling

6. New ideas, enthusiasm
7. Accessibility, responsiveness
8. Budget responsibility

9. Profit orientation (theirs)
10. Loyalty

6. Boilerplate client service
7. Lack of communication, responsiveness
8. Budget overages; low perceived value
9. General business ignorance
10. Chasing the client with the biggest budget

Before you have that "How are we doing?" meeting with your toughest client, better you should take a reality check on this list.

KEEP SATISFACTION SURVEYS SIMPLE

While personal contact is best, there may not be time or occasion to see all the client people that you ought to. The next best client service satisfaction measurement device is a survey, via either e-mail or snail mail.

Here the rule should be simplicity. You're sending the survey to busy people. Unless you make the survey fairly easy to complete, chances are you won't get the response level you'd like. A lot of agencies probably go astray here; there's lots they want to ask their clients, so they make the survey too long and complicated. Of a half-dozen agency client surveys I have in my files, only one really meets simplicity standards.

Says Padilla Speer Beardsley (PSB) CEO Lynn Casey,

We've really tried to simplify our survey. One of the ways to keep a satisfied client is to make sure you get feedback on satisfaction surveys. It's our duty to make it easy for people (to respond). However, if a lengthy, more detailed survey works for you, it will provide more information than ours does.

Exhibit 9.2 is PSB's simple, two-page, client satisfaction survey. (The survey is e-mailed to clients annually or after a major project. A "heads up" letter advises the client that the survey is coming.)

EXHIBIT 9.2.
Padilla Speer Beardsley Client Satisfaction Survey

Rate your level of satisfaction with the work performed by PSB. (Note: Levels of satisfaction are rated as "Very Satisfied," "Satisfied," or "Very Dissatisfied," or levels in between.)

1. Diagnosing your situation or need?
2. Researching and gathering information/data?
3. Addressing your needs strategically?
4. Demonstrating and applying knowledge of your organization/ industry?
5. Communicating changes in scope or direction?
6. Implementing strategy and program ideas?
7. Recommending programs that address your objectives?
8. Staffing your account appropriately?
9. Involving senior team members when needed? (Note the "when needed" distinction.)
10. Initiating new ideas and opportunities beyond the scope of the primary need?
11. Communicating and managing expectations?
12. Providing feedback and progress reports?
13. Demonstrating creativity and innovation?
14. Tenaciously pursuing your objectives?
15. Delivering good value for your investment?

Rate your level of satisfaction with our working relationship.

16. Listening to your ideas and concerns?
17. Working with you and members of your team as partners?
18. Caring about you and your business?
19. Being accessible and available when you call?
20. Keeping promises, e.g., budget and deadlines?
21. Asking for your input?
22. Thinking beyond the task at hand?
23. Paying attention to your needs?

Rate PSB's overall performance in the following areas:

24. Research/situation analysis?
25. Strategic planning?
26. Counsel and advice?
27. Program design and development?
28. Evaluation and measurement?

The survey then asks the client to "Describe a project or situation that occurred within the past year when you believe PSB's service was very valuable, and tell us why. Conversely, describe a project or situation that occurred within the past year when PSB did not meet your expectations and tell us why." (Clients also are asked to check off those PSB services they have used over the previous twelve months. This tells Casey what specific services the client is rating and reminds the client of the breadth of the firm's services.)

Most important, at the end, the survey questionnaire says, "We will review responses with you shortly after we receive your questionnaire."

UNDERSTANDING THE PROSPECT'S/CLIENT'S NEEDS

Bliss Gouverneur, New York, uses an interesting process to both help prepare new business pitches as well as provide the best service to the client after they're on board. In essence, the process helps the firm understand the prospect's/client's needs as well as level of professional sophistication.

The two-part process includes both a questionnaire to provide information about the prospect and a qualitative diagnostic chart to gauge various levels of the client's sophistication about public relations. The first part tells the agency what makes the company tick. The second part reveals what makes the company's people tick, and, more important, what ticks them off.

Through secondary research or personal contact, the agency collects answers to the following questions:

1. How old is your firm/company?
2. How many employees do you have?

3. How many offices do you have?
4. What are your annual sales?
5. What percent of your sales are domestic?
6. What are your primary products/services?
7. What companies buy your products/services (by size, industry, geography)?
8. Who (functional title) at those companies is the buyer?
9. Who is your competition?
10. What is your share/ranking in the market?
11. How do you differentiate yourself from the competition?
12. Please summarize current strengths, weaknesses, threats, opportunities.
13. Do you have a marketing plan?
14. What is the objective of your marketing communication program (raise awareness, increase leads, both, or something else)?
15. Which of these marketing communication tactics have you used in the past: public relations, speeches, direct mail/newsletters, seminars, advertising, telemarketing?
16. Please explain why (or why not) they have been successful.
17. Who are your experienced spokespeople and/or writers?
18. Are you able to publicly name your clients and describe in detail the work you perform for them?
19. What is your expectation of the results that we will generate for you?
20. Who will be our primary contact?
21. Do you have a budget and/or timetable?
22. When would you like our proposal? May we deliver it in person?
23. Is this a competitive situation? If so, who is our competition?
24. How long have you been with the company? To whom do you report?
25. Have you used a PR firm before? What were the results?

After the agency meets prospect/client personnel, a matrix chart (see Figure 9.1) is often developed that diagnoses the client as "process" or "results" oriented; as either a "pro" or a "novice"; and as having a "high" or "low" level of sophistication.

	Process orientation →	Results orientation
High (Level of sophistication)	**Process-oriented pros** • Provide a steady stream of information to client re: program status. • Identify other stakeholders' objectives and clarify how BGA will be measured. • Enlist support to showcase successes to stakeholders.	**Results-oriented pros** • Manage expectations. • Make sure organization is ready to support an aggressive program with content, access, and dollars. • Enlist support to showcase successes to stakeholders.
Low	**Process-oriented novices** • Educate client about the pros and cons of various program elements and implementation approaches. • Make sure liaison understands what it will take from his or her organization to be successful. • Provide a steady stream of information to client re: program status. • Identify other stakeholders' objectives and clarify how BGA will be measured.	**Results-oriented novices** • Educate client about the pros and cons of various program elements and implementation approaches. • Make sure liaison understands what it will take from his or her organization to be successful. • Manage expectations. • Educate client re: enlisting his or her organization's support. • Provide status reports that showcase results.

FIGURE 9.1. Understand client needs. The day-to-day liaison—it's important to understand your liaison's "hot buttons" and PR needs.

For a client defined as "high sophistication, process oriented," account team responsibilities outlined on the chart includes "Provide a steady stream of information to client regarding program status." For a "low sophistication, process-oriented" client, the agency requirement includes "Educate client about the pros and cons of various program elements and implementation approaches."

Conversely, for a "results-oriented, high sophistication" client, the chart includes "Manage expectations." For a "results-oriented, low sophistication" client, it includes "Make sure liaison understands what it will take from his or her organization to be successful."

"The matrix chart, created by group manager Meg Wildrick, gives us behavioral insights that are invaluable in helping our AEs run their accounts," according to partner John Bliss.

ESTABLISHING NEW ACCOUNTS

Laer Pearce, president of Laer Pearce & Associates, Irvine, California, suggests "13 Lucky Steps to Successfully Establish New Accounts" that, he says, are based on mistakes made and remedied.

Here are some good things to remember when you haul in the next big fish, according to Pearce:

> The newness (of a new client) is exhilarating, with all the intensity of puppy love; each party enamored with the other, impressed with the exciting new mix of ideas, personalities, and creativity; captivated by the freshness of it all. But exhilarating as it may be, it is a time fraught with danger. When knowledge is thin, disappointments can run deep. When everything is new, there's nothing tried and true to depend on. New client/agency relationships are a risk until the agency can earn trust and build an interdependent relationship. This is much more difficult than winning the pitch itself.

Pearce outlined 13 steps to make sure that new accounts stabilize into "client-agency relationships capable of growing and enduring":

1. *Screamin' teamin':* Make sure you assign exactly the right people, the right number of people, at the right level. Three rights can make a right.

2. *Know yourself:* Create clear assignments for every one of your team members.
3. *Know themselves:* It's just as important that everyone on the client side knows his or her role in this new relationship. Ask, then write it down for them; ask them to review it and commit to it.
4. *The wedding night manual:* It's important for both partners to sit down and review what I call the wedding night manual. (Not racy), it's a meeting with a detailed agenda designed to get the relationship on a solid footing.
5. *Show me the money:* We require a deposit before we begin work and that the contract is signed before the deposit runs out.
6. *Present; don't e-mail or fax:* Present all initial estimates, plans, and important ideas in person. (Don't e-mail) until (you're) comfortable that a relationship has been established.
7. *Have a success story:* It's important to break quickly and cleanly from the gate. Quickly complete one project so (you) have an immediate success under (your) belt. Pick the right goal; then achieve it.
8. *It's who you know:* Get to know the potential client's boss and co-workers during the review process and really turn up the heat as soon as the account is in hand. Think of it as flight insurance, keeping the account from taking flight if (your) client contact splits.
9. *ASAR:* Don't allow yourself to fall into the ASAP mode. (Chances are you'll eventually disappoint the client.) Accept only deadlines that are ASAR, "As Soon As Realistic."
10. *Don't bring Annie Sullivan:* No miracle workers allowed. Your new client's expectations run much deeper than time of delivery. You want these expectations to be on the high side of realistic, not the low side of impossible.
11. *Get some face time:* Schedule regular client meetings. Build weekly or twice-monthly meetings into the early phases of the budget.
12. *Baby steps:* (Avoid long-term planning until a relationship is established.) Start with baby steps, a short-term action plan with clear definitions of success. Then, when there's trust, move on to the Big Plan.

13. *No walk in the park:* Aggressively probe for red flags and immediately act on them. Periodically, ask your new client if they are satisfied with the work you're doing or if they question any of your procedures, charges, or programs.

And then count on things changing. Pearce believes there is a "six-month wall" in a new relationship. He recommends assessing your standing with the client carefully as you approach that wall to make sure that you pass through it with your client-agency relationship intact.

DEALING WITH PEOPLE WHO ALWAYS WANT A DEAL

To be able to provide clients with outstanding service, you must be paid fairly for your work. So, how should you handle the occasional prospect or client who wants to bargain with you over your costs; i.e., can you do the same amount of work or more for less money?

The answer to that question, consultant Alan Weiss, PhD, president, Summit Consulting Group, East Greenwich, Rhode Island, says is "No. Once you make a single concession on price, you've enabled a behavior which will inevitably cost you money and probably drive you crazy."

Writing in his e-newsletter, *Balancing Act* (at www.summitconsulting .com), Weiss says such requests generally come from owners of small companies who are used to haggling with everyone including their coffee vendor and employees of larger company purchasing/procurement departments who see their way to fame and fortune through cutting back on the fame and fortune of suppliers—namely, you.

Weiss recommends that you never offer a concession without a quid pro quo. (Gain something in return for what you're giving.) He notes that once you lower your fee, no matter how slightly, or delay a client's payment dates, no matter how little, you have opened Pandora's box. To cope with clients bent on gaining a deal, he suggests the following:

1. *Be prepared to deny the request and walk away.* If you don't call the client's bluff, you don't belong in the card game.

2. *Focus on the value proposition and the ROI.* When buyers are especially resistant to the price, but indicate they would go ahead with a price reduction, they're really saying that they believe you can help them, but they're not sure how much and want to hedge their bet.
3. *Turn the tables.* Ask the client if his or her organization concedes price on the company's product or service. If they indicate that they sometimes do, ask what they get in return: volume business; payment in advance; introduction to more clients? Then negotiate the same quid pro quo for your firm.
4. *Offer nonmonetary "concessions."* Some people just need the ego fulfillment of having received something for nothing or heavily reduced in price. Offer anything from a free book, to complementary quarterly updates, to free newsletter subscriptions. Provide something to salve their ego so it's not a "win/lose" proposition.
5. *Never allow an underling to reopen negotiations on any topic.* Never enter into a debate with a subordinate or nonbuyer, which is the equivalent of conceding a little bit on fees. If they find they can engage you, they'll take you on with a myriad of trivialities.
6. *Always provide options,* even to small businesses. If the buyer says, "I love option three, but the fee seems a bit high," reply, "That's why we have option two."
7. *Stop work if you're not paid on time.* "Deal-seekers" are famous for delaying payments to squeeze out extra work. If you're not paid in advance and a payment date has passed, allow 10 days and then stop working. Otherwise, you'll be in permanent debt to the company store.

PROFILE 9: STEVE HAWEELI

President, Wordhampton PR
East Hampton, New York

Steve Haweeli has a lot going for him.

- He owns the largest restaurant PR firm on Long Island; however, his largest client is a security firm.
- His restaurant clients don't mind that they compete with one another. More than 50 restaurants, wineries, and other attractions participate in the annual preseason Hamptons' Restaurant Week, which the agency created but from which it receives no revenue.
- Steve frequently takes a dip in the ocean before going to work, then showers off outside the building he owns and dresses for the day. He also can dash to the beach during the day to cool down if things get too hot.
- His firm's heavy workload between Memorial Day and Labor Day largely pays for the rest of the year.
- Despite the fact that his firm could only be described as a "small boutique," he has an extremely sophisticated approach to managing the business. He installed TimeSlips time and billing system several years ago and knows whether each relatively small fee client is profitable.
- His firm also is profitable; he pays himself and his small staff well and provides good employee benefits.

All this evolved from 17 years as a bartender and maitre d', an almost accidental venture into writing direct mail for Manhattan restaurants, and a request to write a press release. To which he had to ask, "What's a press release?"

Haweeli obviously is a quick learner; he spotted the market in the Hamptons and in 1992 opened Wordhampton PR. From charging $50 for his first press release and having no idea what his hourly rate was or should be, he has progressed to the point where a client paying $10,000 for a season's effort will be profitable.

He advises agency principals to "Install a time management system immediately and charge a realistic fee for your work."

Chapter 10

Management Strategies for Success

Every successful public relations firm principal walks a narrow tight rope. You must adroitly manage dual—and potentially conflicting—responsibilities. You must ensure that your firm provides the best possible client service. To accomplish this, you must manage, monitor, and/or participate in current client assignments. Simultaneously, you must protect and advance your bottom line by controlling costs, encouraging high staff productivity, and taking every opportunity to increase income and profits from current and new clients.

Assiduously following the track laid down by the following 10 management strategies will help ensure that these dual responsibilities are fulfilled and that the potential conflict is managed in a win-win fashion.

DEVELOP A PRACTICAL
LONG-RANGE BUSINESS PLAN

If you have not already done so, develop a long-range business plan to provide a direction for your future growth and a benchmark to measure your success. If you already have a plan, review it carefully and critically to make sure that it still fits your firm and accommodates changes in your firm's structure, goals, or markets. And then work the plan.

Your business plan should extend at least three to five years and should include such ingredients as

- a description of your firm;
- an analysis of your market;
- a portrait of your competition;
- an overview of current and planned services;

doi:10.1300/5561_10

- a marketing and sales plan;
- a personnel profile; and
- a pro-forma financial statement.

Don't write the plan and then abandon it in a file drawer. Refer to it regularly as a guide for your daily activities and as a perpetual reminder of your goals.

Update the plan at least annually. Incorporate changes in your organization; note additional current or potential markets; add, delete, or change the description of your competition; add new services you provide, and delete those that you no longer offer; update the description of your personnel, noting staff strengths and weaknesses and the type of personnel you may need in the future; revise your marketing plan to promote new services or reach new objectives; and project a realistic view of your firm's financial potential.

Analyze those aspects of your plan that have been productive and look for ways to strengthen them. Eliminate parts of the plan that have proved to be impractical or unrealistic.

Invite your key senior people to help develop or revise the plan. Involve your total staff in the success of your firm; make sure that everyone understands and supports your goals for the firm, the direction the firm is taking, the obstacles you face, and the part they play in overcoming the obstacles and achieving firm goals.

Be sure that everyone understands and appreciates what achieving these goals can mean to their own personal growth and security. Invite all employees to an annual "job holders" meeting to review the past year's progress and the next year's potential candidly and in detail.

ESTABLISH REASONABLE
REALISTIC GROWTH GOALS

Do you want to run a small, profitable firm where you can retain substantial hands-on contact with clients or build a larger firm where your management skills will be as valuable or even more valuable than your professional public relations skills? Decide if, how, and in what direction you want your firm to grow.

Project both profit and income goals. Growth goals of 15 to 20 percent annually are reasonable and realistic. Be sure to write your goals down. Research indicates that spelling out goals in writing helps ensure their achievement.

DEVELOP A STRATEGIC POSITION
OR MARKET NICHE

Public relations industry pundits foretell a future in which there are a few (perhaps 15 to 20) very large firms with global capabilities (usually combined with huge advertising agencies and other communications firms in a mammoth holding company) and thousands of successful small and medium-sized independent firms serving local, regional, and national needs and special market niches.

Unless you realistically expect to expand globally, pick your target market/s early on and concentrate your efforts on achieving recognition and success in those markets. However, be alert for opportunities and flexible enough to move quickly into new areas or phase out of markets that are drying up.

As part of your business plan, develop a strategic position for your firm. Describe what your firm is; what you want it to be; the kind of clients you want; and the markets you currently serve and those that offer opportunities.

Analyze your current capabilities and those you will need to move into opportunity markets. Delineate your strengths and corporate culture, the things that make your firm unique and memorable. Explore steps you can take to ensure that clients and prospects perceive your firm in step with reality. Community perception of your firm may lag as much as two years behind reality.

Ask your staff members to write a short description of your firm's unique characteristics and position, as they see them, or throw out the question during a staff meeting. Compare their appraisal with your own. Make sure all your employees can describe your firm in a similar manner. And consider asking your clients to describe the way they see your firm.

Write a 25-word description of your firm's strategic position and post it on your bulletin board. Decide what you will say when a prospect asks you to tell him or her the most significant thing about your firm—the thing that sets your firm apart from competition and is most important to your clients.

Promote your firm's strategic position, and make sure that everything you do aligns with, supports, or strengthens that position.

CONDUCT AN ONGOING MARKETING PROGRAM

Do for your firm what you do for your clients. Budget for and conduct an ongoing self-marketing program that includes such elements as publicity, literature, direct mail, and personal contact. See Chapter 4 for detailed self-marketing recommendations.

ESTABLISH A REPUTATION FOR INNOVATION, CREATIVITY, STRATEGIC SAVVY, AND MEANINGFUL RESULTS

Companies looking for a new public relations firm usually base their decision largely on three factors: personal chemistry or the culture compatibility between the prospect and the firm; the firm's strength in strategically driven creativity; and its ability to produce and demonstrate meaningful results.

Creativity tied to strong corporate or marketing strategies will win the prospect every day. "Big Ideas" or special events that do little more than generate unfocused media attention pale in comparison to a unique creative approach supporting a tight, targeted strategy. And more and more companies demand the latter.

In addition, clients increasingly refuse to put much value on or accept results whose only evidence is a book of clippings and a cassette of TV news clips. Instead, progressive public relations firms have developed an expanding array of techniques to measure and evaluate both "process or input" results (measured in terms of the total media impressions generated in support of specific objectives) and "outcome or impact" results (measured in terms of public changes in awareness, attitudes, and behavior).

Successful firms continually and persuasively merchandise their strength in strategically driven creativity as well as their ability to produce meaningful results that demonstrate the client's return on investment.

One excellent way to merchandise your strategic, creative, and results capabilities is to enter your best campaigns in local and national professional competitions. However, entering a competition deserves a full commitment of time and effort to ensure that your entry properly documents the details and success of the program. Any lesser, last-minute effort is a waste of time and money.

ENCOURAGE AND ENSURE
HIGH STAFF PRODUCTIVITY

One of the most common problems encountered by small and medium-sized firms particularly is low productivity, i.e., staff members billing less than an average of 85 percent of their time to clients. Low productivity can result from a number of factors, including

- poor management planning;
- faulty resource allocation;
- overstaffing;
- lack of enough business;
- well-meaning but overzealous management intentions to create good working conditions; and
- poor employee motivation.

It is not uncommon for a firm's average productivity to sink as low as 60 percent. Consider that, at only 60 percent billable, a single account executive billing at $150 per hour could cost your firm as much as $70,000 annually in lost income.

Ensuring firmwide high productivity, of course, requires that enough work is available on a continuing basis to keep people busy and that efforts are made to smooth out the cyclical nature of the agency business.

An ongoing marketing campaign (especially important when you are the busiest), proper and practical anticipation of client needs, and allocating work loads across all employees can do much to ensure high productivity.

However, consistent high productivity depends most critically on establishing and maintaining excellent staff morale and motivation. Employees need to understand, be recognized for, and be proud of their contribution to your firm's success. They need to develop a strong sense of their own self-worth. And they need to be trained and encouraged to anticipate high and low work loads and to balance their own productivity by getting help in handling peak loads or asking for additional work when their own client load is about to drop off. A high level of staff interdependence is essential to overall high productivity.

Here's a formula to help you determine the number of hours that professionals should be available to work annually:

2,080	Number of hours in a year at eight hours daily
(80)	Average two-week vacation (ten days)
2,000	
(80)	Average number of holidays (ten days)
1,920	
(40)	Average number of personal/sick days (five days)
1,880	Average number of hours available to work annually
@ 85%	Productivity/utilization goal
1,600	Billable hours at 85 percent

Based on an eight-hour day and 85 percent utilization, staff members can be expected to bill a maximum, on the average, of about 1,600 hours a year to clients. For planning purposes, use the conservative average of 1,400 hours for an eight-hour day.

At this writing, the average annual income generated nationally per professional is about $186,000. Higher hourly rates and tougher productivity requirements by larger international firms probably push the average to this figure. Most smaller independent firms, however, will do well to set a goal of at least $150,000 average income generated per professional. Determine your firm's specific average income per professional based on your average hourly rate and productivity average. The higher income generated per professional, the higher your agency profit will be.

Staff members will appreciate knowing their worth to the firm, and they need to understand and support your productivity expectations. Anything less than an average 80 to 85 percent productivity across the board means that your income and profit are less than they could and should be.

TRACK INDIVIDUAL CLIENT PROFITABILITY

To ensure overall profitability, you must be able to track and control the profitability of individual clients. You need to be aware of and able to root out profit leaks. If you don't already have a system to accomplish this, check out the variety of available time and billing software systems that can provide this information.

Most such systems are based on two major factors: the salary/benefits-cost-to-income ratio for each client and a standard percentage share of firm overhead assigned to each client. Depending on client needs, you can control individual client profitability by adjusting the salary cost ratio. The lower the salary-to-income ratio percentage, the higher your profits will be. Ratios below 30 to 33 percent will ensure good profitability. The Golden Rule (Golden as in "dollars"), of course, is to ensure that, while maintaining excellent client service, the most highly qualified, least costly, staff members do most of the work.

Flat fees or retainers, though comforting from a cash flow standpoint, can quickly and easily become unprofitable through overservicing. If you can't make an account profitable, consider resigning the client!

CHARGE A FAIR AND ADEQUATE PRICE
FOR YOUR SERVICES

Public relations firms are forbidden by law to discuss or exchange information on the hourly rates that they charge in any way that could be construed as price fixing. The reality is that most firms have a pretty good idea of prevailing rates in their area. And the fact is that you don't do yourself any favors—you won't gain many additional clients—solely by charging rates lower than the area standards.

Clients, particularly those more experienced and sophisticated, seldom fret over an agency's hourly rates. They are more concerned with the results that can be produced within their budget. If a client is worried about hourly rates, he or she can always find someone, such as a freelancer, who is willing to work for less money.

Don't sell yourself cheap. Charge competitive rates, but don't be afraid to raise them. Clients raise prices on their products for a multitude of reasons. And most clients do not expect you to operate as a nonprofit organization.

Bear this in mind. A $5.00 per hour increase in your rates can mean at least an additional $7,000 income annually per person!

CONTROL COSTS

It's this simple; the best way to control costs is to avoid mistakes, whether by management or staff. Committing your firm to too much or too expensive space, costly furnishings, or excessive salaries are management mistakes that can be avoided with a little forethought. (Most firms use a salary-to-income ratio of 50 percent as a goal and try to hold rent costs between 7 and 12 percent of income.)

Constantly and carefully examine and justify every overhead item. Arrange for the best possible deal on insurance and other employee benefits. Watch travel and entertainment expenses. Charge all possible costs back to your clients.

Train and motivate employees to avoid human mistakes that cost you money. Reprinting a client brochure or redistributing a press release because of a typo or incorrect information takes a chunk out of your bottom line. (And doesn't do a whole lot for client relations or your agency's professional reputation.)

USE YOUR TIME EFFICIENTLY AND PRODUCTIVELY

Sooner or later, as your firm grows, to control and ensure firm growth and profitability, you will need to spend less time on client service and more time on firm management.

The closer you are to reaching or topping $1 million in annual income, the more attention you should pay to managing your business. (A firm owner with profit problems once told me that she "hated to waste time looking at time sheets." Once she did—and corrected the problems she uncovered—her profit problems also were corrected.)

Carving out time for agency management tasks provides the flexibility and latitude to monitor and manage critical profit factors as well as develop and lead a proactive marketing program. Schedule regular and uninterrupted time to address problems and opportunities. Try not to spend more than half your time on client service; use the rest to manage and market your firm.

Follow these 10 management strategies religiously and relentlessly—and provide the best possible service to your clients—and your growth and profitability will be ensured.

Without attention to good management principles and practices, your firm's future will be dimmer than you'd like—even with excellent client service.

It's your choice!

PROFILE 10: JONNI HEGENDERFER

President, JSH&A
Chicago, Illinois

Headquartered in a Chicago suburb, JSH&A Inc. matches competitive strength, creative wits, and sterling reputation with large downtown international firms. Named a runner-up "Boutique of the year" by *PR Week,* the firm offers clients a unique brand of LIF™Style public relations and proudly proclaims, "We look at how people really live." ("LIF" derives from "Life Influence Factors," which, president Jonni Hagenderfer says, "generate consumer preferences and drive decisions.")

JHS&A backs up this claim with research to study socioeconomic, age, and gender groups, such as seniors and women, examining how people live, the things that are important to them, and how that relates to their buying decisions. This approach has helped the firm win a number of big name consumer clients including Jim Beam Brands, McDonald's, and Allied Van Lines.

In a second specialty, the firm provides issue management counsel and service to such companies as Clarke Mosquito Control.

In 1989, Hegenderfer left her post as a Golin/Harris International senior vice president for an opportunity to have more control over her future and the challenge of creating a business with her personal vision, values, and priorities.

From the first year's $75,000 fee income, the agency has grown to more than $2 million. Hegenderfer's early lessons included learning to keep close track of time and expenses and make sure bills get out promptly. While she squirms at the difficulty of self-promotion, her firm advertises widely and uses direct mail productively. JSH&A's unique approach to LIF™Style PR is regularly featured in business and trade magazines and local newspaper articles.

Hegenderfer advises new PR firm principals to create a network of business consultants and "supporters" who can provide insight into running a small business. To earn client accolades, "Do the jobs that no one else wants, but that are important to clients," she suggests.

Chapter 11

Managing Time and People

As the principal of a successful public relations firm, you should, at all times, be able to answer two basic and critical questions:

1. What are my three most serious problems; how am I/how will I deal with them?
2. What are my three best opportunities; how will I take advantage of them?

Unfortunately, you may be so involved—so dedicated—to serving the daily needs of your clients, scratching out whatever business that falls in the door, and performing routine duties, such as paying bills and meeting a payroll, that you fail to take time to think thoughtfully about long-range problems and opportunities. Or to establish priorities to help you solve your problems and take advantage of your opportunities.

Establishing and adhering to priorities require that you manage your time—and that of your staff members—aggressively and productively. The more efficiently and aggressively you manage your personal time, the more valuable you will be, both to your clients and to your agency. To help become more efficient and effective, keep a running list of your three most serious problems and your three best opportunities as they relate to either your clients or your agency. Keep this list flexible and current.

PRIORITIZE PROBLEMS AND OPPORTUNITIES

Assign priorities to your problems. Here are three suggested priority categories:

doi:10.1300/5561_11

1. *Pressing:* Solve it now, this instant, or face disaster.
2. *Probable:* It's a problem, but you have a jury-rig fix on it, and it probably won't explode immediately.
3. *Potential:* You can see this one coming, but you have a little time to get ready for it.

How do your current problems fit these priorities?
Do the same with your opportunities. Here are three ways to prioritize opportunities:

1. *Immediate:* If you don't jump on it now, it will disappear forever.
2. *Real:* It's there, but you have a little time to decide how to approach it.
3. *Potential:* This one may or may not exist unless you make it happen.

Okay? Ready, get set, go! Move on that fat opportunity.

DO IT NOW

To manage your time more aggressively, start with a "do it now" attitude. Attack even the most difficult or disagreeable tasks quickly. As the man said, "If you have to swallow a frog, don't look at it too long." Don't let distasteful tasks linger; get them out of the way quickly.

Live with a daily "to do" list tied to your priority problems and opportunities. Decide what has to be done and when, and list priorities. Focus on the 20 percent of your effort that reaps 80 percent of the results. Teach and delegate routine work instead of feeling comfortable doing it all.

Revise your lists daily; change priorities as required. Analyze "to do" lists against priorities. Take 15 minutes each day to plan the next day. Continually ask, "What is the best use of my time *now?*"

DEAL WITH PAPER

Computers were supposed to create paperless offices and make waste baskets obsolete. Didn't happen! Despite all the electronic marvels, paper continues to accumulate. And there are still only three things you can do with a piece of paper: Pitch it, file it, or act on it (even if you only send it to someone else). Number three is preferable.

Lots of people love paper. Piles of it on their desk give them a feeling of security. Rotund Royal Plenty was the former *Philadelphia Bulletin* business editor and a crackerjack investor relations pro in my Philadelphia PR firm. But the piles of paper on his desk left room only for one 8 1/2 by 11 sheet of paper on which he scratched edits. Royal claimed he couldn't get used to not sweeping his desktop clean to the floor every night after writing his daily newspaper column. So he just left it there. But he could find everything he needed. In his honor and to shame other careless souls, we created the "Royal Plenty Trash Award" and hung the engraved plaque outside erring practitioners' sloppy offices until they got the message.

The message is, make short work of paperwork. Here are some suggestions that you may have heard before:

- Pick up each piece of paper only once; try to do what has to be done with it the first time.
- Avoid new memos; write informal replies on the same sheet of paper.
- Don't let paper clutter your desk; throw away all the paper you can; file what you must keep; a good memory saves file-retrieval time.

USE TIME WELL

It's an old cliché that once time has passed, you can never get it back; that time is gone. The way you use your time will have a big impact on the success of your agency. Here are some suggestions:

- Avoid interruptions and delays; answer your own phone and make your own calls (unless you're under a deadline).
- Set ground rules with your receptionist about handling calls and unscheduled visitors when you're busy or in a meeting.
- Be punctual; expect others to be.
- Put dead time to use; do something productive when you're traveling in a plane, waiting in a lobby, or otherwise twiddling your thumbs.

- Get in the "inside-lunch" habit.
- Make the most of meetings: set agendas and distribute them in advance; make sure every meeting generates action to solve problems; if there's nothing for an agenda, cancel the meeting.

And, finally, stop believing in the virtue of "busyness" for its own sake. Don't mistake activity for accomplishment. Don't credit the most harried individual—even if that's you—with being the hardest working. Vow to work smarter instead of just harder.

MANAGE STAFF PRODUCTIVITY

A PR firm's primary source of income is the time its employees invest in behalf of clients at varying hourly rates. Ensuring that employees maintain the highest possible level of billable time (high productivity) is one of your most important responsibilities. High productivity hinges on pleasant working conditions, good employee morale, and strong staff self-motivation. Both junior and senior practitioners should be empowered with the responsibility and authority to do whatever is necessary to meet performance standards and achieve client and firm goals.

ALLOCATE STAFF RESOURCES

Allocating the human resources of your firm properly—deciding who is going to do what and when—is an essential element of good agency management. Whether you do it for one, several, or all your clients, you must plan, assign, and balance work loads so that you can balance income flow and avoid problems caused by the cyclical nature of the agency business.

Proper allocation of work loads also helps keep average staff productivity high and provides a guideline to determine both short- and long-term staff needs.

Remember the importance of averages when you are allocating staff resources:

1. Everything works on averages over a period of time.
2. Allocation of staff time should be based on the average income generated by individuals or the average billable hour potential.

Determine overall and individual staff productivity averages. Taking into account average individual productivity and average hourly rates, determine the amount of income that the average practitioner can be expected to generate in a year. Multiple this figure by your total number of professional staff members. This represents the total time that can be assigned to clients and the total income that can be generated at your current staff level.

3. Example: As noted earlier, at this writing, a professional staff member can be expected to generate an average of about $150,000 per year in income. (Your hourly rates, billable averages, and competitive situation will determine your actual income generated per professional.)

Here is how the formula works (Note: The figures are conservative and rounded off):

1,880	Average number of hours an individual is actually available to work in 12 months based on eight hours per day. Subtract vacations, holidays, sick days, and other time off from the 2080 total number of hours in a year. (See Chapter 10.)
1,600	Average number of hours an individual can be expected to bill to clients at 85 percent billable.
$150,000	1,600 hours times average hourly rate of $95. (Your average hourly rate may be higher and/or your billable average may be lower than 85 percent.)

Tables 11.1 and 11.2 show the staff allocation matrix that I used for about fifteen years while managing agencies. I thought that I had invented it until I discovered that other firms used the same system. The matrix can be used in both short- and long-range planning for both multiple and single clients and projects. It also takes into account staff capabilities, available staff time, and specific client needs and budget.

The matrix can be designed and applied in pencil (to be changed frequently) or designed as a computerized Excel "what-if" template. Here's how the matrix works:

TABLE 11.1. Resource allocation matrix—Multiple clients.

Client	Mgr.	Helen	Ralph	Shirley	Paul	Time shortage	Time allocated	Annual budget/ fee
SMI	5,000	40,000			15,000		60,000	60,000
ABC	15,000		40,000	20,000	25,000		100,000	100,000
JON		10,000			30,000		40,000	40,000
WID				25,000			25,000	25,000
XYZ	10,000		10,000		20,000		40,000	40,000
COM			20,000		10,000		30,000	30,000
HOS	10,000	30,000		10,000			50,000	50,000
PIC	5,000	20,000		15,000			40,000	40,000
PEN				35,000			35,000	35,000
INK	10,000			15,000		15,000	25,000	40,000
DRI	10,000					30,000	10,000	40,000
PRO	10,000		(Pro bono—not billable)				0	0
NBD	45,000	10,000	(New business—not billable)				0	0
SHO	10,000		60,000		20,000	10,000	90,000	100,000
NET	20,000	40,000	10,000			30,000	70,000	100,000
FOL	10,000	20,000		60,000		10,000	90,000	100,000
Total	160,000	170,000	140,000	180,000	120,000	95,000	705,000	800,000

Note: Figures represent billable hours converted to dollars.

Problems:

1. Helen is overbooked; so is Shirley.
2. Ralph and Paul are underbooked.
3. Shirley is assigned to too many accounts.
4. Paul may be too junior or too specialized.
5. You are about two-thirds of a person short to meet all client needs and earn all the income budgeted over this twelve-month period.

Solutions:

1. The manager may have to reduce time spent on new business to spend more time on client service.
2. Shift some of Shirley's accounts to Paul, or replace Paul if he can't handle additional work.
3. Reduce or eliminate Helen's time on pro bono work.
4. Don't accept any project work until you get increased staff flexibility.
5. Line up freelancers to handle projects or heavy loads.
6. Look at the timetable of scheduled activities to determine if and when an additional experienced professional will be needed. Begin recruiting and interviewing.

TABLE 11.2. Resource allocation matrix, individual client—SHO.

Activity	Mgr.	Ralph	Paul	Time shortage	Time allocated	Income
Planning		2,000	5,000		7,000	7,000
Supv.	5,000	10,000			15,000	15,000
New prod.		20,000			20,000	20,000
Features			10,000		10,000	10,000
Releases			5,000		5,000	5,000
Press conference	3,000	10,000			13,000	13,000
Media tour		4,000			4,000	4,000
VNR		4,000			4,000	4,000
Brochure				10,000	0	10,000

Note: Figures are billable hours converted to dollars.

Problems: No one has time to write the brochure; Paul is also scheduled for some heavy writing chores on client COM that will conflict with his writing chores here.

Solution: Bring in a freelancer to handle writing assignments on several accounts, including the SHO brochure.

1. The ingredients
   a. List all your clients by three-letter initials down the left-hand column.
   b. List your professional staff members across the top.
   c. List client budgets or fee income down the far right column.
2. The process
   a. Determine the amount of time required or available from assigned individuals for each account. (Use either hours or hours converted to dollars.)
   b. Assign dollars (or hours) per individual to meet individual client needs.
   c. Note both continuing needs and special short-term projects.
   d. In the second from the right column, add the total time allocated to each client against budget.
   e. Add the assigned time for each individual at the bottom of each column.

f. Determine shortfalls, overages, and problems.
g. Update the matrix weekly, monthly, and annually.

Look ahead, on a structured basis, at both broad needs and individual client activity periods. Both management and staff members can be involved in projecting the amount of time required to service an account as well as the expected income. Making adjustments in staff assignments on a weekly, monthly, quarterly, and annual basis lets you spot and handle problems before they occur—and helps ensure smooth agency operations and satisfied clients.

DELEGATE RESPONSIBILITY AND AUTHORITY

One of the hardest things for many agency principals to learn or accept is delegation. They like to keep their hands on the wheel at all times. Can't let go. However, to be the most efficient and effective, you will need to delegate both responsibility and authority: responsibility to do the job and authority to get it done.

The need to delegate applies to account executives as well as senior management. Letting someone else do it, when you're sure you could do it better, can be a bitter chore. You can find lots of *reasons* why "I have to do it myself":

1. I have to make sure it gets done right.
2. The client wants me to do it.
3. No one else has the time.
4. I have to do it so we won't go over budget.
5. I can do it better than anyone else.
6. It's faster to do it myself than to show someone.
7. I need something to do to look busy.
8. I don't want anyone else to know how to do it.
9. I don't want anyone else to know agency secrets.
10. I don't get to have any fun.
11. I like to do it.

If you've found yourself using any of these reasons (even subconsciously) to avoid delegating a task or responsibility, catch yourself by the back of the neck and give yourself a good shake.

Why Delegate?

Delegating responsibility and authority to other people frees up your time for things that only you really can do or, at least, do better than others. Remember the rule that says you make the most profit when the most highly competent, least costly people do most of the work.

In addition, and more important, people need increased independence and increased responsibility in order to grow. They grow by being taught, tested, and critiqued and by observing, experimenting, and doing. By delegating responsibility and authority to others, you will set a pattern for your senior people to follow and for others to copy.

How to Delegate

Let's be clear about it; delegation does not mean lowering quality standards. Repeat: delegation does not mean lowering quality standards! Follow these steps to ensure that quality is maintained while people are encouraged to stretch their minds and professional muscles.

1. Review the client's needs. What level of skill will be required to complete the task?
2. Evaluate the practitioner's ability, and determine the amount and level of supervision required.
3. Set standards for the assignment; outline the results required.
4. Inform and instruct the practitioner; establish a realistic timetable for completion of the project.
5. Be flexible on the method and approach to be used. There are many ways to do things, not all of them the same as you would use. And that's not all bad.
6. Evaluate the effort. Be positive. Discuss changes. Offer suggestions and guidance. Do not redo the job yourself (unless you are absolutely out of time and budget).
7. Protect the agency; provide a protective but inconspicuous oversight. Let the less-experienced person function on his own as much and as long as possible. Monitor; be aware of progress toward deadline. Don't threaten or pressure.

8. Be willing to risk—up to the point where you decide that you must step in immediately to avoid disaster. I cannot tell you what that point will be. However, you will know when you hit it. Go just a bit beyond your first warning before you step in or yank the assignment away.

PROFILE 11: ANNE KLEIN

President, Anne Klein & Associates
Mt. Laurel, New Jersey

Klein left the Sun Company in 1982 after 16 years of corporate, nonprofit, and agency PR experience; the shrinking oil industry made her job security appear tenuous. However, she left with a one-year contract from Sun for her new PR agency. Operating from offices in the basement of her home, the firm's first year income hit $43,000; it's grown to 10 employees and more than $1 million in revenue.

Anne Klein & Associates handles a wide range of communications challenges, including market positioning, community outreach, and change communications in addition to issues, crisis, and reputation management. (Klein's expertise in crisis communications can be seen in her insightful contribution to this book's chapter on "Crisis Planning for PR Firms.")

Lessons learned during her firm's early years, according to Klein:

The owner of a firm cannot do everything or be involved in everything; working from home can only last so long if you want to grow; and managing the finances and growing the business are as important as delivering excellent service.

We live by the rule "good enough is not good enough." But I learned that clients won't pay for the ultimate (in service).

I also learned that no one can build your business for you. You can listen and learn, hire consultants, but, in the end, you build your business in the image you have for yourself. Before you start your firm, be sure you like to sell, have a strong network of potential referral sources, and, above all, have a good professional reputation.

Love your existing clients; be visible; court your colleagues and potential clients. Schedule more time off of short duration rather than one long vacation—you can never look tired.

Chapter 12

Systems and Procedures

Flying an airplane by the seat of the pilot's pants went out of favor with the advent of aircraft that could fly faster than pilots could think. PR firm principals face much the same type of problem.

Things move too fast in the agency business for you to guess where you've been and where you're going. While you are still trying to figure out whether you made any money last month, the waters of disaster may be lapping at your nose.

To keep your firm on the right track, you need administrative systems and procedures that generate business progress data, ensure tight cost controls, track profitability and productivity, and help you report promptly and properly to clients. Such systems can range from an online computerized daily time report to a method of establishing hourly billing rates that return a specific profit to a method of evaluating your firm's overall performance.

Unfortunately, principals with great entrepreneurial instincts and professional strengths may lack the self-discipline to see the value of or adhere to such administrative parameters. Big mistake!

CLIENT AGREEMENTS

In addition to trust, confidence, and chemistry, the foundation of every client-agency relationship should be a signed agreement stipulating the beginning date of the relationship, the terms of the agreement, the services to be performed, the financial arrangements agreed upon, a "hold harmless" clause, and the conditions under which the agreement will be extended or terminated.

doi:10.1300/5561_12

There may be occasions when the signing of such an agreement is delayed while the client's legal counsel earns his or her pay. However, you tempt fate by investing any substantial time or money in the new client's behalf until all signatures have been applied.

I learned this lesson painfully when my agency began working for a state-mandated but farmer-funded organization while the client's legal counsel "studied" the contract we had proposed. Weeks went by with no signed contract. "You know how lawyers are," the client contact explained several times. By then, we had invested thousands of dollars worth of time in the client's behalf.

Then, we were called into a meeting with the organization's executive director. Barricaded behind his desk, the client solemnly advised us that state law forbid any work to be done for his organization by outside agencies before a contract was signed. With a straight face, he said that since he had not signed a contract, he obviously had never assigned us to do any work—this, despite an inch-thick file of conference reports. (We learned later that the executive director was madly back-pedaling to forestall being fired for violating state regulations.)

However, he said, his attorney would be happy to negotiate an agreement with our attorney. Stunned, and sitting on $75,000 worth of unpaid invoices, we submitted to the negotiation charade. *Three months later,* we signed a 10-page agreement! The next day we received a letter terminating our services. (We envisioned the client breathing a sigh of relief at his close call with a pink slip.) We ended up collecting about half of the amount due.

Moral number 1: Never begin work for a client who hesitates to sign an agreement immediately.

Moral number 2: Never be a client's first PR agency, if you can avoid it. The hassle can drive you bonkers.

You should consult your attorney in the preparation of an agency-client agreement format that follows your state laws. Exhibit 12.1 is a sample letter of agreement that you may want to adapt for your use.

Some clients may object to individual paragraphs, such as the interest penalty clause, in an agreement like this. Depending on how strongly you feel about such clauses, you may want to question whether you should establish a relationship with a client who nitpicks an agreement. And when your new client says he hasn't signed the agreement because "Our attorney still has it," believe that about as much as the one about the check being in the mail.

EXHIBIT 12.1. Sample Agency-Client Agreement

Dear _____ :

This letter, when signed by both parties, will constitute the agreement between us with regard to our representation as your public relations agency.

1. We agree to serve as your public relations agency in connection with the implementation of a public relations program in your behalf. As your agency, we will provide you with counsel on the public relations aspects of your policies, programs, and goals. In addition, we will perform other public relations and marketing-related activities.
2. For our services and outlays in your behalf, the basis of our compensation shall be as follows:
   a. For all counseling, planning, writing, and placement services, we shall be entitled to:
      • A minimum advance fee of $ _____ per _____ for staff time charges.
      • Charges for services of our staff members will be made at then-standard hourly rates for officers and staff as they are required to carry out the programs and activities approved by you. Staff time charges incurred in any month will be applied against the minimum fee. Any staff time charges incurred above the minimum will be billed at then-existing standard rates.
   b. On all artwork and mechanical items purchased by us for you on your authorization, including printing, typesetting, photography, artwork, and specialty items, you agree to pay us our cost plus the standard commission of 17.65 percent.
   c. You will reimburse us at cost for such outlays made by us in your behalf as travel, telephone, telegram, facsimile transmission, messenger, copies, freight, postage, taxes, and similar expenditures.
   d. At our option, we may require advance payment by you for large out-of-pocket expenditures. You agree to pay same promptly upon request from us.

3. The following billing and due dates shall be in effect unless otherwise specified and agreed upon between us:
   a. The monthly fee will be due and payable within ten (10) days from date of receipt of invoice.
   b. Travel costs, messenger, postage, and other similar expenditures (see 2.c above) will be invoiced as incurred. All invoices are payable within ten (10) days of receipt of invoice.
   c. Payment for production invoices is due ten (10) days from receipt of invoice.
   d. On invoices for which payment is not received within 30 days, you agree to pay us simple interest computed at the prime rate plus 1.5 percent per annum on the amount outstanding after 30 days of the invoice date until such payment is received.
   e. In the event that you question the validity of a charge by us, payment for only that portion under question may be delayed without penalty, provided you express your objection in writing within twenty (20) days of the date of the invoice.
   f. At our option, we may suspend work on your account should any invoice remain unpaid beyond sixty (60) days from date of said invoice.
4. We agree that any and all contracts, correspondence, books, accounts, and other sources of information relating to your business shall be available for inspection at our office by your authorized representative during ordinary business hours upon reasonable prior notice by you to us of your desire to inspect same.
5. Following in-person or telephone conferences between your representative and ours in which decisions are made concerning actions or work to be performed, we will submit a conference report summarizing decisions made. Unless you object in writing (or via e-mail) to the conference report within three (3) business days, that report will be considered an accurate summary of the conference.
6. The terms of this agreement shall commence on _____ _____ and will continue unless and until terminated by either party on not less than ninety (90) days' prior written notice

to the other, delivered by registered or certified mail. The rights, duties, and responsibilities of the parties hereto shall continue in full force until the expiration of the term.

7. Upon the expiration of this agreement, no rights or liabilities shall arise out of this relationship, except that any noncancelable contract made on your authorization and still existing at the expiration of the term shall be carried to completion by us and paid for by you in accordance with the provisions herein, unless mutually agreed in writing to the contrary.

8. Upon the termination of this contract and receipt of final payments, we shall transfer, assign, and make available to you or your representative all property and materials in our possession or control that belong to you.

9. We agree to indemnify you with respect to any claims or actions for libel, slander, defamation, copyright infringement, idea misappropriation, or invasion of rights of privacy arising out of any materials that have been prepared by us on your behalf, except that if any such claim or action is based upon materials supplied by you to us, then, in such event, the aforesaid shall not apply, and, in turn, you will indemnify and hold us harmless with respect thereto. In addition, we agree to indemnify you with respect to any other claims or actions based upon the contents of any publicity material prepared by us without your approval, and you agree to indemnify us with respect to any such claims or actions based upon the content of any such materials that have been supplied by you to us.

10. We covenant and agree that we:

    a. Shall keep confidential any and all information concerning your business and operation that becomes known to us by reason of the performance of our services as your public relations agency and that you advise us in writing that you consider to be confidential in nature.

    b. Shall not disclose any such confidential information to any person outside our employ unless to do so is required in connection with the performance of our services, and, in such event, we agree to utilize our best efforts to obtain from any such suppliers a similar agreement to maintain such information as confidential.

    c. Shall obtain from our employees who in the performance of services on your behalf may become privy to any such confidential information, a similar covenant and agreement to keep confidential all such information.

11. You agree not to hire or retain directly or indirectly any person employed full time by this agency during the terms of this agreement or for one year after termination of this agreement unless we approve in writing or you pay the agency equivalent of twice the employee's annual salary at time of separation from this agency. "Indirectly" includes you hiring or contracting with another firm that employs an individual employed by us.

If the above meets with your approval, kindly indicate your consent by signing where indicated below.

           Very truly yours,
           AGENCY NAME
           By _____
           Title _____

ACCEPTED AND AGREED:
By _____
Title _____
Date _____

ESTABLISHING CLIENT-AGENCY EXPECTATIONS

There are few more teeth-grinding, nerve-fraying, sanity-sapping experiences than trying to work efficiently, effectively, and profitably for a client who has no public relations experience or experience in working with an agency.

Mental trauma can occur especially when you are the client's first agency. In such cases, the words *realistic* and *expectations* seldom appear in context or in client-agency discussions.

Another threat to agency principals' mental balance is the client executive who, although several layers removed from his or her company's day-to-day PR activities, wields control over PR programs, budgets, and invoice approval and who can wipe out a recommended program with an infuriating shake of his head or drive you silly by nitpicking invoices to bits.

It also may be true, as some bitter souls contend, that clients begin to hate (and/or fear) their agency immediately upon hiring it. Your client contact may have had a bad experience with a previous agency and is anticipating a similar disappointment. He may not have been comfortable with his role in the agency selection process or may doubt his ability to move the agency swiftly and productively into the traces.

The PR executive may have promised senior executives that the agency could and would produce great wonders. Everyone may be waiting eagerly for your first big media hit. They also may be holding their breath in anticipation of your first big bill. And you're still celebrating the win!

If you should become embroiled in one or more of these unhappy circumstances, you are likely on the way to becoming an endangered species. The truth is that too-great, often-unrealistic expectations are the norm and too frequently the cause of serious client-agency fall out.

One of the best ways to prevent or diminish such friction is to teach the client what he or she can realistically expect from the agency and what the agency expects from its clients. Do it early on, before the relationship has time to sour. As Tom Gable, chairman, GCS Public Relations, San Diego, California, puts it in his firm's *Client Service Manual:*

> Since agencies toil in the field of communication, they should be clever enough to tactfully share with clients some instructions that reflect the client's part in building strong unions. While this sharing won't necessarily be accomplished in a single document or afternoon, the points should be made. For instance, an agency can suggest that its clients:
>
> • Pay bills promptly. If there is a question or concern, deal with it right away.
> • Adjust expectations to reality and rely on the agency for "reality checks" as to where the company is headed vis-à-vis the market and its competition.
> • Be a partner with the agency; work together for mutual success.

- Allow the agency to make a fair profit on the business.
- Avoid seeking something for nothing. Expect to pay for program development and creative thought.
- Set clear business objectives upon which the agency can build its program in the client's behalf; a client should not expect the agency to write its marketing and business plan (unless hired and paid for that purpose).
- Be responsive and available, both for approvals and media contact.
- Respect the professionalism of agency staff and match it internally.
- Appreciate that the agency will never know as much about your business as you do; nor should it be expected to. Benefit from its independent point of view and ability to translate the essence of your business for multiple audiences.
- If not a public relations executive, learn the basics of the profession. (Reprinted with permission of Tom Gable.)

RELATIONSHIP COVENANT

You also may want to insert a "Relationship Covenant" into your standard letter of agreement. The covenant could read as follows:

We understand that you expect the agency to invest a consistently high level of skill, creativity, and professional performance in your behalf so as to generate a substantial return on your investment and advance your business objectives. We also understand that you expect to receive timely, honest, and descriptive invoices that are supported by meaningful back-up information. We are committed to the fulfillment of these expectations.

In return, we will expect high levels of understanding, support, patience, and professionalism as well as realistic performance requirements from you. We expect to be paid promptly.

The realization of these mutual expectations will provide the core and sustenance of a mutually satisfying and long-lasting relationship between our organizations.

Clients are seldom reluctant to outline their expectations (if they know them) or to complain when they are not met. It therefore seems appropriate and realistic that agencies follow suit. Performance and commitment on both sides are keys to good client-agency relationships. But the client may never know what you expect in terms of his performance and commitment . . . unless you tell him.

TECHNOLOGY IN PR FIRM MANAGEMENT

I am indebted for the following section on the use of technology in PR firm management to long-time friend and client William Boehlke, a principal in Connecting Point Communications, a San Francisco technology specialist firm. When in doubt, ask an expert. Says Bill:

> Surveys of clients indicate that the perception of low value for the money is the greatest marketing problem faced by our industry. In response, PR firms must continue to identify ways to achieve more results for the budget dollar. I believe that you must plan to invest roughly ten percent of fee income in technology (for capital equipment, supplies, and labor) every year in order to improve client service, maintain profit margins and give clients more results for the money each year.
>
> Your staff should be working on networked personal computers, with a cluster of servers delivering shared services. Despite the people we see typing in Starbucks, I think the age of the laptop has passed. They are expensive. They break almost annually if you're traveling with them, and they get stolen. You can give each of your staff two more powerful desktop computers for less money than a comparable laptop. The combination of the Internet and handheld devices does the same work in different ways.
>
> Instead of laptops, consider combining desktop machines with Blackberrys or comparable devices from other manufacturers. I like the Blackberry because I use Microsoft Office, and the Blackberry gives me a cell phone that delivers my office e-mail and calendar information. In addition, your users should have what are called roaming profiles, so they can log on to any computer on the network and have it act as their personal machine. Then, if they are traveling to a remote office, there's no

need to carry a laptop unless they are planning to do a lot of writing from a hotel room. You can handle that need with a single shared laptop that people check in and check out.

A network is still the single most important prerequisite for a substantial return on your investment in technology. The network is the infrastructure that lets you do things that make you more productive. You need high-speed Internet access as well as a local area network.

When considering Internet service providers, be sure to ask what service level they provide. Once you have electronic mail, Web-based research, and perhaps even your telephone service on your network, your business needs a broadband connection to the outside world every day. Consumer services like DSL and cable are priced like relative bargains. The cost comes once every couple of years when they go down and you're out of business for a couple of days because their only obligation to you is that they won't charge you for the time you don't have service. That's not good enough when you have a report that has to go out. Business class service like T1 costs more every month, but the provider contracts with you that the service will be there.

You and your clients need to be connected because public relations is collaborative; a single copy of all shared information must be immediately accessible to the professionals who need it, inside the firm or at your client's. Shared information should be delivered through one or more centralized databases. In the early days of public relations, practitioners considered the Rolodex a strategic asset. Today, the database does the same job, better. Every practitioner should have access to the complete history of all the firm's contacts with the rest of the world.

Research is another area where technology continues to have a big impact. Your people should have World Wide Web access to media coverage, preferably on a fixed cost basis so you can let everyone use it without risking a huge bill. When information is free and easy to access, it gets used for activities ranging from coverage reviews to competitive analysis.

Your computers also can help you manage your business better. Job cost software has come a long way in the past decade. It's more than daily information about what your employees worked on and billed to your clients. Software should keep you current on the status of all your sales opportunities. It gives managers a quick way to make detailed work assignments to staff members, helps keep everyone on track to produce the results you told your clients to expect, and can even help you coordinate your recruiting activities with your new business pipeline.

The breakthrough productivity opportunity for agencies today is the telephone. Stockbrokers record every telephone call with the outside world, for training and to verify transactions. So should you. Your people are on the phone much of their day, and you need to know that they are delivering quality work.

Integrated telephony is not as hard or as expensive as it used to be. A call is just another computer task if you move to digital telephony. That makes tying your computer system and telephones together affordable now for most firms. Look for Voice-over IP technology and prepare to be amazed at the possibilities.

Information technology will help agencies deliver more results for the same client budget dollar every year. Firm principals who plan to grow beyond a few clients should have a plan for managing this area of their business, or they won't stay in business. (Reprinted with permission of William Boehlke.)

COST ACCOUNTING
("THE GOSPEL ACCORDING TO HARRY")

A few years ago (actually, more than a few), when I was learning to manage a profitable public relations firm, the guru of "Cost Accounting and Budgetary Control" was Harry Cooper, vice president, finance, Hill & Knowlton. Cooper wrote a monograph published by the Public Relations Society of America's Counselors Academy that outlined the basic systems and procedures needed by a well-managed public relations firm.

Some forty years later, the "Gospel According to Harry" is still being sung by the choir (without many of the choir members knowing where the words and music came from). Cooper's dictums are applied by many PR firms, perhaps by most well-managed firms. If you are a member of the Counselors Academy, I recommend that you get a copy of his monograph, which may still be in print when you read this. If you are not a member, it's worth joining just to get your hands on Cooper's masterpiece.

According to Cooper, your accounting and budget control systems should generate the following:

1. The basis for accurately billing your clients for the services you provide
2. A monthly tabulation of your firm's operating income and expenses (Expenses will be of two types: [A] a cost to the firm or [B] outside purchases that will be rebilled to clients.)
3. The means to determine whether your payroll costs are chargeable (to clients) or nonchargeable (having to do with time off or administrative, new business, or agency chores)
4. Monthly reports of both overall profitability (or loss) and individual client profitability

Four things that you will need to know regularly and accurately are the number of dollars that the firm generates through hourly time billing and markup of outside purchases; the amount of overall profit that the firm earns (both pre- and posttaxes); the amount of profit earned on each client; and the level of productivity (billable hours) for the firm and individual staff members.

TIME REPORTS

Since the days when B.C. Neanderthal and Associates hunter-gatherers chiseled a record of their billable hours on stone tablets, public relations agency practitioners and support staff have historically fought—and often neglected—the necessity to account for their daily time in small increments, usually of 15 minutes. Frequently, the agency principal and other senior executives are the most guilty of this infraction. (Some years ago, a Ketchum PR account executive temporarily overcame her distaste for the task by compiling her time sheets a week in advance—until I caught on to her sudden promptness.)

The fact is that almost everything that is basic about the financial life of a PR firm rests on daily time reports filed by everyone from secretaries to the CEO.

Individuals' time reports can be submitted on traditional paper time sheets or via an online computer software program tied into your accounting software. As with many things, agencies seem to follow no particular pattern in their requirements for reporting staff time. While agencies may opt for daily, weekly, or semimonthly reports, I recommend that time be reported and imported into your software program daily. At the least, employees should maintain a daily record of the way they spend their time, if only through cryptic scrawling on a desk calendar.

As every agency employee learns quickly, it is difficult enough to remember, in some detail, what you were doing 24 hours earlier without trying to recall exactly what you did a week earlier.

Both time that is chargeable to a client and time that is not chargeable should be reported. Sometimes (sometimes too often), time will be invested in behalf of a client but not billed to that client. In such cases, the nonchargeable time becomes part of the cost of servicing the account. Therein lies the source of the dreaded "write-down" or "write-off" in which time, and related dollars, that should have been billed to a client are wiped from memory, lost forever in a sea of red ink. Nonchargeable time, of course, also can be expended in justifiable agency support activities such as publicity, promotion, and new business solicitation.

Paper time sheets and online computer systems generally require individuals to record such data as an employee number; client codes—usually three initials; a job number; the amount of time invested in specific projects; a brief description of the service provided or work completed; and a record of time off (vacation, holiday, illness) and other nonchargeable activities. Employees are required to account for a minimum number of hours each day, depending on the normal working hours of the firm (7, 7.5, or 8 hours).

If an employee works more than the standard number of hours in a day, these additional hours also should be recorded. Weekend hours are recorded in the same way. Account people who need—or take—more time to complete a project than a client's budget permits may be tempted to put in the extra hours in the evening or on a weekend and not report the time so that the extra time does not become visible or billable. Not a good idea; in fact, a bad idea!

Such behavior reduces agency income and leads to an unrealistic picture of account profitability by indicating that fewer than the actual number of hours were required to complete the project. It also paints a false picture of the employee's productivity and prevents future budgets on similar projects from being adjusted upward.

Employees must be directed to report their time candidly and accurately without being concerned that their time sheets—perhaps indicating a number of unbillable or excessive hours—may reflect badly on their performance or on their job or financial security. Encourage employees to maintain high productivity and stick within client budgets. However, understand and accept that there always will be instances when, for understandable and acceptable reasons, the employee can do neither.

Such things as a sudden budget cut, an incorrect budget estimate, a client decision delay, or any number of uncontrollable circumstances can leave a practitioner with a lot of unbillable time on his or her hands. In such cases, accurate time reports will give you reliable information on which to base management decisions.

TIME AND BILLING SYSTEMS

At this writing, Windows-based time and billing systems are used by most agencies. An old standby, Windows-based TimeSlips, is the most popular agency time and billing software. However, coming up fast on the outside is a new contender, a whole slough of Web-enabled timekeeping systems including Web versions of Windows-based systems. Advantage software (available in both Windows and Web versions and used mostly by larger firms because of its cost and complexity) leads this cagtegory. But even TimeSlips is available in a Web-enabled version, TimeSlips eCenter.

This may surprise you: a minority of firms still use paper time sheets although most of these post time results to an electronic time and billing system.

Here are other Windows (or Mac) systems used by various agencies:

- Quickbook Pro
- Excel
- Traverse
- Adman
- TimeKeeper
- Clients and Profits (integrated accounting and timekeeping)

- Mind Your Own Business (Mac)
- Account Edge (Mac-based accounting system)
- Timepiece
- Advantage (in both Windows and Web versions)
- Silent Partner (Windows and Web versions)
- BigTime

Other Web-enabled systems used by firms include Get My Time, 600 Monkeys, and BillQuick.

Some agencies, primarily larger ones, have developed proprietary systems or modified vendor systems to meet their specific needs.

At this writing, the majority of agencies are not yet enthusiastic about Web-enabled systems. Most still use Windows-based systems, haven't considered switching, and don't intend to.

A discussion of the advantages and disadvantages of Windows- and Web-enabled time and billing systems, according to a survey of agency principals, follows.

Advantages of Web-Enabled Systems

Web-enabled systems can be accessed remotely from home or while traveling (generally considered the most important benefit). They create less traffic and take up less hard drive space on your local servers. They are easily supported; easy to customize, enhance, or change; easy to import data to your accounting software; and easy for Macs to use. Lower costs are incurred for equipment/server space. Finally, they are flexible in every way and useful for an agency with multiple locations.

Disadvantages of Web-Enabled Systems

If the vendor site or the Internet is down, you have no access to your numbers. You have to rely on the vendor to back up the database. You have no control over technical issues or software glitches. These systems require higher monthly fees and you do not own them. You must rely on a third party for ongoing support/upgrades. Your databases and the security of your firm's information are left in the hands of the vendor. In addition, you can't produce summary reports from the Web. For most reporting functions, you need to be on a Windows system.

Advantages of Windows-Based Systems

You can locally back up and deal with software problems. If the Internet is down, you can still access time sheets. Your time sheets and numbers are protected behind your firewall, and you are responsible for the security of the database. All data are stored in-house. You have more control over who can access your information, and the fees for ongoing service are minimal. Because the reporting function is critical, we also have the Windows version of the Web-enabled software. In addition, the Windows version ties into Crystal Reports, a more sophisticated and comprehensive program used to produce productivity and profitability reports.

Disadvantages of Windows-Based Systems

You cannot access your information away from the office. The system is usually a canned program that can't be customized. It must be compatible with your accounting program.

Cost Comparison

I asked Detroit-area computer consultant Pete Shinbach (pete@ birminghamgroup.com) to compare the costs of the two systems. Here are his comments:

It's difficult to compare online versus desktop time and billing software costs because of the variables.

For example, it's usually cheaper to buy software than to subscribe to an online service. That's because the online subscription entails a monthly charge that, after time, exceeds the purchase price of whatever time and billing software you select. And that holds true even with the additional costs of upgrading that software. But there are other costs to maintain the software that aren't incurred with online subscriptions;

- You have to pay someone to install and maintain the software.
- You have to pay for upgrades and maintenance releases.
- You have to have systems in place to back up the data files, which you probably already do anyway.

Conversely, a software program, such as TimeSlips, offers advantages over online services: better practice management and analysis reporting; superior ability to customize rates, project tracking data, billing details, formats, and other elements of agency business management. None of these, however, has any direct cost benefits.

In addition, the desktop products have much better data security and access capabilities. They can be set up to prohibit account managers from changing billing rates or creating new client/project files; restrict access to other people's or groups' information, etc. Online services may have some of these capabilities but not to the degree that the desktop products do.

Along these lines, I've found that most of the online services include capabilities that many PR firms simply do not need but which they have to pay for as part of their subscription. For example, most online time and billing services have a lot of features that would be used for ad buying or some billing practices used primarily by other industries (e.g., architects, software consultants).

Another consideration, which may or may not have an effect on agency expenses, is the ability of the time and billing software to share data with the agency's accounting, general ledger software. Online services may not have this capability and, thus, result in considerably more work for your agency's bookkeeper who will have to manually reenter all the time and expense data from the online service into the firm's accounting program.

Finally, if you don't have a high-speed Internet connection— e.g., DSL, cable modem, etc. —it doesn't make much sense to subscribe to an online service. It would cost you too much billable time and run your phone bills up. (Reprinted with permission of Pete Shinbach.)

Pete's analysis seems to suggest that unless your staffers spend one heck of a lot of time on the road or working from home, the primary benefit of remote access would not be worth much additional cost.

However, I'll bet that, within five years, many, even most, independent PR firms will have switched to or added a Web-enabled time and billing system for the pure joy of having a new electronic toy. Oh, yeah, and so people can submit time sheets remotely. But how's that going to get time sheets submitted any quicker? What's that old adage, "Out of sight, out of mind?"

SETTING HOURLY RATES

Public relations agencies use different systems to establish hourly billing rates. Agencies may try to simplify the process by applying variations of an inaccurate but historically popular "X times direct salary cost" method combined with "what the market will bear."

Unfortunately, this simplistic approach does not take into account rising overhead expenses, in particular, today's high cost of technology and employee health care benefits.

As Harry Cooper said all those years ago: "Good financial planning demands that the overhead factor *must* be taken into consideration in the setting of any client billing rates. . . . It also demands that all items of overhead are controlled and maintained at the absolute minimum level." Well said, Harry! Especially in Cooper's time when many PR firm principals were taking the easy way out by using two and a half times direct salary as the base for hourly rates. Today, that formula more likely ought to be upward of four or five times salary costs. And it would still be wrong. Harry had it right then . . . and now.

Although more complex than the "X times salary cost" system (which actually is more of a guessing game than a management system), the most practical and profit-generating system that I know of—that I first read about in Harry Cooper's monograph—utilizes the following three factors as the base for hourly billing rates:

1. Annual salary costs (including benefits), plus
2. Overhead percentage, plus
3. Profit percentage desired.

This total is then divided by the expected number of annual billable hours per person to arrive at the hourly rate that is required to achieve the desired profit percentage.

An individual's annual salary costs include both his actual salary and an expression of benefit costs, either actual individual costs or a percentage share.

To determine your overhead percentage, divide your total overhead costs (including nonchargeable staff salaries, i.e., secretaries, receptionists, etc.) by your total direct salary costs. This overhead percentage figure—generally plus or minus 100 percent—is added to salary costs for an individual or a group of employees. (The more you reduce overhead costs and the overhead percentage, the higher your profits will be and the lower your hourly rates can be to reach the desired profit.)

To set hourly rates that will generate 25 percent profit, add a 33 1/3 percent profit factor to the sum of salary and overhead costs. To achieve 20 percent profit, add a 25 percent profit factor; for a 15 percent profit, add a 20 percent profit factor.

Divide this total by the number of expected annual billable hours to arrive at the appropriate hourly rate.

Here are two examples of the system at work:

Salary cost	Over-head @ 80 percent	Sub-total	Profit factor @ 33 1/3 percent	Total	Annual billable hours	Hourly rate
$50,000	$40,000	$90,000	$30,000*	$120,000	1,500	$80
$100,000	$80,000	$180,000	$60,000*	$240,000	1,200	$200

*Equals 25 percent of "total."

For convenience, instead of establishing different rates for each individual, you can group employees by title or salary increments (e.g., every $5,000).

This system works best when average numbers are used and in agencies with ten plus employees. You may find that the system results in hourly rates that are too low competitively for junior people and too high for senior people. This is easily resolved by raising junior rates and lowering senior rates competitively while maintaining the same total projected profit. A prime benefit of the system is that it permits you to look ahead at various levels of profit your firm can earn based on your hourly rates.

While this is a commonly accepted system, firms use a number of other methods to set hourly rates. However, all of the alternate methods utilize the same basic data. The primary variation is in the number of hours that practitioners are expected to bill annually. (For some reason, PR agencies cannot agree on a standard for the average number of hours that a practitioner should reasonably be expected to bill annually.) Here are several examples of other systems:

- *National firm:* Determines annual salary costs for a practitioner by adding a 4 percent salary increase factor and 22.5 percent for cost of benefits to actual salary. Divides by 1,540 hours to arrive at an hourly rate.
- *West Coast firm:* Multiplies salary by 128 percent for benefits and divides by 1,612 hours. Then adds a 70 percent overhead factor to arrive at the hourly salary cost. For most midrange account people, who spend all their time serving clients, a 50 percent profit factor is added to reach the billing rate. Account coordinators and senior people who spend less time actually servicing clients are not billed at as high a profit factor. Here is how the system works:

$50,000	Annual salary
14,000	28 percent for benefits
64,000	Divided by 1,612 hours
40	Cost per hour
28	Plus overhead of 70 percent
68	Total hourly cost
34	Plus profit of 50 percent
100	Hourly billing rate

- *Midwest firm:* Divides direct salary costs by 2,080 hours and adds 20 percent for benefits. Uses these factors plus a 150 percent overhead factor to monitor client profitability. However, billing rates are pretty much set by what the market will bear.
- *West Coast firm:* Uses four times direct salary costs to set hourly rates. Rates are set by job title.

Harry Cooper's system is still the best!

REPORTING TO CLIENTS

One of your most important responsibilities is to establish and maintain a good flow of information to and from your clients. Get in the habit of putting things in writing. Confirm client decisions and instructions. Keep your client contact informed of details of ongoing programs as well as of meetings and projects that he or she might not be involved in regularly.

A good two-way flow of information prevents misunderstandings and offers excellent CYA benefits. Sometimes, you might think that all this is too much bother . . . or that it's costing the client too much. (I've even seen the rare client who didn't want a lot of reports. Such clients were told that a full reporting system was an agency policy.)

However, I guarantee that the day will come when you will be grateful that you have a record confirming that the client gave you certain instructions or approved a specific project or cost . . . some time in the past. Long after you both have forgotten the details of the project.

Here is a good rule to follow: Any time a client provides information, gives you instructions, makes a decision or approves something, *confirm it in writing and send the client a copy* via e-mail, fax, or the U.S. Postal Service.

The Paper Flow

Here is a quick review of the "paper" (includes fax and e-mail) that should flow from your firm to your client's. Copies of these reports should be distributed as broadly as possible within the client organization to not only ensure that senior executives understand the progress of the public relations program but also to merchandise the agency's accomplishments.

Conference Report

This report confirms the understandings reached, instructions given, or approvals granted in every meeting, conference, and contact between agency and client personnel—whether in person or by telephone. It usually follows a standard format, often on "Conference Report" letterhead or form with spaces for the client's name, the meeting date, and the conference report date. The format may contain sections for "Activity," "Action to be taken," "Action timetable," and "Action responsibility."

Conference reports confirming client financial commitments are especially important. Reports should be completed and sent to the client as soon as possible, no later than 48 hours after the conference.

Be sure your clients understand that the agency will act in accordance with information contained in conference reports unless the client refutes the report contents within a reasonable time, usually two to five days. (See client agreement example.)

A former client was fond of scheduling weekly meetings with the full agency account team. Before distributing the conference reports we wrote after each meeting, we sent a draft version to the client. He could make sure that we had described the meeting the way he "remembered" it. Sometimes, after the client's "corrections," it seemed like we hadn't all attended the same meeting.

Monthly/Quarterly Status Report

This report covers the progress and status of the agency's assignments over the past month or quarter. The report should accompany monthly invoices or follow shortly. It provides an opportunity for the client to evaluate agency charges against results and work in progress.

A thoroughly detailed status report can answer or defuse a client's questions about the invoice. It also helps increase the agency's visibility and appreciation within the client's organization and can help increase the client contact's stature within his or her company.

With the client contact's approval, the report should be distributed broadly within the client organization. This helps merchandise and increase respect for the agency's work.

The report also serves as a control mechanism for agency senior account managers by indicating the account team's progress for the client and the work that remains to be completed. It also ensures that senior agency executives—who may not be involved in all daily work for the client—can respond logically and calmly to a client complaint.

The first page of each status report should be a brief "Highlights" section made for quick reading by senior client executives. Write tersely. Summarize significant accomplishments; sell the value of the program and the agency's activities. Provide enough detailed information to reflect the firm's total effort and results achieved.

Media Contact Report

This report informs clients of routine contacts with media and reminds them that you are working in their behalf even when they may not see very much happening.

It also ensures that the client is not caught off guard if a reporter mentions a conversation with an agency representative when he calls the client and that no media request is accidentally overlooked.

Prompt and detailed reporting of your activities in clients' behalf is essential in maintaining a positive professional relationship. A good flow of agency reports also helps merchandise agency accomplishments and emphasize account stewardship.

AGENCY PERFORMANCE AUDIT

Here is a way to take a hard look at the overall performance of your firm. You can use the "Agency Performance Audit" (see Exhibit 12.2) to gauge how well you are serving your clients and managing your business.

Each performance area has an arbitrary 10-point value with a total of 160 points. Give your firm an objective and honest score in each area. A 10 means you are doing everything you should and/or as well as you possibly could in that area. Total the points. And look at your firm in the mirror.

Ask your staff members to rate your firm the same way; combine and average their scores. They may not be able to answer all the questions. However, their opinions will be revealing. Compare the way staffers rate your agency with your own opinion. That may be even more revealing. Agencies also use the Performance Audit as the basis for discussion at staff meetings or retreats.

EXHIBIT 12.2. Agency Performance Audit

	Perfect Score	Your Score
Creativity in behalf of clients	10	___
Innovation in behalf of clients	10	___
Strategic planning for clients	10	___
Concern for clients' interests	10	___
Success in producing client results	10	___
Success in retaining clients	10	___
Agency long-range planning	10	___
Agency strategic positioning	10	___
New business effectiveness	10	___
Account management	10	___
Agency financial management	10	___
Agency personnel management	10	___
Vendor relations	10	___
Facilities and equipment	10	___
Rate of profit/income growth	10	___
Agency's general reputation	10	___
Perfect score	160	___

MIRROR, MIRROR ON THE WALL . . .

140 and above	Excellent
120-139	Pretty good
100-119	Fair
80-99	Woeful
60-79	Awful
Below 60	Get a new job!

After you look at your firm in the mirror, on a separate piece of paper, write down the action required to improve each area that scored lower than seven or eight. Indicate the person responsible for the action, if it isn't you. Follow up to make sure the action is taken. Six months from now, grade your firm again. Repeat the test every six to twelve months.

RATIO ANALYSIS:
A MEASURE OF FIRM SOLVENCY

At a minimum, PR firm principals need five basic pieces of financial information to manage their firm properly: cash flow, individual staff productivity, overall average staff productivity, individual client profitability, and overall agency profitability.

In addition, here are several financial ratios that New York CPA Rich Goldstein recommends you analyze regularly to "better manage your firm for growth and profit." (A ratio expresses the mathematical relationship between two quantities.)

- *Liquidity:* The measurement of the degree to which your firm can meet its short-term obligations. Often expressed in terms of working capital, it shows the excess of current assets over current liabilities. Expressed as a ratio, it is current assets divided by current liabilities. The higher the ratio, the greater the liquidity. A ratio of 1:1 means the agency has $1.00 in current assets to cover each $1.00 of current liabilities. A quick look at your accounts payable aging schedule will tell whether you have a weak current ratio. Are you, in effect, asking vendors to finance your agency because you can't pay them on time?
- *Quick ratio:* This is cash plus accounts receivable divided by total current assets. It shows the dollars of liquid assets available to cover each dollar of current debt. This ratio is often used by lenders and creditors to determine the ability of an agency to repay loans and is an even sterner test of a PR firm's liquidity than the current liquidity ratio. Similar to the working capital ratio, the higher the ratio, the greater the liquidity. Focusing on billing and collection, managing current liabilities better, and replacing current debt with long-term debt will help improve current and quick ratios.
- *Current liabilities to net worth:* This contrasts the amount due creditors within a year with the funds permanently invested by the firm's principals. The smaller the net worth and the larger the liabilities, the greater the risk.
- *Total liabilities to net worth* (also expressed as debt to equity ratio): This ratio is the most comprehensive that measures the relationship between total debt to total net worth. It expresses the

degree of protection provided the creditors by the principals. A ratio of 1:1 indicates higher long-term debt participation by creditors as compared to net worth by principals. The higher the ratio, the higher the risk to creditors.

- *Fixed assets to net worth:* Shows the extent the principals' equity has been invested in fixed assets. Generally a smaller ratio is desirable in both of the above cases. However, because of a trend by PR firms to lease equipment, a higher ratio may be acceptable.

PROFILE 12: MARINA MAHER

President, Marina Maher Communications
New York, New York

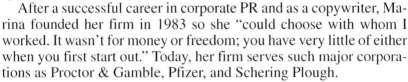

When corporate executives got a sales call from Marina Maher in the early 1980s, they probably heard busy office sounds in the background. Actually, that was Marina sitting at her dining room table busy pitching potential clients while her IBM electric typewriter ran on "automatic" to simulate a "busy" office.

Such a creative strategem isn't necessary anymore; Marina Maher Communications hit about $9 million in revenue in 2004. The firm serves consumer product and health care clients with a "lifestyle" focus and a specialty in marketing to women.

After a successful career in corporate PR and as a copywriter, Marina founded her firm in 1983 so she "could choose with whom I worked. It wasn't for money or freedom; you have very little of either when you first start out." Today, her firm serves such major corporations as Proctor & Gamble, Pfizer, and Schering Plough.

Marina says, "We understand female psychographics and what influences their purchase decisions or changes their behavior." MMC is the only agency of its size to staff a fully dedicated Media Department with Lifestyle Trends expertise to identify pop culture trends that have potential impact on the firm's clients' products as well as the media.

Ahh, but in the beginning! According to Marina, "One of my biggest mistakes was that I did not know how to hire people; I hired people whom I liked, not necessarily those who could do the job well."

Starting over, she would "invest earlier in a good administrative infrastructure: Finance, HR, IT, etc. Such a solid infrastructure can make a real difference in your agency's operation."

Advice to new principals: "Stay focused. Pick what you do well and stick with it. Hire people smarter than you. Keep your sense of humor; you will definitely need it."

Chapter 13

Forecasting Income
and Managing Profitability

One of your most important management tasks is to accurately forecast the amount of income that can be expected from clients during a given period of time: a month, a quarter, six months, or a year. You will need this information to anticipate cash flow and profit (how much money you will take in and how much you will keep) and to plan staff schedules and anticipate hiring additional employees.

There are important distinctions between forecasting and budgeting. (See Chapter 14 for an in-depth discussion of client budgeting.) Forecasting describes the amount of income/revenue that your firm expects to generate in a given period of time based on work that actually will and/or can be completed. Accurate forecasting is an essential aspect of both short- and long-range business planning.

Budgeting is more pragmatic. It outlines the maximum cost of client projects and the total income available to the firm.

There are both similarities and differences between budgeting and forecasting. They are both based on your ability to estimate how much staff time will be required to complete specific client activities and, therefore, how much agency income can be expected in payment for that work. Large amounts of commission or markup on production projects also should be included in income forecasts.

Budgeting establishes the cost parameters within which you must work. To produce an accurate income forecast, you must predict precisely how much work you will actually do within a specific time period and within budget parameters. The budgeting process may cover a longer period of time than forecasting.

For example, the client may have approved a total budget of $50,000 to cover the introduction of a new product over a three-month period. Forecasting requires that you estimate how much in-

doi:10.1300/5561_13

come the agency will receive during each of these three months based on the pace and amount of work required each month. For example, $10,000 the first month, $15,000 the second, and $25,000 the third.

And this means being able to establish and maintain realistic staff work schedules. (See Allocating Staff Resources in Chapter 11.)

Forecasting income requires knowing the amount of time that you and other staff members will have available to invest in specific client projects within a set time period.

Forecasting income also requires an understanding of the activity that can be completed within a given period—because the client has approved it and/or budgeted for it and staff time is available—as well as the activity that must be completed within that period because it is time sensitive.

Time-sensitive activities include such projects as a special event tied to an athletic contest, a new product introduction that must precede the advertising campaign, or press material related to a specific holiday season or special publication issue.

Of course, variables such as unforeseen or last-minute assignments, opportunities, crises, the client decision-making process, and other client idiosyncrasies will always have an impact on how much and what type of work is performed and, therefore, will affect the amount of income that is actually earned in any given period.

FORECASTING FACTORS

Here are some other factors that can impact the accuracy of your income forecast:

1. *Client manufacturing schedules:* Will the product be ready in time?
2. *Client legal/approval process:* Will the legal department forbid or delay the release of the copy or require extensive rewrite?
3. *Client marketing and advertising plans:* When is the client's advertising campaign scheduled to break?
4. *Time schedule/availability of client contact:* Are the client's priorities the same as the agency's? Is your client contact busy with so many other responsibilities that agency projects are delayed?

5. *The experience/status of your client contact:* Is your client contact experienced enough or respected enough within his company to push your work through and get approvals?
6. *Corporate financial status:* Are the corporation's sales falling off to the extent that PR budgets may be stretched out or eliminated?
7. *Economy:* Is a weakening economy likely to affect client spending?

For the most part, you have no control over any of the above factors. On the other hand, you do have some control over the amount of agency staff time that can be harnessed within a time period to meet client needs.

You can juggle your staff time commitments to meet varying client priorities. If you expect to be up to your earlobes in the logistics and promotion of a major special event for one client that must happen in a specific time period, you may have trouble completing work for other clients during that time unless you anticipate the problem and take steps to solve it. (See Allocating Staff Resources in Chapter 11.)

Being able to accurately forecast activity and income for one client will help ensure that required work can be completed for other clients. Anticipating client needs well in advance—by forecasting anticipated income—also may indicate that you will need to change client schedules, if possible; change staff assignments; or call on freelancers to help you through the time bind. Spreading the workload out among staff members ensures that not only are client needs fully met but that available income is actually earned as anticipated.

Despite all the gremlins and glitches that can affect income forecasts, try to make your crystal ball view as accurate and timely as possible, neither overly optimistic nor pessimistic. On the other hand, it also is a good idea to be conservative when forecasting income. It's much easier to deal with more income than expected than the reverse.

If you have acquired the ability to develop realistic budgets, the chances are good that your income forecasts also will be realistic. And vice versa.

MANAGING PROFITABILITY

In addition to reliable income forecasts, your firm's profitability depends on vigorous and consistent control of such profit drains as high salary to income ratio, high overhead and operating costs including rent (your second largest expense after salaries), low staff productivity, and unbillable client time. Nonbillable expenses, such as agency promotion, new business development, travel, and client entertainment must be budgeted and contained.

Establish and live within a realistic overall firm budget. Charge fair, competitive, and profitable hourly rates. And, track the profitability of each client. Either turn around or resign unprofitable clients.

THE FIVE MOST POPULAR WAYS TO LOSE MONEY

The five most popular (most common) ways that public relations firms lose money (or reduce profits) are

1. low productivity,
2. write-offs,
3. unprofitable clients,
4. human mistakes, and
5. excessive salary costs.

Low Productivity

Billable averages below 85 percent of the time practitioners are available to work may be the leading contributor to less than desirable or possible income and profit.

Agency billable averages as low as 60 to 70 percent are not uncommon. Consider this: a single account executive billing only 60 percent of his time at $150 per hour can cost your firm as much as $70,000 a year in lost income!

A Midwest firm principal admitted that his firm's low productivity over a two-year period, including a 62 percent billable average during the second year, had reduced the firm's income and led to flat earnings. Additional income was available from clients but went unearned because employees had not hustled enough to generate the extra revenue.

An unfortunate side effect of this kind of problem, of course, is that when practitioners are not hustling—have little or no sense of urgency—the quality of client service often suffers. Fortunately, in the above case, the firm avoided client criticism.

The only acceptable excuse for low productivity is lack of enough business to keep practitioners busy. In that case, the responsibility for low productivity rests primarily with the firm principal, who is burdened with the need to both generate new business and ensure that current clients are well served.

The simple fact is that a PR firm will only be as successful as its employees are motivated to get off their duffs and produce. Employees must be trained to understand and be enthusiastic about the fact that they represent the agency's primary source of income. (Or, as Joey Reiman, well-known Atlanta, Georgia, marketing consultant, told a PRSA Counselors Academy conference, "If employees are not fired with enthusiasm, they will be fired with enthusiasm.") However you choose to motivate employees, with a hammer or honey, only you can provide the needed spark.

The Midwest firm mentioned above boosted productivity abruptly with a giant, guaranteed-amount, all-or-nothing, first quarter bonus carrot. Total income had to meet management's goal. Either everyone got a bonus or no one did. Not my favorite motivation method and likely to be difficult to maintain on a continuing basis. However, in this case, the jump start worked. The firm has never again paid an all-or-nothing bonus but continues to reward individual employees for extra performance.

Write-Offs

Referred to as "write-offs," "write-downs," or "cuts," the unhappy practice of not charging clients for all the staff time that has been invested in their behalf can cost your firm hundreds of thousands of dollars annually. (Are you wincing because I just struck a nerve?)

Here again, you must bear the onus for the problem. You must ensure that your staff maintains high client service quality but does not overservice clients unnecessarily and does not make dumb mistakes. Remember that clients deserve excellence and are willing to pay for it but are not willing to pay for perfection. (Here is that dual responsibility to manage the potential conflict between your clients' need for the best possible service and your agency's need for the most possible income and profit!)

Establish and sick to realistic budgets. Insist that employees invest no more time in clients' behalf than can be billed. Insist that employees do not do client work on their own time without charging it to clients. (Whether it actually gets billed to clients is a later decision.) Hire practitioners who are competent, have a sense of urgency, can adhere to budgets, and have the confidence to stop work before they invest too much time.

Unprofitable Clients

Not all clients are profitable. (Or had you already discovered that?) If you are stuck with an unrealistic low fee, the client's work requires too much time from senior people, or you consistently write off large amounts because of overservicing, excessive client demands, or faulty budgeting—and there is no way to turn the account around, to make it profitable—consider resigning it.

If an account is unprofitable because you budgeted wrong in the first place, you may be stuck with it unless you have a very understanding and generous client. Perhaps you can plead temporary insanity, throw yourself on the client's mercy, explain your loss on the client's account, and gain additional funds. But don't count on it.

If program parameters change, i.e., the client decides to take a different direction or otherwise changes the ball game, you must confront him with two alternatives: increase the budget or eliminate some previously scheduled activity to bring the budget in line.

On the other hand, there may be good reason to keep an unprofitable client on the books, at least temporarily. The client's check may help pay your rent and electric bill. It may be a good name to have on your client list. Or you may be able to do good work for the client that helps you get other business.

I once found it impossible to nudge a machine tool manufacturer's profitability much above 4 percent because of the amount of time required from two high-salaried people. However, it was a well-respected company, and the work and results we produced for the client were converted to case histories that helped win other business. So the client stayed on the books.

The difference was that I knew exactly the amount of profit the client was generating, why the profit was low, and whether anything could be done about it. With that information, I could make an informed decision about the company's future as an agency client.

Two other examples: A Los Angeles firm resigned a major food service operators owners' group shortly after winning it because the client demanded the agency assign eight full-time people, in addition to the firm principal, to a $330,000 annual fee. A Washington, DC, firm consistently handled large, highly visible public events that were minimally, if at all, profitable. However, because of the events' high visibility and the good results produced, the firm was awarded other more profitable business. On the other hand, a midsized firm walked away from a $360,000 account because, the president said, "We couldn't do good work, and we couldn't make any money."

Unfortunately, many principals do not know the profitability of individual clients and cannot make informed decisions. Available computer software time and billing programs can take care of that.

Human Mistakes

Blunders that lead to eating out-of-pocket expenses can cost thousands of dollars. (I know. I well remember $10,000 in out-of-pocket costs that we washed down the drain because a tiny technical typo snuck through both agency and client proofreading, not to be discovered until the brochure was printed. The client said it was our mistake, even though he had signed off on the brochure, because he had given us the correct data in writing. I had to agree with him. But it ruined my P&L statement for that month and most of the rest of the year.) Staff training and motivation, careful proofreading, proper vendor instructions, and tight supervision are the answer.

Excessive Salary Costs

Your salary to income ratio should average no more than 50 to 55 percent (60 to 65 percent if you include payroll taxes in your salary calculations). Your ratio will soar higher than it should if you have too many employees, do not have the proper balance between junior and senior people, salaries (including yours) are higher than industry averages (or your cash flow can accommodate), or your hourly rates are too low.

The answer to all of these problems is proper planning, budgeting, and management.

LIVE WITHIN A REALISTIC BUDGET

If you have not developed an annual budget for your firm, here is a realistic guideline to help you reach that magical 20 to 25 percent pretax profit level (see Table 13.1). It's also a reminder of the types of expenses that you should anticipate and include in your firm's annual budget.

Base your budget on the amount of income (not your firm's total billing, which includes rebilled costs) that you conservatively expect to earn during the year (fiscal or calendar). You can easily reduce the budgeting process to quarterly or monthly increments.

Your actual costs for individual expense categories may vary from these percentage guidelines. However, stray too far above these suggested cost-to-income percentages and your bottom line results will be more bleak than you would like.

Monitor your actual costs against these guidelines on a regular basis, at least quarterly, preferably monthly. Change budgeted dollar figures as your income and expense projections change.

A good way to prepare your first budget is to break down the previous year's expenses into the categories listed in Table 13.1 and use that not only as a guide in preparing a 12-month budget but also as an indication of where better cost controls may be needed.

Set Expense Budget First

To get a little more control over the profit you earn, you might want to try this interesting approach. Instead of estimating your expected annual income and expenses to see what kind of profit you might have left, reverse the process. Deduct your desired operating profit from your projected income to determine the amount left for expenses. And then control expenses tightly to ensure the profit you want.

While you can't control your firm's income because of the influence of outside parties, namely, clients and prospects, you do have a good bit of control over your firm's expenses. For example, suppose you're projecting next year's net fee income of $2 million and you want an operating profit of at least 15 percent ($300,000). Subtract the $300,000 profit from the $2 million income, and calculate your expenses as a percentage of $1,700,000, the amount of money you'll

TABLE 13.1. Suggested annual agency budget categories.

Expenses	Percent of projected income	Comments
Salaries and benefits	50	Over 55 percent and you're in big trouble!
Travel and entertainment	2	Nonbillable client expenses
New business development	1	2 or 3 percent may be more realistic with a very active new business program
Unbilled (mistakes!)	1	Expect, plan for them!
Operating expenses (rent, utilities, telephone, maintenance, messenger, depreciation, etc.)	13	Break out individual expense categories. Keep rent within 7 to 10 percent of income
General and administration (stationery, supplies, insurance, postage, dues and subscriptions, employee recruiting)	4	Break out individual expense categories
Payroll taxes	4	Depends on local rates
Total salaries and expenses	75	Attainable!
Pretax profit	25	Nirvana!

have with which to operate your firm during the next year and still return the profit you want.

Prepare your operating budget based on 85 percent of your estimated next 12 months' income. If you manage your costs tightly so that they don't exceed 85 percent of your total income, you'll return a 15 percent operating profit. It's that simple.

Table 13.2 lists some budget percentage guidelines based on a study of advertising agencies with gross incomes of $2 million or less. They should apply equally well to PR firms. Change the individual percentages to fit your own specific circumstances. Applying

TABLE 13.2. Budget percentage guidelines.

Item	Percentage	Cost ($)
Travel and entertainment	2.7	45,900
Rent, light, maintenance	9.0	153,000
Postage, shipping	0.9	15,300
Supplies	3.7	62,900
Depreciation	2.3	39,100
Telephones, etc.	2.4	40,800
Data processing	0.8	13,600
Agency self-promotion	1.4	23,800
Operating insurance	1.5	25,500
Memberships, subscriptions	1.8	30,600
New business	1.0	17,000
Misc. operating expenses	1.8	30,600
Processional services	1.7	28,900
Payroll-related costs/benefits	9.5	161,500
Employee payroll	38.5	654,500
Principals' payroll	18.5	314,500
Bonuses	2.5	42,500
Total	100[a]	$1,700,000

[a]Total is 100 percent of 85 percent – total income less 15 percent profit.

these percentages as a guide to a $1.7 million operating budget is shown in Table 13.2. (You can use the same expense percentages as a guide to help guarantee a 15 percent operating profit for your firm, no matter what your expected income. If your income estimate increases or decreases during the year, change your budget.)

TRACKING PROFITABILITY

To keep your firm moving forward, you need information on two types of profitability: overall agency results and individual client profitability.

Some years ago, I asked the general manager of a national firm's Chicago office whether his firm tracked individual client profitability. He said he didn't need such information because he knew that his office was profitable.

Contrast that misguided opinion with a letter from the president of a West Coast firm: "At your suggestion, our CFO developed hard data on profitability per client. We've since resigned seven accounts that were too small or were a pain. That allowed us to take one of our best people and assign her to a large account where she's doing a great job."

Here is a compelling truth: Just because your firm is profitable does not mean that all of your clients are profitable or as profitable as they could be or that your agency is as profitable as it could be. There may be leaks in the bucket!

Tracking the profitability of both your agency and each client—and doing something about problems in both areas—should be a monthly priority.

There are only four basic factors that need to be considered in tracking individual client profitability: income; salary/benefit costs (the actual costs to you of the time invested by employees in serving a client, whether the time is actually billed to the client or not); non-overhead expenses incurred in behalf of the client that cannot be rebilled; and your firm's overhead percentage.

Hourly salary costs are determined by dividing the total cost of an individual's annual salary and benefits by the total number of hours for which he or she is paid annually. For example, 40 hours a week equal 2,080 hours a year.

As we've noted previously, your firm's overhead percentage can be determined by dividing your total overhead costs (including non-chargeable staff salaries) by your total annual direct salary costs. Generally, your overhead percentage will range between 80 and 100 percent of salaries depending on how well you control costs.

Each month, multiply the hourly salary costs of all the people who worked on an account by the total number of hours charged against that client by each person (whether or not billed to the client). That will give you the total salary cost for each client for the month. (In this case only, don't worry about unbillable time, that is, the number of hours that staff members neither charge against nor bill to clients.)

Next, multiply each client's salary costs by your overhead percentage. That will give you the expense overhead cost to be borne by each client. Each client carries the same overhead percentage. For example, $24,000 in salary costs times an 85 percent overhead percentage equals $20,400 in overhead costs to be applied to that account. You also should factor in other nonrebillable client costs such as travel, entertainment, and any client-oriented vendor costs that cannot be rebilled to a client.

When you subtract the sum of salary costs and overhead expense share, plus miscellaneous client costs, from each client's gross income, you will arrive at profit or loss.

Here are two examples of the process:

Monthly income	Salary/ benefit costs	Overhead @ 85%	Total	Profit	Profit percent
$10,000	$6,000	$5,100	$11,100	($1,100)	(LOSS)
$10,000	$5,000	$4,250	$9,250	$750	7.5

There are several ways to shrink salary costs and increase profits: reduce the number of hours charged against a client but not billed; reduce the number of hours billed against a flat fee; or reduce the number of more costly hours invested in a client by more expensive senior employees.

Quality standards and client service needs must, of course, always be your highest priority. However, remember that you earn the most profit when the most highly competent, least costly employees do most of the work. In addition, if the overhead percentage in the second example above rose to 95 percent, the profit on the account would drop to $250. That's a 67 percent drop in operating profit because of a 10 percent increase in overhead costs. Factor that difference into your firm's numbers. The result should be strong motivation for controlling overhead costs.

Tracking client profitability can be computerized either by using a software program that you or a consultant develop or by using vendor software such as TimeSlips or Advantage to do it automatically.

Ask your accountant, financial officer, or a computer consultant to recommend or design a computer program that will track and report both overall agency profitability and the profit or loss on individual clients.

New Clients May Not Be Profitable in the First Year

Okay, so winning new business is great for the soul, the ego, and the cash flow. And, at the least, it will help pay your overhead or replace departing clients. But did you ever consider the fact that it may be difficult or even impossible to make money on the new client the first year, if you really take into account what you actually invested to win the business and learn it?

Let's take a hypothetical new client with a $100,000 fee budget. If your before-tax profit goal is 15 percent, that means you ought to be able to return at least $15,000 to your bottom line from this client.

Here's how much it could cost in time invested at regular hourly billing rates, not to mention out-of-pocket costs, just to win the account:

Title	Hours invested	Cost
President	20 @ $250	$5,000
Vice president	30 @ $150	$4,500
Account coordinator	40 @ $100	$4,000
	Total cost	$13,500

In many case, perhaps most, additional time will have to be invested during the first couple months to learn the client's business. And you're probably going to write off that extra time above the fee or budget. Here's an estimate of possible write-offs during just the first month:

Title	Hours invested	Cost
President	5 @ $250	$1,250
Vice president	10 @ $150	$1,500
Account executive	10 @ $100	$2,000
	Monthly write-off	$4,750

Total cost of winning new business

Proposal preparation	$13,500
Learning the business	$ 4,750
Total	$18,250

That's why the best way to grow your business or replace departing clients is to generate increased income from current clients.

Recovering Client Rebillables

A PR firm principal (a relatively inexperienced one) once asked, "Is it worth the time involved to bill clients back for expenses like telephone, copies, publications, messenger, and fax charges?" Simple answer: yes!

It's always worth billing all reasonable expenses back to clients. Either track the exact costs (which can be largely automated) or charge a percentage of the time bill to cover such costs. (These days, at least 6 or 7 percent of the time bill, added to each invoice to cover miscellaneous postage, copies, telephone costs, etc., would seem fair. Large mailings or copy runs would be billed separately.)

Charging expenses back to clients adds cash directly to your bottom line. For example, how many copies do you make monthly? Only 2,000 copies per month charged to clients at 25 cents each puts $6,000 back into your pocket annually and helps pay for your copier. (The average cost per photocopy page charged to clients in 2005 was 33 cents.)

Occasionally, there may be a question as to whether an item is an agency or client expense. For example, if you take a client to lunch, that's obviously the agency's expense. However, if you take both a client and an editor to lunch, that's the client's expense. (You probably won't get anyone to admit that when they take a client to lunch they eat the up-front cost, but bill the client an extra half hour that day to cover the lunch cost. But it happens.)

Remember, there is no such thing as a free lunch. Rule of thumb: Anything you do or spend in behalf of the client gets billed back to him.

Eliminate Write-Offs

The time that employees invest in client programs but that, for any number of reasons, cannot be billed to a client can make a really sour impression on your bottom line.

Let's say, for example, that last month your billable fee income *should have been* $100,000 based on time invested in your clients. You had $50,000 (50 percent) in salary costs, including your own, and $35,000 (35 percent) in operating expenses, leaving an operating profit of $15,000. Pretty good, you say. That is, if you *could have billed* all the invested time to clients.

Instead, you had $10,000 in time invested and/or out-of-pocket costs that you couldn't bill to clients and had to write off. So you actually only billed clients $90,000, with the same $85,000 in salaries and expenses. So, instead of a profit of $15,000, you had an operating profit of only $5,000—an operating profit of 5.5 percent instead of 15 percent. Not as nice a picture. Money down the drain!

As we've noted before, writing off unbillable time or expenses—because of sloppy budgeting, human carelessness, or overinvestment of staff time—is one of the biggest single contributors to lower-than-possible PR firm profits.

Such gaffes not only take money out of your pocket, but also reduce the amount of cash available for employee salaries, benefits, and bonuses. That fact alone should make staff members pay attention when you talk about the importance of reducing or, even better, eliminating write-offs.

Sometimes you may need to invest time in nonbillable client services. New client start-up or staff education can result in legitimate write-offs. But don't over-do it.

Avoid getting so enthusiastic about overservicing a new client that you have trouble backing down after the first few months, particularly on a flat-fee client. Don't put up with employees who can't or won't work efficiently and effectively. (One individual getting away with doggin' it can make everyone else wonder why they're running so hard.)

Make sure that projects are budgeted accurately. Train staff people how to budget. Consider installing a computer budgeting system with online historical data and a standard budgeting form that contains all the elements of any project.

Make sure that employees understand exactly how much time has been budgeted to complete projects. Encourage and train people to complete work within budget and to know when to stop work. One of the most important things you can train inexperienced people in is to have the self-confidence to stop work before they've invested more time in a project than a client will be willing to pay for.

Hold staff members responsible for careless mistakes or inaccurate or incomplete budgeting. Show employees the negative impact that write-offs have on the amount of bonus money available. Make it clear that every dollar lost through write-offs directly reduces the bonus dollars in their pockets.

Most important, make the elimination or drastic reduction of write-offs a personal priority! Do not permit employees, even senior people, to write off significant sums unless they have an excellent reason and your written approval. (In my agency days, any write-off more than $100 demanded my personal approval and a darn good reason.) When it comes time for bonuses, reward those who keep write-offs under control. (One year a West Coast firm, with a severe write-off problem largely because of overservicing clients, based its bonus plan for senior people on rewards for reducing write-offs.)

Remember, it's a lot easier to boost your profits by eliminating write-offs than it is to earn increased income to produce the same result. Once you've generated income, it's a shame to pour it down the drain needlessly through carelessness, inefficiency, stupidity, or lack of management concern and attention.

Estimate and Recover New Business Costs

It's no secret that with the heavy competition for every piece of new business, the cost of obtaining that business has been soaring over the years.

The good news is that the majority of agencies appear to be coping with increased costs by comparing the expected return on investment (ROI) against the projected costs to win the business and not entering the fray if the pay-off doesn't appear worthwhile. Or, as one agency president noted, "We plan to make at least twenty percent profit on net fee income on all our accounts. If it costs us more than twenty percent to pitch, we're giving up our entire first year's profit."

That's the good news. The bad news is that, according to my surveys of agency principals, one in four agencies does not estimate how much it could cost to pitch a new piece of business, doesn't look at possible profit, and has little or no idea how much they spend chasing the brass ring. That's unfortunate.

So if you're not already following good cost control procedures when you go after new business, here are some steps I recommend you take immediately.

Estimate Costs

Develop a system to estimate the time and out-of-pocket (OOP) costs of pitching a piece of business. For example, a West Coast technology firm estimates its potential time investment in the following areas: lead generation; company research and preparation; proposal development; internal meetings for preparation and review; travel and presentation; and budget/proposal refinement.

The firm's marketing director estimated that to win a $100,000 account his firm would need to invest about 55 hours at an average hourly billing rate of $250 or about $13,750.

Track Salary/Benefit Costs

Track the amount of time and out-of-pocket dollars that you actually invest in pitching an account. The majority of agencies who track new business time assign a job number to the prospect and calculate time costs by multiplying staff hours by hourly billing rates. I'd like to recommend a more accurate way of toting up staff costs.

Measuring staff time costs using hourly billing rates tells you how much income would have been generated if staff hours invested in new business had been billed to clients. That also could tell you how much income was lost assuming you had enough client work to keep people fully billable. That's a "what if" kind of thing. But it does not tell you the actual cost of pitching the business. Only calculating your investment in employees' hourly salaries and benefits against new business time gives you the real cost, which, of course, will be smaller than utilizing hourly billing rates.

To follow such a system, plug employees' hourly salary costs plus a percentage for benefits into your time-tracking software program. To get hourly salary costs, divide an individual's salary by the number of hours in a year for which he or she is paid. If your shop works an eight-hour day, you pay people for 2,080 hours a year. Your accountant can give you a percentage for benefits.

On that basis, using an average salary of $75,000 (fairly high because of expected heavier time investment by senior people) with an hourly salary cost of $36 plus 10 percent for benefits (chances are most agency benefit percentages are higher than 10 percent), the technology firm's actual costs to win that $100,000 account would be $2,200—compared to $13,750 based on hourly rates.

Recouping New Business Costs

Assuming that, on the average, it's going to cost you $11,000 (based on hourly billing rates) to win that hypothetical $100,000 account, as our surveys have indicated, you need to make sure you recoup some or all of your investment to provide a brighter P&L.

Is it legitimate to recover new business development costs? Certainly. Within practical limits and assuming it doesn't make you go over budget. In most cases, you will be recovering the costs of "spec" research and planning that you had to do to win the business in the first place. And that gives you a head start on achieving results for the client, which they won't object to. Here's how agency principals have described the way they recover new business costs:

- "This relates mostly to recovering some research and creative costs. Depending on the potential account, we will conduct preliminary competitive research, a media and analyst audit, and develop some initial creative recommendations on positioning plus major media opportunities. We include these in our recommended budget for the new client. Then, on a case by case basis, we build on what's already been done and recoup some of our investment in research. Same for creative and media relations. You can't just bill previous time. A key question: has the work added value to the client program, and is it something they wouldn't have had otherwise?"
- "Many ideas become billable as we employ them."
- "We bill for research and planning in the first of couple months."
- "We capture all development costs associated with a pitch in an account (that's tied to the new client). On every client billing sheet that goes to an AE each month, our controller suggests an amount of development time to be recovered or notes the amount of development costs and asks, 'Did we recover anything?' For example, if we come in under budget on a project, such as an annual report, we'll recover part of the development costs. The client is satisfied because we hit the budget. If the client is exceedingly pleased and we're going to 'value bill' him or her, we might capture some of the development costs under 'value bill.' We make a value judgment on how much we recover." (The agency also insists that clients pay all overbudget costs, unless the agency was responsible for the overage.)
- On the other hand, the CEO of a large Midwest agency said, "Many of our larger clients are working with corporate 'transparency' guidelines that make it difficult to do this unless we ne-

gotiate it up front, and that can factor unfavorably in a decision to hire us in these budget-conscious times."

The guideline to recouping new business costs should be, as noted above, "Has the work added value to the client's program, and is it something they wouldn't have had otherwise?"

UNIVERSAL RATES UNIVERSALLY UNLOVED

For a number of years, agency principals have discussed the use of blended or universal hourly rates (a single averaged hourly rate applied across all staff levels). These discussions have usually revealed that few people really like the concept. At this writing, the majority of independent firms do not use a blended rate.

However, in the past several years, with increased influence by corporate procurement officers on agency contract negotiations— particularly for very large contracts and with clients' emphasis on cost control—the discussions have been revived. You may be asked to supply a blended rate one of these days.

According to one agency principal,

> Blended rates have become somewhat popular with those organizations that are handling PR agency fee negotiations via their purchasing/procurement departments. When this happens, the blended rate issue is far from the biggest problem. It puts agencies in a vendor role rather than a valued consulting role.

Here's how the few agencies that do use a blended rate do the math:

- "Divide total estimated client fee by total estimated staff hours."
- "Calculate a weighted average of all staff working on the business, and then discuss with the client to come to an agreement on a fair rate that provides value to the client while still ensuring a profit margin for us."
- "We just estimate the plan based on the individuals required to implement. We take the total dollars and hours per the hourly estimate. Then give the client the budget based on a single rate. This is a silly and inefficient way to do things! It just opens us up to questions during a potential financial audit. I would rather bill

things as they are, based on the individual doing the actual work."
- "We divide costs, including salaries, benefits, and overhead, plus twenty percent profit, by the average hours worked in the previous year."
- "Average of billable rate of people working on the account."
- "Quite often, it's dictated by the client's budget and their desires."
- "Estimate the variety of service level; calculate overall profit margin of at least fifteen percent."
- "Taking the hourly rate of each person assigned to the account and then doing an average."

Then there were those candid agency heads who said the following:

- "Who knows? It seemed right; it was the same as competition."
- "It's often based on what we feel the market will bear. It's typically higher for crisis work."
- "We made it up."
- "What we believe the market will bear."
- "If pressed, we say $175."

There's nothing very scientific about most of the above. But that's what can happen when agencies are forced into doing something they don't agree with.

Here, based on our surveys, is how agency principals describe the advantages and disadvantages of a blended rate. Even principals who hate blended rates can see some advantages.

Advantages of a Blended Rate

- Principals express various versions of it's easier to calculate, estimate, budget; simpler for bookkeeping; simpler for clients to understand.
- "The advantages are only for the client."
- "It demonstrates to clients our commitment to their business and hopefully continues to grow their business with us."
- "You may be able to have lower priced personnel perform the work, but that will eventually catch up with you in the audit."

- "It encourages clients to seek senior management involvement and provides fewer billing questions/issues." (Note: This is counter to the way most principals feel about the problem of senior people doing more work than juniors.)
- "Some clients may find it psychologically difficult to see the comparatively higher value/rates of those with the most experience."
- "Some clients are more inclined to use an agency that has a lower hourly rate rather than what the project will cost."
- "Everyone works on the business; more collaboration; clients don't nitpick hours; ease of billing."
- "Eliminates client whining."
- "It's a lazy way of budgeting for those who have a math handicap."
- "It provides easier billing; higher margin on junior staff; rates don't scare clients from senior staff."
- "Makes time sheets easier, but does not provide profitability analysis per employee."
- "Clients believe they are saving money."
- "Clients can quickly calculate the number of hours per month (the agency invests) in their account."

Disadvantages of a Blended Rate

- Most principals agree that the biggest downside of a blended rate is the negative impact on the agency's profit if there is imbalance between the amount of time invested by senior versus junior staff members. One principal said: "An agency could take a beating if the senior people spend more time than the juniors."
- "Promotions within an account team on a specific contract will cause dramatic increases in blended rates from year to year if the more senior positions on the account did not exist before. Therefore, this process will require more explaining to the client each year."
- "If all rates were the same, why would a client want to talk to a junior person at all?"
- "The lost revenue potential is significant."
- "Could leave money on the table."
- "It commoditizes the PR function."
- "It can be more difficult to remember to make sure that work is done at the absolutely best level in the organization."

- "It does not accurately reflect the business."
- "It does not reflect the true value of time; either the firm or the client is cheated."
- "Clients feel $110 for admin work is a rip-off; they don't like it. The cost does not reflect the nature of the work."
- "Every time you added or subtracted team members, you'd have to reassess the blended rate to accurately reflect the current experience level and cost of personnel. Since you can't change rates on clients every time there's a staff change, there would be hesitancy to add anything but a low-cost individual, which would result in a loss of quality and then, of course, loss of clients."
- "It's hard to make money (on a blended rate); difficult to justify rewarding employees with unique skill sets with higher pay; inherently feels unfair."
- "Overvalues certain tasks; undervalues others."
- "Another way to cut profit."

Further Thoughts on Blended Rates

- "(We submitted a blended rate) to win a piece of new business and we lost. We won't do it again."
- "If we are in a competitive bidding situation and the determination will be made by a blended rate, we see this as a danger signal that suggests we are dealing with a very unsophisticated prospect. If we decide to pursue the prospect anyway, we qualify our answer by telling the prospect that the 'blended' rate is based on certain assumptions about the scope of work. Generally, that gets us to the next threshold. At that point, we determine if questions about a blended rate are motivated by the politics of the corporation or by the naïveté of the unsophisticated prospect. If it is the former, we most usually can cope with it. If it is the latter, we most usually cannot."

"WE HAVE MET THE ENEMY AND HE IS US": POGO'S WARNING

Agencies are often their own worst enemies when it comes to increasing client billing, according to Ken Makovsky, chairman, Mokovsky & Company, New York. Makovsky listed "Pogo's Six Commandments" to help agencies increase client billing:

1. *Recover your sales investment:* To recover sales costs, Makovsky recommended:
   A. Track sales costs;
   B. Add an additional 2 to 4 percent to hourly rates to cover sales costs;
   C. Maximize staff utilization;
   D. Reduce overservicing;
   E. Seek more noncompetitive bids;
   F. Get paid for planning; and
   G. Ask the client to pay sales costs.
2. *Tighten the receivable cycle:* "Don't be your client's banker." Makovsky recommended:
   A. Ask for 10 to 20 percent of the annual fee up front to hold on deposit until the end of the contract; bill the monthly fee against the deposit; have the courage to ask the question;
   B. Know your client's payment cycle;
   C. Deliver time and activity reports to clients on time;
   D. Get an advance on expenses, particularly if expenses are going to be significant.
3. *Connect with clients on budget issues:* "Executives in our business who are fearful of going to the client before exceeding a monthly or annual budget are really the people that Pogo was talking about. Don't be afraid to talk to the client about money. If you don't ask, you won't get."
   A. When going over budget, get the client to approve additional funds or slow down activity.
   B. Educate clients at the outset on how the agency operates and what the budget is for; clients are buying time for specific activity.
   C. Anticipate overruns with the client before they take place.
   D. In the contract, ask for a fee review after the first or second quarter.
4. *Deal with procurement officers on your level, not theirs:* Procurement officers want to come up with one universal rate for everyone in the agency that allows for a twelve to fifteen percent profit." Makovsky's suggestions:

A. Meet with the marketing manager or brand manager—whomever is seeking the benefits of PR—along with the procurement officer. Explain the strategic value of the agency's offer. Establish a two-tier rate, one for strategic planning and one for execution.

B. Consider reducing a universal rate to obtain a larger revenue contract.

5. *Strategically employ value billing:* Value billing, although controversial, is a sure way to deal with low fees and high costs. If you provide the value, many clients are willing to pay for it.

A. "During contract negotiations, ask the client, 'If this particular problem was resolved, what would it mean to you?' Include a contract clause that enables the agency to bill for full value of services rendered. Value billing is usually tied to media coverage performance." Makovsky's example: "A *Wall Street Journal* corporate profile or a three-minute CNN feature segment on the client was worth a $50,000 bonus.

6. *Market return on public relations investment to clients:* Do a good job of marketing your results back to the client and particularly to the individuals who hold the purse strings. Companies that recognize the value of their public relations investment will invest more. The more likely an organization is to measure stakeholder attitudes and public relations influence on reputation or product success, the larger is the PR budget. When "ad equivalency" is used (to justify PR), budgets are lower. Measuring PR results by ad equivalency (the value of a print ad occupying the same amount of space as a published article) is without a doubt the worst possible measurement technique. But sometimes it's the only thing that clients understand. (Reprinted by permission of Ken Mokovsky.)

PROFILE 13: PHIL MORABITO

President, Pierpont Communications
Houston, Texas

With an MBA in marketing and several years of New York City agency experience as credentials and an aversion to big city commuting, Phil Morabito migrated from New York to Houston, Texas, in the late 1980s to start his own firm. (Morabito claims that although he's attended a few rodeos, he still doesn't own boots or a cowboy hat.)

Morabito operated as a sole practitioner for five years before his firm took off and he snagged enough business to begin hiring staff. Today, Pierpont Communications (named for a street near his elementary school in Rochester, New York), with a second office in Austin, Texas, serves more than 50 clients, ranging from small businesses to Fortune 500 corporations, and does about $3 million in revenue annually.

From his early days, Morabito has been an avid self-promoter as a way to build business; his firm continues a strong program of self-marketing. In addition, the firm has been named one of Houston's fastest-growing firms, and Morabito has been recognized as "small business entrepreneur of the year."

"I learned early to surround myself with good people," the transplanted New Yorker (and father of four children) says. "I tackled the new business effort and hired strong account service professionals and a strong operations professional to run the day-to-day financial and administrative needs of the firm."

In Houston's turbulent economy, Morabito also has learned how to survive a recession. He advises: "Get your costs as low as possible; get your staff productivity to record levels (but don't kill your people); market your brains out; get realistic about sales—teach senior account service people how to sell; and cut your losses—don't hang on to more staff than your business will support."

Chapter 14

Client Budgeting

Three of the most important elements of good client service are strategic thinking, creativity, and budgeting. Often, budgeting gets 10 percent of the attention and causes 90 percent of the problems. Accurate budgeting requires careful planning, awareness of project variables, consideration of staff experience and skills, and close attention to production details. And, most important, careful attention to the client's needs.

Conversely, although individual agencies may apply certain rules of thumb, there are very few guidelines that can be applied to all budgeting situations. Moreover, budgeting is seldom taught; it is usually learned by doing.

THE CLIENT'S NEEDS

Former Sears Roebuck and Company PR executive Ron Culp told an audience of Chicago PR counselors: "We view the client-agency relationship as a matter of complete mutual trust. Every budgeting problem that has ever arisen has been the result of a breakdown of that relationship."

There are three ways to destroy a good client relationship, Culp said:

1. "Surprise the client, even in routine matters. In budgeting, this includes everything from underestimating to overpromising. Agencies should budget precisely, realistically, and completely. Clients hate to see TBD (To Be Determined) in a proposed budget," Culp said.

doi:10.1300/5561_14

2. "Confuse the client by changing the game plan unexpectedly so that it impacts on costs and the budgets. Always involve the client in the decision process if circumstances make a change necessary that could impact on the budget. Give the client as much detailed budget information as he needs."

3. "Cheat the client or appear to do so. The direct way to cheat, of course, is to bill the client for services or goods not performed or provided. The indirect approach is to add secondary vendor mark-ups without the client's approval. Other ways to cheat the client are to (a) operate on the theory that if it's in the budget, we should spend it; (b) consider that a contingency fund is available for day-to-day projects; and (c) propose or adjust budgets based on the perceived depth of the client's pockets."

SURPRISES KILL A BUDGET

When preparing a budget, you can never plan too much or pay too much attention to details. Here are two horror stories from the long-ago files of a national public relations agency.

Horror Story 1

To introduce a new food product, the agency planned to send samples of it to food editors across the country so that they could taste it—frozen yogurt, at that time a new supermarket freezer category.

Unfortunately, when budgeting for the shipment of the samples, the agency was not aware of and did not plan for the fact that the product had a melting tolerance of just five degrees.

As a result, the product had to be packed in special containers that could accommodate dry ice and still meet air express regulations. The actual cost doubled budget projections.

The budget melted but the product didn't.

Horror Story 2

Although the agency had budgeted for the client to exhibit at a major trade show, no one knew that the exhibit was scheduled to be used at another show that ended two days before the start of their show.

To make sure that the booth was at the convention site in time, the agency had to Federal Express a 10' × 20' booth. The shipping charges alone were $8,000.

The booth looked great, but the budget looked terrible.

Moral: Surprises kill a budget! Always ask the right questions and then ask them again.

THE TEN BIGGEST BUDGETING PITFALLS

Here are the 10 biggest and most common budgeting pitfalls. Make sure that you avoid them.

1. Underestimating the time and manpower required
2. Wanting to look good for a client or superior and purposely low-balling projected costs
3. Misrepresenting a project to vendors and receiving incorrect cost projections
4. Budgeting for a project without thinking the whole project through
5. Not informing the client of budget problems until *after* the project is well underway or completed
6. Not taking the time with a client at the beginning of the project to fully explain all the expected expenses and the exact components of the project
7. Identifying a good opportunity during the project and not asking the client for more money to take advantage of the opportunity; either trying to squeeze the opportunity into the budget or passing it up
8. Setting unrealistic timetables that cause you to put in overtime and/or overstaff a project
9. Not budgeting for contingencies
10. Not giving complete budget information to all members of the account team

Most Common Budgeting Problems

Of these pitfalls, agency principals say that the three most common and most serious budgeting problems are the following.

Underbudgeting

Deliberately underbudgeting or lowballing because you are afraid that you might frighten or even lose the client if the projected cost is too high is a mistake. In most cases, such concerns are unrealistic.

Clients can always find someone who will work cheaper than your firm, if that's what they want. On the other hand, it's important to apply what Lou Williams, president, L.C. Williams and Associates, Chicago, calls "a sense of anticipation," anticipating the cost level that will make the client's ears turn red—and not exceeding that level.

To stay within a realistic budget, you can reduce the scope of the program or give the client a selection of overbudget items that can be substituted for elements included in the budget.

Warning: Don't be tempted to squeeze the budget just to get the business.

Faulty Time Estimates

Failure to accurately estimate how long it will take to complete a project or a program is different from deliberately underbudgeting to get a job or not anger a client. Both of these approaches are bound to result in either having to write off the cost overage or asking the client for more money—neither of which is a pleasant experience.

Incomplete Budgets

Don't forget important elements of the budget, such as postage or shipping costs or agency markup on production costs. It's very embarrassing to have to ask a client for more money because you forgot to include a production cost in the budget. But it hurts worse to have to eat your mistake. A little embarrassment can make up for a lot of red ink.

THE BUDGETING PROCESS

Budgeting ought to be really simple. There are only two things that you have to worry about: how much time it will take to complete a project or a program and how much the client will have to pay for out-of-pocket costs and internal agency expenses. Doesn't that sound easy? If only it was.

Budgeting for out-of-pocket costs can and should be relatively simple. As long as you provide accurate and complete information, you can usually rely on vendors for accurate cost estimates. As long as you remember to include all possible out-of-pocket expenses in your budget, you're home free.

Estimating the amount of staff time that will be required to complete a project or program is a different kettle of fish.

A critical factor in preparing a budget is the level of experience and skill of the person or persons who will actually do the work. Unfortunately, the person developing the budget usually has more experience than the person or persons who will carry out the project and can do the job faster. That can cause problems.

Should the senior person budget for as much time as he or she knows it would take them to personally complete the assignment? Should he try to guess how much time it will take a junior person, or should he ask the junior person how much time he or she thinks will be needed?

Like so many things in the agency business, the right answer is an average, an estimate of the average time that it should take a relatively experienced person to complete the project. And experience will usually tell you what that ought to be.

But then there are the variables, those things that you can't plan for but that will happen as sure as Murphy's Law decrees that if something can go wrong, it will.

Unfortunately, it is very difficult to teach people how to budget because of the huge variety of projects that a firm can be asked to handle, some of which it may never have handled before, and the possible variables that can affect costs.

Individuals often learn to budget on their own through experience, trial, and error. A better way to learn is to work with an experienced person in a client or classroom situation. Many firms have written guidelines, based on past experience, that can be very useful, although not infallible. It follows then that the more experience you have, the better your judgment and instincts will be. And the easier it will be for you to produce accurate budgets.

The most practical approach to budgeting is to apply the averages and add a safety factor. Estimate the average cost of specific projects, and then add a fudge factor for variables and unforeseen circumstances. Or, as one agency principal said, "If I think an article ought to cost $2,000, I'll budget it for $2,500, just to be sure." On the other hand, in such a case, you could safely budget 10 articles at an average of, for example, $2,000 each, because some of the articles will cost more and some less than $2,000, and the averages will work out.

How to Develop a Budget

Translate your personal experience into an estimate of the time required to complete specific projects, news releases, brochures, special events, etc. Consider the required investment of time as if it was being expended consecutively and continuously.

You have a press conference to be budgeted. How much time will be required for management/supervision, research, brainstorming, planning, writing, photography, client approvals, rewrite, media contact, travel, event and production supervision, and reporting and merchandising results? Consider the skill level of people who may be involved. How much time will be required for client meetings and executive counseling?

Then consider the agency's experience or the average cost for similar projects, if such information is available.

Multiply the number of estimated per-project and total hours by your average hourly rate. Add another 20 to 25 percent to this sum to allow for Murphy's Law. When estimating production costs, include out-of-pocket expenses for items such as the following:

- Design and illustration
- Freelancers and consultants
- Photography
- Printing
- Mailing and handling
- Food and refreshments
- Audiovisual material
- Travel
- Model and/or spokesperson fee
- Equipment rental
- Markup (if any)

Include agency expenses for the following:

- Telephone
- Fax
- Copies
- Clipping and video service
- Publication subscriptions
- Postage, shipping, messenger
- Editorial and client entertainment

Admittedly, the budgeting process described here is little more than a few homemade, hand-me-down, shot-in-the-dark techniques based on hopefulness and educated guesses. But that's the way agencies have done it for years. The majority still do.

AND IN THE END

Three broad rules will help guide you through the budgeting labyrinth:

1. Always get the client's approval of the budget in writing or confirm a budget decision in a written conference report.
2. Never invest any time in the client's behalf until the budget is approved.
3. Clients will almost never object if you come in under budget.

PROFILE 14: CARL MUELLER

President, Mueller Communications
Milwaukee, Wisconsin

With a background as a newspaper reporter and editor, governor's press secretary, congressional staff aide, assistant university chancellor, and chief of staff for Milwaukee's mayor, Carl Mueller started his firm in 1985 with two partners and $160,000 income the first year. Today, his two former partners run agencies of their own. Mueller heads a $1.4 million firm that serves diverse clients ranging from the Wisconsin drug and grocery retail outlets of Jewell-Osco to M&I Bank, Harley Davidson, Covenant Hospital System, and the commissioner of Major League Baseball.

Mueller is active in a number of local organizations including the Greater Milwaukee Committee, a prominent civic organization of local business executives and political leaders. His company is one of the best known and most influential public affairs agencies in Wisconsin.

The firm's "Core Values" set it apart from competitors, according to Mueller: *Creativity*—Think outside the box; *Professionalism*—Honesty, integrity, and accountability; *Quality Service*—Excellence in work performed; *Respect*—For each other, for clients, for the competition; *Share Our Success*—Give back to the community through volunteerism and philanthropy.

However, all was not smooth sailing in the early years. Mueller says personnel mistakes created the biggest and hardest lessons to learn. He advises, "Start with the right people and set high standards. Don't waste time trying to fix bad personnel decisions. Focus on the business of your company and develop personnel carefully. Get professional help to run your business."

Chapter 15

Recruiting, Training, Retaining Employees

It's true; your inventory goes down in the elevator every night and, hopefully, comes back up in the morning. Efficiently and effectively recruiting, training, motivating, and retaining good people are keys to building and maintaining a healthy agency.

Public relations firm principals complain that finding and keeping qualified employees at a reasonable cost—particularly at more experienced levels—is a major and constant challenge. The need to attract and retain the best possible employees puts great importance on sophisticated recruiting techniques, supportive training methods, and superlative motivational and morale-boosting efforts. In boom times, such as the late 1990s, when client budgets were fat and agencies scrambled to find enough talented staff to meet client needs, finding and keeping good people was even more critical.

HIRING SMART

How's this for a painful scenario? Two new clients just rolled in the door, and you just lost two of your best people to a competing agency. You're working your butt off trying to keep up with client needs and still run a profitable agency. And there are these two applicants who are breathing, aren't afraid to look you in the eyes, and don't have this morning's breakfast on their shirt. You're tempted to hire them. However, you don't know a whole lot about them, haven't had time to check references, and you're a little suspicious of the samples they offered. But what the heck, they're breathing. And you're bordering on being desperate.

doi:10.1300/5561_15

Wait a minute! Consider the damage you could do by hiring the wrong person. According to psychiatrist/hiring consultant Dr. Pierre Mornell, "If you make a mistake in hiring and you recognize and rectify the mistake within six months, the cost of replacing that person is two and one-half times the person's annual salary." Translation: making the wrong decision on a $50,000 account executive could cost you $125,000, according Dr. Mornell!

Despite neverending client pressures and the constant shortage of really good people, you can save yourself a peck of grief by following the suggestions in Dr. Mornell's book, *45 Effective Ways for Hiring Smart: How to Predict Winners and Losers in the Incredibly Expensive People-Reading Game* (Ten Speed Press, Berkeley, California). Packed with real-life problem hiring case histories and a plethora of savvy advice, the book makes easy and fascinating reading. You'll go, "Yeah, I know that," and then "Wow! How come I never thought of that? That's a great idea!"

Here are 14 of Dr. Mornell's 45 effective ways that fall under the "How come I never thought of that?" category. (At least for me.)

Preinterview Strategies

1. Before the initial interview, pick up the phone and call the candidate. How hard or easy is it to reach the candidate? Does the candidate return your call at the specific times that you suggest? Is he or she an articulate communicator in the first two minutes? What else can you tell about the candidate in the first two minutes?
2. Ask the candidate to visit your Web site before the interview. If he has anything on the ball, he's likely to think of this himself. Then ask for the candidate's observations (about the site).
3. Cast the widest net possible. Let a broad range of people know that you're looking for better candidates. Use unconventional ways to communicate your staffing needs. And remember, the best candidate may not be looking for a new job.

Interview Strategies

Dr. Mornell suggests that you remember three basic things about interviews:

(1) Interviews test how well people interview, not necessarily how well they'll do the job; (2) A good con artist can fool you every time; (3) Interviews in which you induce stress seldom work. Putting a candidate on the defensive will only demonstrate his or her style of defensive behavior.

1. Look for the passionate candidate. When passion is present, the sky's the limit. When passion is missing, all bets are off.
2. Ask all your questions at once. Write them down for the candidate. This allows you to settle back and watch a candidate's behavior as well as listen to his or her words.
3. Have fun during the interview. Ask some "Columbo" type questions, for example: "How are you going to lose money for me?" Listen for what the candidate leaves out of his response.
4. Assign a miniproject to finalists. Three-quarters of the way through the interview, give the candidate a task to perform. Ask her to comment on a client problem you're working on.
5. Seek closure by announcing the five minute warning. Tell the candidate, "We have about five minutes more." Men and women invariably say something that's really important at this point, regardless of how much time you've spent together.
6. Ask for a legal release. Some questions are tricky and may be illegal. (The book provides the draft of a release form authorizing you to ask personal and performance questions of previous employers. Check your attorney on this one.)
7. Throw a few curveballs at the end of the interview. Ask questions such as, "Where are you less than perfect? How do you let others down? Where do you get angry?" (The book also includes four pages of other questions you can ask a candidate as well as a list of puzzles to test a candidate's ability to visualize problems in a new way.)
8. Ask the candidate to call you back at a specific time. Fifteen percent of the candidates miss the call.
9. Assign a take-home project. Give finalist candidates a postinterview project that evaluates attention to detail as well as the ability to analyze problems and suggest solutions.
10. Consider what psychological tests have to offer. Many firms use the well-known self-administered Myers-Briggs Type Indicator. There are two critical things to know about any psychological test. First, an interpretation can be very insightful,

neutral, or unhelpful. It all depends on the interpreter's expertise. Second, tests are especially helpful when they correspond with a candidate's history, interview impressions, postinterview behavior, and reference checks.

Postinterview Strategies

1. Ask a candidate's references to call you back. Try to reach them at a time they probably won't be available. Leave a message saying, "X is being considered for a position at our firm. Your name has been given as a reference. Please call me back if the candidate was outstanding." Dr. Mornell says this technique is fast and legal. "No derogatory information has been shared; no libelous statements have been made; no confidences have been broken." (This may be one of the most insightful and helpful tips in the entire book.)

RECRUITING GOOD EMPLOYEES

Here are eight strategies to help make your search for competent practitioners more cost-effective and productive:

1. Use Employment or Search Firms Selectively

A $50,000 account executive, hired through an employment agency or executive recruiter, can cost you $15,000 or more in fees and then be unprofitable for months while he or she learns to become productive or billable.

On the other hand, there undoubtedly will be occasions when a good professional recruiter can find a well-qualified practitioner or special-skills professional either locally or in another part of the country when you cannot or do not have time to conduct a proper search. You will need to decide whether your time constraints are so severe or your staff requirements so urgent or specific that you must look to an outside source. In such cases, the investment, while hefty, can be worthwhile.

If you do not use an outside source, however, how do you find the people you need? There are a number of good methods, some of which are more long range than others, but all of which will pay off.

2. Make It Easy for Good People to Find You

Aim everything you do at three groups of people: your clients, prospects, and future employees.

Become highly visible. Promote your firm in ways that potential employees will notice. Get people talking about you and your agency. Become involved in professional associations. Make speeches, appear on panels, write articles, and announce your new business wins locally and nationally.

Make sure that the public relations community is aware of your firm's growth and stature. Growth is attractive to prospective employees as well as to prospective clients.

3. Create a Pleasant and Satisfying Workplace Atmosphere

To reduce turnover as well as attract new people, establish and nurture a workplace ambiance that ordains your firm with the reputation as a good place to work.

Here are some things you can do to help build that kind of reputation:

- Compensate employees fairly.
- Push responsibility and authority down to the lowest possible level.
- Involve staff members in as many aspects of the agency as possible.
- Provide opportunities for personal and professional growth.
- Recognize good work and reward top performers.
- Conduct regular and meaningful performance reviews.
- Support staff development with training, seminars, and professional conferences.
- Hold staff lunches and outings.
- Be realistic and reasonable in staff productivity requirements.
- Inform employees about agency, client, and new business developments.
- Be cordial and caring in dealing with staff members, and do everything possible to enhance staff members' sense of self-worth. Word spreads about the good places to work as well as the "sweatshops."

4. Tap Professional Resources

Get to know your fellow agency principals; they usually will be willing to refer qualified employee candidates whom they can't use at the moment. Ask them to refer people with specific experience to you, not just "anyone you don't need." Reciprocate by referring candidates to other principals. Utilize professional association job banks, and offer a reward to staff members who refer new employees (if the new employee stays at least three months).

5. Build a Resume File

Don't discard resumes, particularly if the individual appears to have potential. You may need a specific individual some time after you first receive his or her resume, and he or she may still be available. Maintain a file by experience-level categories such as graduate, mid-level, or senior, or by job backgrounds, such as packaged goods, high tech, food, or business-to-business. This will help you locate potential candidates quickly without searching the entire file.

Keep the file current by regularly deleting resumes more than two years old. Chances are, the individual has moved on by then or rigor mortis has set in. If you should happen to contact someone through an old resume and find that the person has already changed jobs, make a note of the new position. You may be able to hire an individual as much as a year or two after you first receive his or her resume.

6. Be Available

Make time to interview people regularly, even if you have no openings or are not looking for someone with their background. In particular, talk to recent or upcoming graduates as often as you can. They need encouragement and experience handling interviews. Interviewing a near or new graduate will help keep you current on the availability of entry level people and the caliber and curriculum of public relations education. It also will build your file of potential employees and help create a good reputation for your firm.

7. Use Interns Productively

Colleges and universities are an excellent source of part-time or short-time staff members. Provide internships to as many talented university students—not necessarily all PR majors—as you can handle productively and profitably at one time.

Internships will help build a backlog of semiprofessional individuals who are grounded in and enthusiastic about your firm and who may qualify for full-time employment when they graduate.

Use interns part time during the school year and full time during the summer or after graduation. Students can be productive if they have 15 to 20 hours available a week. Pay interns a reasonable salary ($7 to $10 per hour), and charge their time fairly to clients ($25 to $35 per hour). (Note: if you do not pay interns yet charge their time to clients, you are letting yourself in for a possible lawsuit from a disgruntled intern.)

Consider appointing one of your better young account executives on a rotating basis as intern supervisor to schedule the interns' time, act as a mentor, and monitor their training under your guidance. The interns will relate well to the younger person, and the account executive will gain supervision experience. You also may want to let the intern supervisor recruit and hire interns with your final approval. It will be valuable experience for the intern supervisor with little exposure to your firm.

Internships should be productive for both you and the student. Assign interns to meaningful tasks within their capabilities. Do not limit them to clerical assignments or pro bono projects that do not provide realistic training in client service or insight into the reality of everyday agency demands.

Given the proper supervision, talented interns can handle lower level responsibilities well. This not only gives the intern practical training, but spares your more senior people from handling "grunt work" and ensures that the intern is modestly profitable. The intern's enthusiastic report to fellow students or professors about his or her satisfying and stimulating sojourn in the outside world will help attract a continuing stream of good intern and graduate candidates.

Although most prospective interns will be juniors or seniors, you may want to offer limited-duration (three-month) internships to graduates with no commitment of a job at the end. However, require the graduate to commit to remain the entire internship. Keep track of good interns when they graduate, even if you can't use them at that time.

Let colleges and universities in your area know about your internship program. Send professors and intern program coordinators a persuasive description of your internship program that can be posted on school bulletin boards. Speak to university classes and work with student PRSSA chapters.

8. Advertise for People, But Don't Skimp

Don't believe the old saw that "good people don't answer ads." They do, but you must advertise persuasively and in the open.

Place an attractive, well-written, decent-sized display ad in the Sunday business news section of the best major newspaper in your area. Identify your firm. If you are not in a large, metropolitan area, use a newspaper published in the nearest big city. For instance, the *Chicago Tribune* pulls well in Wisconsin.

Don't skimp by inserting a few lines of anonymous type in the classified "Help Wanted" section. Blind ads are not as effective as signed ads; they generally attract fewer well-qualified applicants. (In addition, people may be concerned that the unidentified agency is their own firm.)

Using this approach, you can reach and attract better qualified people who may not even be looking for a new job. Many PR practitioners habitually read the Sunday newspaper business section, including the "Executive Careers" display ads. They may not read the classified ad section.

I tested this theory by running the same attractive, signed display ad in both the classified and business news sections of the *Chicago Tribune* on succeeding Sundays. The response by better qualified people from the business news section was almost double that from the classified section.

In your ad, sell your firm and the opportunities offered. (Remember, prospects also read the Sunday newspaper.) Describe experience and skill requirements. Specify that applicants should not telephone but should write you a letter selling themselves. Individuals who can sell themselves well in a letter usually make good public relations professionals and, in particular, fit well in an agency atmosphere.

Answer all applications quickly with a form letter that you personally sign. You may want to use several different form letters, depending on the applicants' experience and potential. One of these candidates may later become an employee, prospect, or client. Make a good impression now. However, discard resumes that are not accompanied by a letter. Someone who cannot follow instructions well enough to write a letter (and not telephone) probably will not be able to follow job instructions.

Don't worry about receiving a flood of mail that will take too much time to read. In a few seconds, you can scan the first two paragraphs of a letter and decide whether you want to read more or perhaps talk to the individual. A typical well-written ad in a major metropolitan newspaper, for example, can produce several hundred responses. Out of this, you should get at least six or seven viable candidates and another 30 to 50 resumes that you will want to file.

There are other advertising avenues; ads in out-of-town locations, with a good supply of the kind of people that you need, can be effective. National publications, such as PRSA *Tactics, PR Week,* and *PR Services Report,* can generate qualified applicants, but you may find that most of the respondents are from distant locations requiring heavy moving expenses. The *Wall Street Journal* pulls well when you are seeking senior people.

And, of course, promote your staffing needs and your agency amenities on your Web site. Good people looking for a better opportunity will search your Web site for that opportunity.

Over a 10-year period, during which I hired about 60 people, I used a placement firm only twice. All the other new employees were attracted through metropolitan newspaper ads or came in unsolicited largely because of the firm's reputation as a good place to work.

Recruiting the right kind of people is a long-range proposition, a task that must be worked at constantly, not just when an opening suddenly occurs.

TEN QUESTIONS TO ASK TO FIND GOOD EMPLOYEES

Executive recruiter Colleen Aylward, president, Devon James Associates, Bellevue, Washington, suggests 10 questions that will always get the information you need from candidates:

1. Take me through a time when you took a project from start to finish.
2. Describe the way that you work under tough managers.
3. Describe the way that you work under tight deadlines.
4. What is your definition of working too hard?
5. Persuade me to move to your city.
6. How do you manage stress?
7. What kinds of opportunities have you created for yourself in your current position?
8. In a team environment, are you a motivator, a player, a leader, or an enthusiast?
9. In the past three years, what part of your professional skill set have you improved the most?
10. If you were a new employee, what would you do to gain respect from peers in 30, 60, and 90 days?

TWIN MISTAKES AGENCY CEOs MAKE

Some years ago, the president of a fast-growing West Coast firm told me, "I gotta stop hiring people who are just like me."

Two common mistakes agency CEOs make are (1) hiring people who are just like them and (2) *not* hiring people who are just like them. Both mistakes can be particularly glaring when the person you hire is at a senior level or maybe even your number two.

Hiring People Like You

It can be very comfortable to hire someone at the senior level who could be your twin. You have similar backgrounds; you tend to finish each other's sentences; you may even dress alike. You're confident that she will do a good job, will handle clients the same way you would, and will be loyal, hard working, and competent. It's a no-brainer; obviously, you were made for each other.

However, the other side of the picture is that she may very well have the same professional weaknesses or problems that you have. If you're not happy digging up new clients, chances are she won't be either. If you hate "crunching numbers," or worrying about cash flow, you can figure she won't like the business side of your firm either. If you're not very good managing people, she may not be very popular with your staff either. On the other hand, clients will probably love her because she will do a great job of providing the best possible client TLC. Just like you.

If you need someone to direct client service and build business with current clients, to relieve you of the bulk of client service responsibilities, your "twin" may do fine . . . if you let her. And the chances also are good that her clients will be nicely profitable. However, if you need someone to train all the tender young sprouts you've been hiring, you'll need someone who's more patient with green staff members than your twin may be. If you need someone who's good at chasing new business, you'll need a person who is, at least, a little extroverted and likes to stand on her feet and pitch.

The big question, of course, is, "What do you really need at the senior level?" Doctor, lawyer, Indian chief? Have you written job descriptions that list senior responsibilities in depth and the experience required to fulfill those responsibilities? Have you developed senior level experience requirements not to mirror your background but to complement it?

Not Hiring People Like You

On the other hand, do you actually need someone—particularly as your number two—who's pretty much like you? But you're having a hard time accepting this reality?

You may run a well-thought-of agency but with a big, but largely disguised, gap between your experience and staff and client acceptance levels. Chances are, that means in addition to bringing in most of the new business, clients want to deal with you in tough situations, or even day to day, because you're the one they trust—compared to the twentysomethings on your staff.

Don't kid yourself; deep down you may like it that way. It's very gratifying when clients want to talk mostly to you. It's also good for the ego—although it can be tiring—when the youngsters on your staff constantly come to you with problems instead of solutions. I also know agency principals who often slow things down to a walk because all client material must go over their desks. This can cause missed client deadlines and frustrates the staff to no end.

The president of a good, relatively small agency with big-name clients used to write most of the speeches for his largest client, primarily because he liked to write speeches, his client had come to expect it, and he didn't have anyone else as good as he was. Despite what this did to his ability to manage the business side of his agency. Today, that agency is still in business, but the CEO has a strong number two. And I don't think he writes speeches anymore.

Several years ago, I asked a group of agency principals, "What was your biggest mistake in starting your agency?" The unanimous response: "I didn't hire a strong number two quick enough."

Being tied up in client business is fine if you have few or no growth aspirations for your firm and aren't too ambitious about your operating profit. After all, you probably started your agency because you like to do client service work such as counseling CEOs, writing complex speeches and white papers, and pitching the media.

The fact is there are only so many hours in the month, even though you may bill more hours than many of your staff. That means there are only so many clients to whom you can give really good attention. And if there's no one else your client CEOs are willing to talk to, your level of client service may be sagging. It also may mean that your younger staff members whom you depend on for most of the day-to-day client work aren't getting as much training as they need because you're not available. You may find that depending on these young people beyond their experience and competence level without enough guidance and training leads to client service problems as well as staff burnout and turnover. To say nothing of your own potential burnout plus the angry looks and comments you get from your spouse or significant other because of a continuing array of seventy- to eighty-hour weeks.

So, if you can't be spread any thinner, how are you going to grow your business? (It may be okay if you don't want to grow your business and you like things the way they are. Remember, however, that PR agencies often are compared to sharks; if they don't move, they die.)

The first step in growing a business usually means the CEO must back off from "doing PR" and spend more time managing the bottom line and bringing in new clients. That may mean that you need someone with almost the same level of experience and skills that you have, someone your clients can and will respect the same way they respect you. Such a hire may be costly because really good people don't come cheap. In the long run, though, hiring strong senior people—

and giving up being "needed" so much—will pay off in happier clients, better trained staff members, and a bigger, more profitable firm. (And probably a happier spouse or significant other.)

So who do you really need? Someone to help ease you out of client service and let you spend more time developing new business? Someone to watch over agency numbers, monitor salary and benefit costs, answer staff questions, and tend to client invoices and receivables? Someone who's really good at pitching business but who gets bored with client work? Someone whom both your clients and staff will trust and rely on?

Someone like you—or not like you? Think about it.

FLUSHING OUT GOOD CANDIDATES WITH A TESTING SERVICE

At least one-third of independent PR firms use a psychological testing service to help flush out candidates who most precisely meet their job needs. From reviewing such services' online information, interviewing executives of several of them, and talking to agency principals who use such services, I've arrived at two general conclusions: (1) For the most part—except for minor cost differences—such testing firms all provide the same basic services and personnel information; and (2) there's no doubt that the results of such psychological tests can give you a good, solid, valuable peek at whether a job candidate has the right personality and/or psychological quirks to fit your firm. Agency principals who use a testing service swear by its advice.

For about $200 per test (individual services' prices vary) your job candidates will take a paper or online test requiring twenty to forty minutes. They will either answer a series of questions about themselves or, in a two-part test, check off words (1) that they think apply to themselves and (2) that other people think apply to them. Based on the test, the service will send you—usually very quickly—a summary of the individual's personality, both positive and negative aspects.

In addition, the services will probably provide suggestions on ways to manage or ameliorate the candidate's more negative characteristics, including questions to be used in a second interview to probe the individual in depth. The services will also, for an additional cost and in consultation with you, provide a basic personality profile of the type of person who will fit most satisfactorily in your firm. This may include developing personality profiles of all your current employees to arrive at a definition of a "high performer." The tests are race and gender sensitive.

Several years ago, Rembrandt Advantage, a testing service used by a number of firms in cooperation with members of the Council of PR Firms, developed an "Ideal Selection and Developmental Model" for a PR agency vice president/account director. Here is a summary of the "differentiating performance factors" of an "ideal" senior agency executive, as developed by Rembrandt:

- *Problem solving:* Top performers are conceptual and able to work with intangible and abstract issues, challenges, and requirements.
- *Sense of urgency:* Deadlines and high volumes of work energize people with a very high sense of urgency.
- *Sensitivity to rules and guidelines:* Top performers are innovative, tend to use their know-how in new and expanded ways, and find the routine associated with compliance to processes and guidelines frustrating.
- *Motivation to influence:* People who perform high in this drive tend to seek out positions that allow them to actively persuade on a frequent basis; they feel a sense of gratification when they successfully influence others.
- *Reaction sensing/empathy:* People who perform high in this measure tend to be "open minded" and able to incorporate other's feedback into their approach.
- *Verbal communication* (measured by assertiveness and willingness to confront opposition.): Top performers are strong communicators with a solid willingness to stand behind their views even when opposition increases.
- *Stamina:* High-stamina people can put in a full day's work and then some.
- *Self-confidence:* The higher the score in this measure, the better able the individual is to recover from professional setbacks.
- *Social inclination/independence:* People who score high in both of these measures enjoy interacting with the client and are able to do so without sacrificing their views and needs.

- *Personal responsibility:* People who score high in this area tend to follow through on every commitment, sometimes even when new information suggests another approach would be more suitable.
- *Self-discipline:* This measure identifies people who can stick to tasks until they are completed, even if the task is tedious or time consuming.

Here are several testing firms that are used by PR agencies for human resources assessment:

Caliper Profile: PO Box 2050, Princeton, NJ 08543; Tel: 609-924-3800; www.caliperonline.com.

Empowerment Concepts (Rembrandt Advantage): 1276 N. Palm Canyon Drive, Suite 205, Palm Springs, CA 92262; Tel: 800-292-7182; www.rembrandtadvantage.com.

Kolbe Index: 3421 N. 44th Street, Phoenix, AZ 85018; Tel: 800-642-2822; www.kolbe.com.

As one of the services says in its online material, "People rarely succeed or fail due to lack of skills or intelligence—instead, their success or failure is due to personal characteristics such as attitude, motivation and, especially, temperament and behavior patterns." According to agencies that use them, testing services do an admirable job of ferreting out candidates' personal characteristics that can lead to success or failure on the job.

TRAINING, MOTIVATING, AND RETAINING EMPLOYEES

Once you have hired good employees, do everything possible to prevent them from being lured away by better opportunities. Retaining good employees can make the difference between your firm being in the red or black. Outside of lost business—and the two can be related—few things can hurt your firm more than losing good professionals after you've invested considerable time, effort, and cash in recruiting and training them; clients hate it!

One of the most effective ways to motivate and retain good employees is to help them build a strong sense of their own self-worth. Make sure that employees understand that a public relations agency is one of the few places where an individual's personal and professional growth depends almost entirely on his or her personal capabilities and effort.

Corporations and other institutions tend to be highly structured within their public relations departments, starting at the top with a vice president/director and dropping vertically down the chain to the lowest denominator. The only way an individual can move up is usually when a more senior person leaves the company (and with corporate downsizing, the squeeze is even tighter). If you are the sole PR practitioner in a corporation, the chances are few for you to move into other areas of responsibility.

However, as a PR agency grows, opportunities grow to match increased client income.

Teach employees that managing income—not working more hours—is the secret to increased responsibility and personal growth. There are only so many hours that an employee can work in a year and only so much income that he or she can generate personally.

The secret to individual personal growth is gaining increased responsibility for agency income. An employee can personally average only about $150,000 annually in income generated. However, if an account executive is *responsible* for $400,000 in income, it follows that other employees must work for him in order for the income to be generated.

People who are intelligent, highly motivated, interested in building client income, and able to juggle multiple assignments will be excited and ultimately rewarded by this opportunity. This factor sets PR agencies apart from most other organizations in terms of professional and personal growth and increased compensation.

Training Employees

Helping employees improve their professional skills through organized training materials and programs will improve the level and quality of your firm's client service. It also will improve employee morale and help you retain valuable employees. Here are some suggested training ideas.

Orientation/Account Management Manual

A typical manual, given to all new employees, contains information and guidance on agency policies and practices, including

- *Program administration*—conference reports, status reports, time accounting;
- *Managing client money*—expense reports, purchase orders, supplier invoices, client and project job numbers; and
- *Miscellaneous procedures*—telephone system, computer and word processing systems, office supplies, travel arrangements, building access, proofreading system, filing system, document control system, media contact form, and style and graphics standards.

Account Start-Up Manual

To help ensure proper start-up of service to a new client, the manual should outline general operating procedures. It should contain a comprehensive checklist of information and data required from a new client and a list of materials (policies, manuals, marketing programs, etc.) required.

Mentoring/Coaching Program

Junior and new employees are each assigned to a senior person who acts as the junior's mentor. Mentor and employee meet regularly, possibly for lunch at the agency's expense, to discuss agency policies and procedures, client service matters, professional development, and other matters concerning the junior person. Ideally, the mentor should not be assigned to any account that the junior works on so that the junior will feel free to discuss sensitive matters.

In-House Seminars

Specialized professional training is provided either by a senior agency employee or by an outside consultant. (For example, this writer conducts all-day, in-house account management seminars for agency staff members.)

Outside Seminars, Conferences, Professional Associations

Encourage employees to join and participate in the Public Relations Society of America's local chapter. (You also should join

PRSA's Counselors Academy and explore eligibility and benefits of membership in the Council of PR Firms.) Many agencies pay employees' professional organization membership dues and allow expense account charges for lunches, local meetings, and national conferences.

Account Involvement

Provide as much authority and responsibility to employees as quickly as possible, but with senior oversight.

Retaining Employees

There are many opportunities for PR firm principals to gain satisfaction from their job. You will be able to name yours. If you are lucky, one of those will be low or no employee turnover.

I was one of the lucky ones. In 15 years of managing three successful public relations firms, I lost very few employees to better opportunities. In fact, only one person in all that time moved to another PR agency on their own volition.

If you would have asked people why they stayed, the answer might have been simply, "I like it here."

There is no one reason—beyond the generic "I like it here"—to account for extended employee tenure. Perhaps the most important incentive lies with the agency principal.

The principal sets the tone and flavor for the entire organization. You are the spark, the personality, and the pace car for your agency.

If you are fair, open, candid, and nonthreatening, employees will respond positively. If your counsel to clients is creditable, your professional skills admired, and your new business successes appreciated, the examples you set will drive your agency forward. If you are very talented, yet keep a lock on your ego, staff members will follow suit. If you keep your fingers out of the soup, staff members will grow professionally and creatively.

If you take your work seriously, but laugh at yourself, a sweeping sense of humor will pervade the agency. If you believe in working hard, but having fun while doing it, employees will function smoothly under day-to-day job pressures and clients will bask in service satisfaction.

If you ascribe high productivity as a mark of professional excellence, others will pride themselves in their ability to generate agency income. If you encourage employees to cross client lines and seek assignments on other accounts, home economists can write industrial case histories to stay billable and traverse into new spheres. If you refuse to grant sovereignty over individuals to second level managers, demanding that they teach and encourage rather than rule, fiefdoms will run fallow and professional independence will flourish.

If you are aware of individual achievement and lavish laurels on individuals, both achievers and nonachievers will be spurred to greater heights. (Half of my agency's bulletin board was designated a "Glory Board." Employees were encouraged to place laudatory descriptions there of other employees' accomplishments; a client cover story, a major feature placement, client praise, etc. For special exploits, a special ceremony was conducted at a staff lunch or meeting, and a large glittering star was hung around the celebrant's neck.)

If your door remains open and you walk the halls regularly, people will open up to you and will speak their minds. If you foster a strong sense of confidence and self-worth among staff members, practitioners will be encouraged to stretch beyond the mundane and will reach for the top of the mountain; risk taking will be a normal, expected moment in their business day.

I like to think that I was all of these things. We had little staff turnover.

Performance Reviews—Staff and Management

Staff members need to know where they stand with you. Each employee should receive an annual written review of his or her performance. Some agencies tie performance reviews in with salary reviews. Others conduct performance reviews on the individual's annual anniversary but award salary increases on a calendar year basis so that all increases are effective on the same date.

The reality is that employees expect salary increases to be tied into performance reviews. I have always felt that this method resulted in higher morale than separating the two processes for accounting convenience. (When you tell someone they're doing a good job, they want to see visible evidence in their paycheck.)

Whichever method you use, be sure that employees understand your policy.

360-Degree Performance Reviews

The 360-degree performance review, common in the corporate world, has become more popular in the agency industry in recent years.

360-degree performance reviews are commonly defined as the process of evaluating an employee's job performance by gathering specific job performance appraisals from an employee's managers, direct reports, and co-employees. In general, agency principals and managers as well as employees find 360-degree reviews with their accompanying multiple feedbacks to be very effective in improving employee performance. Because feedback is gathered from a number of people—managers, supervisors, and peer employees—professionals find the results of the review more convincing and acceptable than traditional evaluations based on a single management perspective.

Here's how several small or medium-sized agencies use 360-degree reviews:

- *Houston, Texas firm with 16 employees:* Our 360-degree reviews are a takeoff of what a larger organization might do simply because when a team of four rates each other, it's pretty obvious who on their team said what. (Four teams of four employees.)

  We use our client "report cards" to gain feedback on how each team is doing. In the annual employee evaluation, we get employee feedback. Supervisors give their feedback on their people; then every person in the agency meets with me to review their evaluation and to give me their evaluation of their supervisor and of me. Then I meet individually with each supervisor to give them my evaluation and that of their team. This way, the employees can say what they'd be afraid to say directly to a supervisor, and I can present their input in the form of coaching to the supervisor.

  As we grow, this system takes a lot of time. However, I think it's one of the most important things I can do to direct the corporate culture and retain great people. All evaluation sessions with me end with a personal career path visioning session where I work one on one with every employee to create a career growth plan. It has occurred that the best thing for an employee was a career plan that required that he leave the agency. I helped him realize a dream, and he is a lifelong friend of the agency for it!

- *Midwest firm, 60-plus employees:* The firm has two 360-degree performance reviews: Peer Evaluation and Upstream Evaluation of Team Leader.

Peer Evaluation consists of three broad subjective questions: What do you like most about working with this individual? What suggestions do you have that you feel could improve the effectiveness of your working relationship? What special quality, if any, does this individual possess, in your opinion, that reflects what we value?

Questionnaires are sent to all members of a team, either account or administration, for comment. Unsigned responses are forwarded in confidence to the team leader's manager for compilation and discussion with individuals.

Upstream Evaluation of Team Leader consists of 14 multiple choice questions such as "During my work with this individual, I found that he or she"

—Develops and maintains strong relationships through good business and communication skills: (Check one) Consistently, Usually, Sometimes, Rarely, Not rated (Not enough information)

—Effectively delegates workload, responsibility, and authority: (Check all appropriate) Delegates work appropriately; Gives me assignments that challenge me; Gives me assignments that overwhelm me; Gives me assignments that are not challenging enough; Not rated.

—Gives me recognition for my contributions and efforts: (Check one) Often, Occasionally, Seldom, Not at all, Not rated.

The firm's president says, "We used (the two questionnaires) for the first time with the round of annual performance reviews just completed. The Peer Evaluation Questionnaire worked extremely well, probably because of its simplicity. The Upstream Evaluation produced mixed results. I'm not sure subordinates were as candid as they might have been."

- *A Canadian firm with 18 employees:* The firm's 360-degree performance review program is called "Road Map to Success." The performance review, conducted every six months, is divided into three parts:

1. *Individual personal goals*—set at the beginning of the year and tied into agency corporate objectives. Employees are measured on how they contribute to where the agency wants to be.

2. *Four corporate "values"*—with objectives and desired behaviors tied into each value. Individuals are measured against how well they perform against the objectives under each of the values.

3. *Professional and personal development*—areas requiring development are identified for each individual and plans made to achieve the development.

Performance feedback on an individual is requested from all agency employees. The president says, "If I'm doing a review of one of our vice presidents, I'll send an e-mail to all employees saying, 'So and so is coming up for review. Help me understand how he or she is doing versus our values.' People respond in confidence to me with unstructured comments. Everyone knows what behaviors we're looking for so it's easy for them to relate to that. I also might ask questions about how a person is fulfilling his or her responsibilities in specific areas. All the comments are then combined and communicated to the individual being reviewed." The same system is followed in review of other account staff members.

- *West Coast technology firm, 35-plus employees:* Typical probably of many technology firms, the firm's performance review process is totally online. "It's not a pure 360 review," says the CEO, "but it permits a number of people to contribute to an individual's review. Anybody a manager feels is appropriate to feedback can be brought in. If someone has been loaned out to another team, you'd want members of that team to contribute. One of the benefits of the online review is that the person being reviewed can see his or her review as well as a profile of the top ten percent of the people in his or her job category. The individual can figure out whether he or she is in the top ten percent."

The agency conducts two types of reviews: Performance Review and Competency Assessment.

A Performance Review evaluates how senior people, primarily managers, perform against business objectives for growth and profit. "The first time an individual gets business objectives is at the manager level with five to eight years of experience," the CEO says. "In most cases, the manager has incentive compensation tied to achievement of business objectives. The Competency Assessment evaluates how competent an individual is at delivering the client service for which he or she is responsible. The Competency Assessment wants to know things like how well you understand the techniques, how well you manage your clients, and how well you drive your client to do what is needed for the agency to succeed. We do more Competency Assessments than Performance Reviews because we have more junior than senior people."

Junior people such as assistant account executives are evaluated on such factors as Drive, Orderliness, Resiliency, Resourcefulness, Sociability, Teamwork, Creativity, Economic Fundamentals, Daily Contributions and Processes, and Realization (understands and utilizes the firm's operational systems and processes that bear on public relations tactics and the time and billing process).

"People are evaluated numerically in 20 individual categories. If the minimum rating for a specific category is a '3' and the goal is '4,' and you put down a '5' for yourself and I give you a '2,' we need to discuss the difference of opinion.

"The output from the process is 'Here's how you're doing versus the requirements for the position' plus a development program. Our HR department (which monitors individuals' reviews online) is responsible for arranging appropriate training, and the people are responsible for completing their development. "All the computer is doing is automating the completion of the form, doing some extra calculations, and letting multiple people input to the form without the form having to be passed around. There still has to be a conversation between the manager and the person being reviewed."

How Am I Doing?

Here's a 360 review of a different nature. The staff of a medium-sized West Coast firm evaluated the firm's two owners using my 25-point "How Am I Doing?" questionnaire (see Exhibit 15.1). I tabulated the anonymous responses and reported to the principals.

The results confirmed several suspected and relatively serious management and administrative problems. The owners took steps to correct the problems. And here's the kicker; a follow-up survey six months later showed that the staff felt that the problems had largely been corrected.

Employees may know how you rate their performance, but have you ever asked your staff to *evaluate your performance* as a manager and leader? Have you ever asked employees what they expect from you or what changes they'd like to see in your firm's operation?

Try it. Ask employees to rank your management performance on a 1 to 10 (10 highest) scale in a number of areas. To enhance survey credibility, you may want to have an outside party, such as your accountant or a consultant, tally the results. Staff members also are likely to be more candid in a confidential survey that does not reveal their identities.

Two caveats: To make this work, it is vital that you (1) *discuss the survey results* with your staff in a group meeting, no matter how negative or positive the results may be, and (2) do everything possible to *correct any problems* revealed by the survey. If you do not take these two follow-up steps, the survey is a waste of everyone's time.

PROFESSIONAL EMPLOYER ORGANIZATIONS COME OF AGE

When I first wrote about this concept back in 1991, the vendors were called "employee leasing companies." Agency presidents I talked to then unanimously shot down the idea, claiming it would be bad for agency culture, they'd lose control, and they just didn't like it.

Now the idea has been dressed up in a new moniker; the vendors are known as "Professional Employer Organizations" (PEOs) and operate as a "co-employer" with their clients. (The name change

EXHIBIT 15.1. How Am I Doing Questionnaire

Ask your employees to rank you in these twenty-five areas:

Responsibility	Ranking (1-10)
1. Provides instructions and information necessary to complete assignment?	_____
2. Clearly outlines expectations and objectives?	_____
3. Provides training necessary for growth; is a good teacher?	_____
4. Provides opportunities for growth; challenges staff members to grow and assume additional responsibility?	_____
5. Encourages innovation?	_____
6. Encourages alternate ideas; permits and encourages disagreement on creativity and client service; does not always insist on "doing it my way"?	_____
7. Provides responsibility and authority to complete assignments; keeps hands out of the soup to a reasonable degree?	_____
8. Is open and available for discussion of business or personal problems?	_____
9. Keeps staff informed about agency status/problems/ opportunities/successes?	_____
10. Promotes a congenial, comfortable, collegial working atmosphere; believes in having fun?	_____
11. Is realistic about billable time goals?	_____
12. Discusses office policy or procedure changes with staff and asks for input?	_____
13. Supports staff in client discussions and disagreements whenever possible?	_____
14. Is fair and realistic in criticism of staff performance?	_____
15. Criticizes and/or reprimands individuals in private?	_____
16. Displays a calm, even temperament most of the time; is short on ego?	_____
17. Has established a good reputation for this agency in the public relations community?	_____

18. Is a skilled PR practitioner (when he/she needs to be); has professional skills that I respect? _____
19. Respects others' experience and skills? _____
20. Pays competitive salaries? _____
21. Provides competitive benefits? _____
22. Has established good, practical administrative systems and procedures? _____
23. Deals fairly and equally well with both male and female staff members? _____
24. Has made this a good place to work? _____
25. Is a good overall manager? _____

Please complete the following:

1. The most demeaning, annoying, and/or humiliating rule/pro-cedure/form/regulation/policy that I have to live with is:_____

_____

2. If I could change only one thing about this firm, I would:

_____
_____

To see how employees evaluate your management ability, add up the scores for each question and average them. Compile individual answers to the two questions above. Then rank your performance on this scale:

How Am I Doing?

8-10	Excellent — Apply for your halo.
6-7	Good — Couldn't be much better.
4-5	Average — Needs improvement.
1-3	Poor — Why does anyone work for you?

---

sounds like a PR mind at work.) But the basic concept is the same. The major differences are that today's PEOs offer a greater degree and variety of services and have become more acceptable in our industry, particularly among smaller PR firms. And employees don't seem to mind at all.

In the simplest and legal form, your employees also become the "co-employees" of a PEO, which for a fee handles all your human resource requirements and enables you to provide a greater variety and scope of benefits to your employees because of the PEO's buying power. PEOs generally have thousands of "co-employees," giving them more buying clout than a small agency can muster up.

For the firm not big enough to warrant a full-time HR manager or afford substantial benefits for employees, tying in with a PEO makes a lot of sense. In addition to handling paperwork like payroll, taxes, Social Security and Workmen's Compensation deposits, and the filing requirements of other government bodies, a PEO will

- Organize and manage your 401(k) plan;
- Provide life, medical, disability, dental, and vision insurance for your employees;
- Provide tuition reimbursement for employees;
- Help with recruiting by vetting job candidates;
- Deliver on-the-job training to employees;
- Provide adoption assistance to employees;
- Offer legal advice in sticky employee relations questions;
- Redo your employee manual; and
- Offer a batch of other services.

The biggest benefit of signing up with a PEO may be that your employees also legally become the "co-employees" of the PEO for everything having to do with human resources and employee relations, actually relieving you of a batch of paperwork and liability. While you continue to set salary schedules, employees' paychecks (and yours) come with the PEO logo. From an operational standpoint, however, they are your employees; you hire and fire them and direct all their client service activities. But if they have questions about benefits, for example, they call their PEO rep instead of clogging up your office door. Agency presidents I talked to who work with a PEO claim that their employees have no problem with the fact that their checks come from someone else and that there is no significant impact on agency "culture" by the new relationship. Plus, if you need to handle some queasy employee relations questions, such as dismissing a pregnant employee or an older person, the PEO will guide you through the process and help protect you from legal traps.

The bottom line is that you're relieved of paperwork hassles and, because of the PEO's "economies of scale," you probably can afford a wider array of employee benefits than you could on your own.

There are about 2,000 PEOs providing such services. Administaff, which has a number of PR agency clients, is headquartered in Kingman, Texas, with regional offices around the country. You also can reach the national organization, National Association of Professional Employers Organizations, at www.napeo.org.

Administaff has more than 76,000 "co-employees," providing heavy negotiating power in the benefit cost war. Costs are based on a small percentage of your payroll plus the cost of the benefits and service package you elect. According to Paul Sarvadi, Administaff president, (800-237-3170), the average agency's cost is $150 to $200 per employee annually or 3 to 4 percent of the firm' payroll, depending on the benefit and service package it signs up for and its payroll, tax, and other HR costs. Alan Dodd, Administaff corporate communications director, says its average client has 16 employees and that the program "doesn't really work too well with less than six employees." Your size is a good guideline as to whether you'd be a good candidate for a PEO. You can check this out by taking the Administaff "Company Profile Test" at www.administaff.com.

Here are eight PR agencies that are clients of a PEO (not all Administaff). I'm sure their presidents would be happy to discuss their PEO experiences with you:

- LVM Group: New York, David Grant, President (212-751-2800)
- Hanson, Moser & Associates: Scottsdale, Arizona, Scott Hanson, President (602-957-8881)
- GCS Public Relations: San Diego, California, Tom Gable, Chairman (858-458-5835)
- Carlman Booker Reis: Orlando, Florida, Lori Booker, President (407-834-7777)
- Katcher Vaughn & Bailey: Brentwood, Tennessee, Aileen Katcher, Principal (615-248-8201)
- Public Communications: Tampa, Florida, Jim Frankowiak, President (813-226-2772)
- Vandiver Group: St. Louis, Missouri, Donna Vandiver, President (314-991-4641)
- Identity Marketing and PR: Detroit, Michigan, Tom Nixon, President (248-258-2333)

According to Lori Booker, president, Carlman Booker Reis, Orlando, Florida,

> I'll never manage my firm without a PEO again. Since Administaff took over all the workers' comp and HR liability issues, I've slept better at night. And the first year they took over, my profits increased more than twenty percent. Their online HR site is unbelievable. If I have an employee who needs to learn Access or Excel, they learn it free on the Administaff Web site. If I have someone with leadership/management issues, or phone etiquette problems, I just steer them to the Web site. In today's health care coverage crisis, my twenty-person company has benefits better than their friends at Disney or the local *Tribune* paper. We also have dental and vision insurance and a great Employee Assistance Program.

However, PEOs are not for everyone, according to other agency executives. The senior vice president of a midsized West Coast agency with more than 50 employees who interviewed a PEO but decided against it, said,

> We had three reasons for opting out at this point. First, because we didn't have a detailed plan for multistate growth, we felt that we were still capable of managing the HR function through our in-house HR representative. I think there is more value when dealing with employees in multiple states for tax, legal, and other considerations. Currently we are in California and New York. Secondly, there is a clear benefit in the buying power that these types of firms can have for areas like medical insurance. However, when we compared the benefits against our own current medical benefits, we had a richer plan across the board for the same price. This might be a different story for companies with less than fifty people where they fall into the small group market. Thirdly, we are a high-touch organization with a unique culture where people come before profit. Based on some of our research, we found that employers dealing with these companies often felt that they were directed to a Web site versus dealing with a live body. We wanted more of that control. Even the documents we would have been required to sign for legal purposes made us feel that we were giving away too much control.

PROFILE 15: DAVID PAINE

President, PainePR
New York and Los Angeles

According to David Paine,

We believe that the various elements
of our business—our people, management, clients, suppliers, and profit—
all need to be given equal consideration; there has to be synergy between
all the elements as the company moves
forward and makes decisions about
itself. This unique philosophy of do-
ing business enables us to attract and serve clients well, attract
and retain top talent, maintain very high levels of employee morale, and minimize employee turnover.

With seven years of major PR firm experience under his belt, Paine
started his firm in 1986 with five clients and $179,000 income the
first year. Today, the firm has more than 30 blue chip clients, 60 employees, $10 million in income, and a reputation as one of the coun-
try's most creative and best managed PR firms.

However, in the early years, Paine says he made such mistakes as

Putting growth ahead of profit. Hiring people without sufficient
due diligence to ensure that they possessed the necessary skills,
fit culturally, and would contribute to the quality of the organization. And allowing the firm to run me, instead of managing
the firm.

Advice for agency principals:

Be prepared to see your job change from practitioner to business
manager. Be ready in advance. Study business theory. Learn
how a world class organization runs. And develop your own
ideas. Don't just borrow from what you learned in your early
days working at other firms because, in most cases, the methods
of larger firms are seriously flawed.

Chapter 16

Managing Good and Bad Times: Growth and Recession

Anticipating and managing the priorities and problems that come with growth could be compared to learning to ice skate. It's not as easy as it looks, but it's certainly as much fun as you expected . . . once you get the hang of it.

Public relations firms have been compared to sharks; if you're not moving ahead, you may die. On the other hand, if you move ahead too fast, with your eyes closed and no sense of direction, you may slam your nose on a rock.

You also may

- run yourself ragged;
- lose good people;
- lose clients; and
- lose money.

After surviving several recessions (more on that later), reduced or eliminated client budgets, and disappointing new business pitches, as well as the joys and trauma of fast expansion, over a 25-year agency career, I learned that it is often as difficult to manage growth as it is to cope with more negative aspects of the agency business. I also learned that following a few simple principles will guide you safely through to the promised payoff.

Careful planning, good backup people to manage and maintain quality client service, a solid business plan with well-thought-out systems and procedures, and enough cash or a good credit line should be your most important growth priorities.

doi:10.1300/5561_16

245

A survey of PR firm principals who have experienced fast expansion indicated that the primary problems and priorities of growth revolve almost exclusively around two factors: people and systems.

Strangely enough, having enough funds to support expansion was not usually mentioned as an unsolvable or particularly difficult problem, assuming that the firm was able to establish a good credit line early on and paid consistent and concentrated attention to collecting receivables.

And that the principal didn't try to take all the gold out of the mine for himself at the beginning, but put money back into the business. One principal said, "If you're in this business for the short run, you're in for trouble."

A West Coast principal calculates that every new employee can cost at least $20,000 for computers, furniture, and other items, not to mention salary, before the new practitioner earns a cent for the firm. This firm exploded to more than 30 people and two offices in just under five years. The principal knows that she must be prepared for a serious cash outlay every time she thinks about adding people.

Another owner said,

> Establish your credit line before you need it. Get the biggest line of credit you can. You may not think you need a credit line until one of your clients gets in trouble and pays you in ninety days instead of forty-five, and you have to make payroll. When you're expanding, you don't have time to figure out where you're going to get that next bit of cash that you need.

In almost every instance, the principals surveyed talked about the problems that a lack of good backup professionals—usually a number two person—caused during expansion. The biggest problem, as you might imagine, was poor quality control in client service. (On the other side, clients may complain that agencies spend too much time seeking new business and not enough serving their current clients.)

When expansion hit, principals often were spread too thin to pay attention to everything. A Northern California principal said, "I got too fragmented, lost control, and had huge staff and client turnover."

The owner finally solved his problem by hiring an experienced professional to back him up. Asked how he would handle expansion if he had it to do over again under similar circumstances, he said,

"First, I'd find a super number two person to focus on running current business."

In another instance, a Midwest principal said his mistake was trying to find a senior person on the outside when he had good people inside who could have been promoted to greater responsibility.

A New York city principal said the key to managing expansion was knowing the capabilities and capacity of your present staff and being aware of how much additional business they could handle properly.

Another New York city principal noted that expansion forced him to trust his staff and learn to delegate—not too much and not too little.

Several principals recommended staying a least one person ahead all the time. In other words, having a least one more person on staff than your current business will support. Or, at the very least, keeping your networks warm and being aware of people who can be hired quickly when it becomes necessary to staff up. (The CEO of a major Midwest firm said, "We don't do that nearly as well as we should.")

This means interviewing people regularly, even though you may not have an opening at the time, and building a good resume file.

All of this boils down to one rather obvious fact: if you do not invest early on in the right kind and number of senior people to help you manage growth, you are likely to encounter very rough times and could end up worse off than before you expanded. The best time to acquire or train your backup is before growth problems smother you.

SYSTEMS TO HELP MANAGE EXPANSION

The same philosophy applies to the installation of systems and procedures that you will need to manage expansion. Put your systems in place before you need them! This deserves repeating, because it is so important. Put your administrative systems in place before you need them.

It's much easier to install systems while you are small than to try to impose them when you are larger or trying to handle rapid growth.

What kinds of systems will you need? To start with, a networked computer system. Time and billing software that lets you automate time submission, get out billing before the middle of the month, and track agency and client profitability.

An effective system to keep track of expenses to be billed back to clients is vital. As one agency principal said,

> The more clients you have, the more money can dribble through your hands without the right systems. If you haven't caught on to the right systems when you have two or three clients, heaven help you when you have fifteen.

One principal even said that if he had to make a cash decision between people and systems, he probably would put his money into systems. Some years ago, this firm's computers were not networked. Staff members often had difficulty locating stored information. Information could not be shared easily between practitioners or support staff. Today, that principal says, "Networking my computers was the best investment I ever made."

Another principal said,

> Systems saved us. We always had better systems than were absolutely needed at the time. We watched our numbers very closely and had a handle on profitability long before most agencies do. When we put a stamp on an envelope, we got twenty-nine [now thirty-seven] cents back from the client. We knew the number of hours our people billed and how that applied to clients. When we needed more sophisticated systems, we brought in a business manager.

Other systems that you will need when you expand that, perhaps, you could do without when you were smaller include channels to communicate easily and efficiently with all employees (e-mail) and an organizational infrastructure that defines account management responsibilities.

A New Jersey firm that grew from a four-person home-basement office to an 11-person commercial office in less than a year encountered serious problems. Information was not flowing up from the account staff to management, and the principal had trouble managing and maintaining client service quality control. An outside consultant helped the principal establish a management structure and a communication system that solved the problem.

You also should develop an orientation program and a manual for new employees as well as an account start-up manual to define the standard procedures that must be gone through and the information and materials that are needed when beginning service to a new client.

Train your staff not only to serve clients properly but also to manage accounts profitably. Too often, staff members, particularly younger employees, are totally committed to providing excellent client service, but do not pay enough attention to the agency's need to be profitable. (Remember the two conflicting responsibilities of account management.)

Office space is, of course, another problem that comes with growth. Where are you going to put all the people you hire to handle all the new business? Most principals in the survey recommended always having slightly more space than you need at the moment, but not so much that rental costs become excessive. Doubling up in offices is possible, but seldom comfortable or efficient. Subletting excess space to a noncompetitor is an option. Some independent noncompetitive firms even share the same space.

How do you know when you're ready to expand? There are two ways, one based on projected income and the other on a more philosophical approach.

RESOURCE ALLOCATION MATRIX

Since growth means new clients, new income, and additional employees, you should constantly look ahead and project how all the new business is likely to impact on your staff requirements.

The Resource Allocation Matrix shown in Chapter 11 will help you accomplish this. Applying the matrix will enable you to determine the number of people you are likely to need in the future based on the income you expect to generate from both current and new clients. Using this matrix also will help you plan, assign, and balance work loads, balance income, and avoid problems caused by the cyclical nature of the agency business. In addition, it will help keep average staff productivity high and provide guidelines for short- and long-term staff needs.

THE PHILOSOPHICAL APPROACH

A second way to determine whether you are ready to grow requires personal introspection and answers to some tough questions:

- Does the potential new business have substantial, long-range, profit potential, or is it likely to be only a short burst?
- Is my credit line or cash flow good enough to support the additional cost of serving the new business before it becomes profitable?
- Do I have the right kind of people in place or available to manage expansion as well as maintain client service? Will I have to hire people? What kind of people? How much will that cost in salaries and benefits?
- Do I have the systems in place or in development that I'll need when we get bigger?

Probably the most difficult question to answer is a very personal one. Do I have to expand, and do I want to?

One principal warned, "The big message is, Decide what you want to do. Don't let growth be forced on you if you're not ready or don't want it."

Expansion brings some special business considerations and personal demands that are less important when you're smaller. How much expansion can you handle? Be realistic about how much money you will need to grow and how much of your profit you want to use to expand. In reality, you'll be spending your take-home money.

Don't expand too fast. Determine what your revenue will be and what expenses and profits would be if you stayed the same size. Your formulas are going to change radically when you grow.

Decide how big you want to be. Do you want your firm to have five people or fifty people? Sometimes, small firms win large accounts, are forced to hire additional people, and, suddenly, are bigger than the principal wanted to be in the first place.

"If you don't decide what you want to do," one principal said, "The tail wags the dog; the owner feels victimized; employees feel like a ship without a captain or a rudder . . . and everyone is miserable."

Too often, a principal may not think about the personal impact of expansion. What it means to your personal and professional life in terms of the time you will have to spend with your family or do the kinds of things you like to do—including work with clients.

One of the biggest problems among small and medium-sized firms is reluctance or inability of the principal to separate himself far enough from client service so that he has enough time to manage the business properly and make it grow profitably.

Be very clear about one thing. If you are to manage growth properly and come out of it profitably and with your skin on, you will be required to do less client work and handle more administrative chores. That can be a real problem, particularly if you like to do client work and have trouble giving it up.

Expansion also brings with it a broader need to motivate other people. You may need to be careful about the image you project to your staff. An executive of a large firm had a habit of sighing to relax. He found this to be very cathartic. Unfortunately, he learned that staff members thought his sighs meant that the company was in trouble.

A top executive of a national PR firm felt that he must never display excessive happiness or unhappiness because of what he might inadvertently communicate to employees.

Where you are in your life also is an important expansion consideration. As one female principal put it, "If you feel young and energetic—no matter what your biological age—and are ready to kick butts and take names, that's the time to expand."

So, if you're ready to kick butts and take names, go to it—and good luck.

THE BAD DAYS COMETH

On the other hand, sooner or later, and you can lay money on it, you will wake up one morning and find that the economy has soured seemingly overnight. Clients' budgets have been squeezed or disappear; corporations decide to take work inside that they would ordinarily assign to an agency; new business prospects dry up or take forever to make a decision. It's called a *recession.*

Every one who's been in the agency business for any length of time has experienced a recession; they occur with some regularity. If you started your business in the early 2000s, you found that life was tough. If you were in business during 1990-1992, you'd just as soon forget that those were recession years. And if you were in the business earlier than that, maybe stretching back to the 1980s or early 1970s, you really don't want to remember anything about those recession years.

However, history does repeat itself, and you need to be prepared for it, particularly in the good times.

How to Spot a Coming Recession

Before economists and other pundits make their solemn proclamations and the media clocks three successive bad quarters—accepted signs that a recession has already hit—there are some things you can watch for. When these signs accumulate or occur simultaneously, it's time to nail the plywood over the windows and head for the high ground:

- Excessive nitpicking of bills by clients
- Slower than usual payment
- Postponement of client product introductions
- Cancellation of client sales meetings
- Generally slower decisions by clients or prospects
- Cancellation of a client Christmas party/celebration or employee gifts/bonus
- New business prospects begin to dry up
- Insider selling of shares by client executives
- Female hemline changes (Going up is a good sign. Dropping means gloomy prospects, says consumer mythology.)

During the early 2000s recession, I asked a group of agency principals what they'd learned about surviving recessions. Here's what they told me:

- "Always manage your firm as if you were in a tough economy." (This is probably the most meaningful piece of advice here, perhaps even in the entire book!)
- "Don't panic; take control of your destiny."
- "Don't hold on to money-sucking satellite offices. In any economy, be careful about starting a branch office unless you're pretty sure it will succeed in a reasonable amount of time. At the

first signs of a recession, dump an office that's a drag on your bottom line."

- "When bad times loom on the horizon, terminate the people who aren't pulling their weight immediately. When a recession hits, lots of good people are suddenly available. No need to hold on to rum-dums or malcontents."
- "Diversify into new fields, industries, or services. Don't stick solely to a mature or ailing industry or a service with a limited or drying up demand."
- "Be wary of debt under most circumstances, but be especially cautious of committing to unmanageable debt in bad times. On the other hand, develop good banking relationships in case you need a financial helping hand to tide you over until brighter days arrive." (And sooner or later, they will.)
- "Try to obtain and retain recession-proof clients."
- "Diversify within client organizations; generate business in as many departments, divisions, subsidiaries as possible."
- "Treat suppliers well; develop relationships with vendors who could be inclined to give you a break when times get tough."
- "Control salary costs. Consider bonuses and profit sharing (if any) as a way to hold down permanent, ongoing staff costs."
- "Keep employees informed; build a sense of security during good times that can carry over into bad times."
- "Sell hard; market your firm continually and effectively."
- "Suggest fee reductions and other cost-cutting measures to clients when they are being squeezed."
- "Watch the horizon for signs of an impending recession."
- "Know your core competencies and key employees; watch your cash."
- "Get fee deposits."
- "Strong positioning is the key, as in being in industries that are weathering the recession well such as pharmaceuticals and certain retail markets."
- "Pay extra attention to expense control; strive for incremental business from existing clients."
- "Demonstrating the value of what we do is now more important than ever. A slow economy gives our industry the opportunity to carve out more of the marketing communications pie. We should

aggressively take care of current business and market ourselves to as many prospects as possible."

- "You will never have the attention of the people who work for you more than you do now given how many of their friends have been laid off. The economic realities have hit home to the twenty-somethings. (Remember, this was in the middle of a recession, when as many as 5,000 agency people were on the street.) Now is when you find out who represents the future of your agency by who demonstrates their commitment to doing what it takes to get the job done for clients."
- "Cut staff once, but cut deeply and get it over with. Then hire only if new business is obtained. Review all other expenses."
- "Above all, demonstrate real value in helping to meet clients' business objectives."
- "Stay on top of collections; review financial projections frequently."
- "Stay laser-focused on doing a terrific job for your clients. In tough times, clients most appreciate good work turned around quickly and on-budget. Firms with an inherent work ethic and time management controls do well in a down economy."

On the other hand, remember that eventually all recessions go away.

PROFILE 16: STEVEN PARKER

Chief Executive Officer, The CCL Group Inc.
Halifax, Nova Scotia, Canada

In 1977, six years out of college, Steve Parker started a PR firm that generated $42,000 in income the first year. More than a quarter of a century later, Parker leads a $25 million integrated marketing and communications organization with 10 offices in three countries, 500 people, and $5 million in public relations income.

All this from headquarters in Halifax, Nova Scotia, a city of 330,000 quite a distance from the closest major cities, Montreal, Toronto, and Boston. According to Parker,

> We were an integrated organization before the industry term was even invented. Starting in a small market and wanting to have the best available talent and greatest opportunities, it was common sense to have different services within the same organization. Since we started most of these disciplines from the ground up, we have had relatively few issues bringing them seamlessly together for the benefit of the client. It is far more difficult for organizations that acquire various disciplines, each with their own culture, and try to put them together.

The CCL Group is remarkably diverse, with functions including market research, public relations, advertising, print and Internet design and production, video production, and customer relationship management.

Parker said,

> The increasing importance of public relations with a marketing function helps us because we have the natural ability to integrate marketing and public relations. A growing number of clients come to us expecting that our diversity will lead to more cost efficient ways in which to promote their interests or products.

In most markets The CCL Group uses local people to lead its offices. Additionally, the firm has specialists in its head office in Halifax, Nova Scotia, and elsewhere. Our specialists provide support in the background to regional leaders who know their customers and their markets extremely well.

It is a formula that is working for this Canadian company, which has quietly become a leader among independent communications agencies.

Chapter 17

Crisis Planning for PR Firms

ITEM—A workshop on crisis planning for public relations firms, scheduled for the PRSA Counselors Academy's Spring Conference, is cancelled for lack of interest.

ITEM—At two thinly attended Counselors Academy workshops, a Chicago PR firm president explained how she coped with being forced out of her firm's quarters by a natural disaster.

ITEM —The biggest flood in the history of Des Moines, Iowa, leaves CMF&Z PR with no running water and most staff members ordered to work from home.

ITEM—A construction accident forces Edelman's New York office staff out of their adjoining building for a week. The firm's management concedes that it did not then have a crisis plan in place to deal with a long-term overall evacuation of a central office. The firm's management said they were in the process of developing a plan to handle such a crisis.

Talk about locking the barn doors after the horse is gone! If one of the world's largest PR firms can get blindsided by an unexpected crisis, how easy would it be for you to find yourself in a similar conundrum?

Despite urging clients to prepare for crisis, most PR firms ignore their own counsel. Few principals have taken the time to develop crisis response and business resumption plans. Have you?

DISASTER PLANNING

Three types of potential crises face every PR firm: (1) those that can damage your firm's reputation; (2) those that can damage your

doi:10.1300/5561_17

ability to serve your clients; and (3) those that can impact your financial wherewithal.

Here are some of the potential disasters that can severely damage your firm's reputation (thanks to Anne Klein, president, Anne Klein & Associates, Mt. Laurel, New Jersey, for the list):

- Accusations, correct or incorrect, by a local, state, or U.S. government agency
- Accusations of poor work by a client
- Accusations of unethical behavior
- Agency scandal (discrimination, drugs, sex, etc.)
- Bankruptcy
- Conflict of interest caused by serving clients in similar fields
- Conflict of interest caused by moonlighting staffers
- Controversial clients
- Controversial firm contribution or pro bono work
- Controversial statements about firm's financial stability
- Controversial statements about the firm's work
- Controversial statements about the principal or staff
- Embezzlement
- Employee diagnosed with AIDS
- Employee breach of confidentiality
- Employee misstatement (intentional or otherwise) to a client
- Employee misstatement (intentional or otherwise) to the public or news media
- Employee violates noncompete clause
- Key staffers pitch client, then leave to start own firm
- Lawsuits (employee sues agency or vice versa; firm sues client or vice versa; equal opportunity, age discrimination, wrongful discharge, or sexual harassment charge filed against agency)
- Abrupt/rapid income drop
- Layoffs or other high-impact/high-visibility cost-cutting measures
- Loss of name partner
- Serious illness, injury, or death of principal
- Merger (also merger gone sour)
- Misappropriation of ideas (staff member takes ideas/plans/files from another agency or company and gives them to a competing client; staff member takes your ideas/clients to a competing firm)

- SEC, IRS, or other violations of the law
- Serious media misquote in behalf of firm or client
- Serious media attack on firm
- Third-party (vendor) nondelivery of services
- Third-party poor performance reflecting on firm in the eyes of either clients or public
- Unlawful activities on your property: gang fights, drug deals, drug or alcohol use
- Violation of PRSA Code of Ethics or inquiry by PRSA Judicial Panel

In addition to legal and reputation problems, you also face potential natural and man-made disasters. What would you do, for example, if your

- Computer system fails?
- Computer guru quits?
- Key staff member, working on your largest client, quits or leaves to work for a client?
- Firm has too much staff turnover in too short a time?
- Staff size is suddenly or drastically reduced and income lost because several of your staff members become pregnant simultaneously?
- Building has a major problem and no one can work inside for several days? (What would you remove if you were allowed inside for only a few minutes?)
- Building is damaged/destroyed by fire, including all your records?
- Key equipment/documents are stolen?
- Employee is robbed, attacked, or killed on or off your property?
- Staff member calls to report he or she has been in an accident en route to a client?
- Staff members and client are in an accident and your insurance lacks adequate liability coverage?
- Employee morale is adversely affected by the loss of one or more key clients?
- Client defaults on a multithousand dollar bill?

Here are the types of information that should be in your crisis response/business resumption plan, according to Anne Klein:

- Names of the authorized agency spokespersons;
- Names of those who talk with the media, clients, employees;
- Guidelines for dealing with the news media;
- Guidelines for how to use the fax, copier, phone, e-mail system, and other basic support equipment;
- Guidelines for how the computer system works, where the back-up tapes or disks are stored (preferably off-site), and how to retrieve them and get the system running again;
- Names, addresses, business/home phone numbers, fax numbers, e-mail addresses (where appropriate) for all staff members (including a relative's number for emergency use), outside consultants (accountant, attorney, computer programmers, financial planner, insurance broker, management consultant), suppliers (fax, copier, postage meter, telephone service, alternate communication systems), and all key client contacts including home numbers;
- List of banks or financial institutions including account numbers and contracts;
- Location of principal/s will/s, succession plan, key person, and other insurance policies;
- Location of important business documents and financial information kept with third-party consultants;
- Location of off-site storage facility (including name, address, phone and fax numbers);
- Policy regarding storage/access to central files for client information; and
- Provision for employees to work from home when kept out of the office. (For example, issue each employee a "work at home" kit containing material needed to operate out of the office for at least several days.)

In addition, Gary Myers, former president, Morgan & Myers, Jefferson, Wisconsin, recommends that firms protect themselves against the loss of important records as well as loss of the firm's owner/s. According to Myers,

> In our business, there are very few "natural" disasters that really threaten the viability of the firm. Although they are a pain at the time, you can overcome the physical damage of fires, floods, and hurricanes.

However, there are two real disasters that are very hard to overcome. A crisis avoidance plan for these situations is a must:

- Loss of your accounts receivable records. If you lose these, you're dead. Have redundancy/back-up in all financial records, but especially work-in-progress and aged receivables.
- Loss of the owner/s. Does the firm have an obvious/designated heir apparent? A succession plan? A formula to pay off the surviving spouse? Insurance coverage to cover that eventuality?

In our buy-sell agreement at M&M, the valuation formula is very well spelled out. We also have had independent parties review it periodically and include their evaluations in our corporate minutes. Our buy-sell agreement also specifically states that a surviving spouse is to be bought out and does not become a "partner" in the business. Spouses sign the buy-sell as well as the partners themselves.

DEALING WITH THE LOSS OF AN OWNER

A West Coast firm ran into real problems because a mistake was made in the purchase of key man insurance. In sharing firm responsibilities, the president handled the business affairs while the executive vice president (EVP)/partner managed client service. Although the firm had key man insurance based on the then-current value of the firm, the president, for cost reasons, unfortunately decided not to increase the firm's key man insurance when the firm's business almost doubled in a few months from about $2.5 million to $4 million. Even more unfortunate, the EVP/partner was not informed of this decision.

Then the president died suddenly and unexpectedly.

The surviving EVP/partner became the firm's president and presumed that the firm's buy-sell agreement, tied to the insurance policy, would buy out and pay off the president's family. Not so! Existing insurance didn't cover the firm's increased value.

While dealing with personal mourning over the loss of his partner, the new president now needed to run both sides of the business, comfort a predominantly young staff who had never experienced death, and reassure clients. And then here came the lawyers representing the bank/trustee of his former partner's estate. (The heirs were largely the former partner's teenage sons.) Said the surviving partner,

> It was awful. The bank, which received a percentage of the estate's value, sent in waves of accountants and lawyers. They looked in every bucket we had and basically tried to attach it to the bottom line, including trying to include expense mark-up in the firm's valuation. At its worst point, they were telling me that I owed something like $3 million. The negotiations became very contentious.
>
> I was put in the position of having to say to their people, "If you're going to hold me to that, I'm just going to walk away from the agency—and you'll have nothing." I had to threaten to sue the estate for "breach of fiduciary responsibility" because of the unfortunate insurance shortfall. However, with the help of a very good attorney, I ended up only having to pay the estate an additional $325,000, which I did with one check. And it was done. But the whole thing took a year to settle.
>
> You always expect when someone dies that you'll be dealing with somebody you know, people who understand the spirit of the business partnership. If I'd known that I was going to have to deal with a bank/trustee's lawyers for my former partner's estate, I'd have had another look at the buy-sell agreement.
>
> Unfortunately, nearly twenty years of wonderful memories have been tarnished by a bank's bottom-line greed during a period of mourning.

When was the last time you checked your firm's valuation and the insurance covering your buy-sell agreement? In addition, it's ten o'clock; do you know where your firm's accounts receivable records are?

What would you do if your firm was suddenly slapped with an ugly lawsuit or a fire destroyed your equipment and records? Now is the time to write a crisis plan. Update it regularly; explain it to your staff, and dry run it at least annually. Keep copies at your home and those of your senior people as well as in an off-site location such as a bank safety deposit box. Then you'll be as ready as possible when disaster strikes.

WHEN EMPLOYEES VIOLATE
NONCOMPETE AGREEMENTS

On the other hand, dishonest employees can create a crisis of a different stripe.

This is the tale of three agency employees who violated their noncompete agreements and burned their bridges behind them.

Late one recent year, a senior female staff member left a Midwest agency citing "personal reasons." Several months later, two additional female employees resigned to join the former employee in a new start-up agency.

Ordinarily, this would have been fine. Entrepreneurs deserve to be encouraged. Unfortunately, the three professionals—who had all signed noncompete agreements—entered their new venture via a totally dishonest and professionally dishonorable route. While still employed by the agency, the two later resignees conspired with the former employee to take business away from the agency. And to make matters worse, the trio discussed their plans with each other via the agency's e-mail network, even going so far as to communicate their upcoming move to one of the firm's major clients! (Who handled this unprofessional approach in a very professional manner.) The first resignee also warned the two still-employed people to be sure to "double delete" their messages from their computer hard drives.

The two employees' abrupt resignation came as a total surprise to the agency's president, because the duo had pledged their commitment to the agency numerous times and had been actively involved in planning the agency's future.

The trio's actions were not only dishonest and dishonorable, but were downright dumb. While they deleted material from their individual computers before leaving, all three forgot—or ignored the fact—that the agency backed up its computers every night to an outside service and, therefore, had copies of all the e-mails that had been exchanged between the three women as well as with the agency's client!

Not only that, the trio ignored the fact that they had signed noncompete agreements when hired. The e-mail records documented that the former senior employee conspired with the two "inside" women to create business for her new firm; to steer prospects from the agency to the new firm; to encourage the still-employed women to work for the new firm during their regular business hours; and to attempt to have the agency pay the women's expenses to go to other cities to pursue business for the new firm.

The agency president, of course, immediately consulted his attorney and considered his options. They ranged from doing nothing to taking tough legal action. In reality, after thinking about the situation, getting over his anger, disillusionment, and disappointment, and having his attorney send the former senior employee a "cease and desist" letter with copies of some of the damaging e-mails, the agency president decided that the defectors had more to lose from their disreputable deeds than he did. He had not and was not likely to lose any business to the new agency; it was apparent that except for creating some legal bills for the new agency (as well as for his own agency), he probably couldn't gain any financial compensation for their actions, because they had little or no money and all had family responsibilities. So the aggrieved agency's attorney sent one final letter, threatening to take the trio to court if they did one additional thing to damage the agency. And that's where it rests today, like a ticking bomb hanging over the defectors' heads.

What did the agency president learn from this ugly mess?

> If I've learned anything from this, it's that you want an enforceable agreement that keeps employees from stealing or trying to steal clients. Even if they try and fail to steal a client, they can screw up the relationship and use agency time to do it. It's like paying a crook to try to burglarize your home. A tight, well-written agreement can be a strong deterrent. I'm convinced ours is limited in scope and very enforceable. The traitors haven't succeeded in stealing even a single client.

With little or nothing to gain financially, the president let it drop—like a ton of sand on the defectors' heads. He also made sure that his remaining employees understood the dishonorable actions that their former colleagues had taken as well as the way he had responded. Then he said, "It's time to move on."

I asked a number of agency presidents whether they had taken any action in similar instances. Generally, the response was, "Noncompetes are very difficult to enforce." The consensus was that you're better off having employees sign noncompetes than not, if only as a deterrent to anyone with weird ideas. In addition, be sure to back up all computer traffic including employees' e-mail daily. And warn employees that all such messages are the agency's property to do with what it will.

PROFILE 17: BOB SCHENKEIN

Founder, Schenkein Inc.
Denver, Colorado

Several things distinguish Schenkein Inc. from many other midsized PR firms. First, the agency started in 1973 with $177,000 of PR income, evolved into a full-service advertising and PR firm, and then—bucking a trend—spun off its advertising side. Bob stayed with the $1.5 million PR unit.

Second, the firm is widely respected not only for its client service prowess, but for its unique employee culture emphasizing staff coaching.

And third, beginning in the mid-1990s, Bob put a successful exit strategy in place, a feat envied by many other agency owners.

In the early years, the agency experienced significant growth, which was accompanied by a certain amount of pain due to Bob's lack of agency experience for guidance:

> I soloed on everything; hired a lot of rookies; did not have experienced backup; had no proactive marketing plan; waited for business to walk in the door; tended to accept any kind of client and often stretched the agency too thin trying to keep up with a broad client base; did not build evaluation methodology into our programs; and should have joined a PR agency network earlier.
>
> Today, I'd work first for a large regional or national firm; hire experienced senior personnel sooner; join the PRSA Counselors Academy; and attract a highly qualified partner.

About Bob's exit strategy: in the mid 1990s, he began talking to his two talented top female executives, Leanna Clark and Christin Crampton Day, about eventually taking over the firm. Beginning in 1998, after sacrificing bonuses and salary increases for four years, the duo each purchased 15 percent of the firm. In 2002, they obtained a Small

Business Administration loan, purchased Bob's remaining interests, and assumed total ownership of the firm. Bob stayed on for a couple of years in largely a rainmaker role and retired at the end of 2004, one of the few agency principals to exit the agency business exactly the way he planned it.

Chapter 18

The Rise of Procurement and the Fall of Profits: Winning in Procurement-Led Buying Processes

I've always believed that the amount of profit earned by a privately owned company could be kept confidential, except for IRS eyes, if the owner/s wanted it that way. This confidentiality principle certainly should apply to PR agencies, unless the enterprise is one of the large public multinationals. Over the past few years, that's been changing for many PR agencies, especially those dealing with large corporate clients. It's called "procurement" (or "cost cutting" in a big way).

A BIT OF HISTORY

Some years ago, the CFO of one of my agency clients was required to negotiate new hourly billing rates with the purchasing department of one of the firm's major clients. A most trying situation, I thought: negotiating something as vaporous as an hourly billing rate with an individual whose professional experience encompassed buying—at the lowest possible cost—a variety of physical products. Not a happy experience. But an anomaly in those days, I remember thinking. However, I should have felt a tingle on the back of my neck.

A few years later, the president of a midsized Eastern agency was asked by a large client to supply previously confidential agency information, such as overhead percentages, salaries, and the amount of profit the agency expected to generate on the account. I squirmed at the discomfort the agency president was experiencing in order to supply the requested information without giving away the store.

doi:10.1300/5561_18

AND EVEN MORE RECENTLY

I talked with the CEO of a midsized Midwest agency who told me about the first time he dipped his toes in the procurement waters. This had happened six or seven years earlier. The CEO lived to talk about it, not only talk about it but benefit from the occasion.

It seems he was asked, out of the blue, by a client's purchasing department, for some pretty basic information about the agency's costs, i.e., how much did it cost to do various kinds of projects? When the agency CEO inquired why the purchasing guy was inquiring, he was told, "I want to put together some material before we call you in." And at that, the red flags went up. Everything the agency CEO had been hearing about cost-cutting moves directed at "widget" manufacturers was evidently being rolled out against service firms, namely, his PR firm.

But this CEO didn't panic. He thought, *Here's an opportunity to teach the purchasing guy a little bit about the agency business.* So he made an appointment with the purchasing guy and spent an hour or so educating him on the agency business, the kinds of things agencies do, and why it's sometimes hard to quantify that.

The agency CEO said,

> I was lucky. I was able to get in on the ground floor of something new. I consider myself very fortunate compared to what's going on today. The basic advice I would give to anybody going through this is, "See if there is a way to help educate and support the procurement department, to be part of the process instead of having the process done to you."

The agency CEO said he also learned to make sure there was an opportunity to talk about achieving efficiencies in the agency-client relationship and how to work toward that versus just focusing on the agency's cost. The agency CEO continued:

> And then [when we were asked for a proposal], we held our breath and discounted in good faith that first time around [reduced the agency's cost] on a couple of our staff experience levels because we knew that they were looking at sixteen other agencies; every one of which wanted our business.

Unfortunately [in our proposal], we forgot to account for the fact that we were going to have a rate increase the following year.

So, after retaining the business over all the other agencies, even though its bid was not the lowest, the agency had to hold to its rates for a couple years and watch its margins go in the tank. The CEO noted,

> What I got off easy on, was that all these guys [the purchasing officials] wanted to know was that we were in the ballpark. I told them what they should know and that they should look at whether the agency is in line. And that's what they went on.

The agency supported its cause by providing a wealth of industry statistics such as typical margins, salaries, billing rates, etc.

I asked the CEO, "Do you feel like you have a pretty tight control on how much profit you can earn now from this client?" He answered,

> We do now. I've heard that the firms that are having the hardest time with this [procurement problem] are the ones that have finally managed to work their retainer relationships to their advantage [and now they're confronted by clients wanting to cut costs]. We've chosen not to ask for retainers unless the client really wants it. We have pre-fixed budgets, and there's always budget money if we come up with a good idea. We know what the game plan is; we know what it's going to take to get it done; we know who's going to do the work; and we know what the hours are. So our margins are pretty much built in. We don't up-charge, and we try not to write off.
>
> These days, it's not whether the agency is in line; it's how low can they go. That's why I believe I had a kinder and gentler experience—as jarring as it was—[than agencies are having today].

I asked the CEO, "What do you hear in talking to other agencies about how they are adapting to or accepting or handling this new procurement thing?"

Oddly enough, it's become kind of a bond, a common bond among agencies that typically may not share much with each other. We are all fighting a common problem that requires—to the extent that we're not under nondisclosure agreements—a lot of brains to be brought together to solve the problem. What I worry about is that if we don't take some industry positions on this, it's going to be every agency for itself, and all we'll do is prove the self-fulfilling prophecy of a commoditization of our business. I'm sure it's going to expand, and we'll be caught more. I'm thankful that we earned our stripes on this a few years ago.

WINNING IN PROCUREMENT-LED BUYING PROCESSES

Here are recommendations on dealing with procurement officials from Rick Miller, now CEO, but formerly head of PR for Northlich, a large integrated communications firm in Cincinnati:

Few things strike fear into the hearts and balance sheets of agency principals like the newest ingredient in the agency evaluation game: *procurement.*

Surveys have shown that 80 percent of large advertisers use some type of procurement process to make agency proposal decisions. And, recently, they've begun to use it in public relations agency relationships, too.

Whether we call it procurement, purchasing, or strategic sourcing, it's borne of the corporate imperative to cut costs, improve governance, and clarify accountability. Wall Street demands it, so management specifies it for all major cost centers.

Procurement has migrated from a finance-led function that sought to drive down costs of commodities to capturing savings in areas such as travel and technology. Today, communications, often accounting for 30 percent or more of sales and marketing costs, is another expense that cannot be ignored. By tracking mountains of communications data cheaply, procurement processes offer clients the promise of huge savings potential.

As expertise in applying procurement principles has grown, along with the nagging suspicion that inefficiency haunts client-agency processes, large outsourcers such as Pfizer, Procter &

Gamble, and Eli Lilly have begun looking at professional services, including those provided by agencies.

Forward-looking procurement managers have backgrounds in communications and apply value-based thinking. For their companies, the idea is not to slash budgets, but to deploy resources more effectively. They view the process as *strategic sourcing* and work to create long-term, best-in-class relationships, not re-bid business every year.

For agencies, the concern is financial transparency and constant pressure to deliver more for less. Some agencies refuse to open their books; others feel procurement processes penalize them for efficiency.

Rhetoric aside, how can you win the procurement battle? Here are six ideas:

- *Treat the procurement officer as a prospect.* Find him. Learn his background—finance, IT, PR, or another area— and expectations. Embrace him. Invite him to spend several days at your firm. Include your own CFO as a key member of your team.
- *Learn what will penetrate a procurement officer's radar.* She may build short lists of preferred agencies based on her own analysis of awards, agency growth, capacity, competencies, and referrals from internal clients. Don't overwhelm her with information about your firm. In two pages, explain why you are relevant, demonstrate your intellectual connection, and articulate your specific contribution to building her customer base.
- *Introduce efficiencies to ensure that client and agency click.* Bidding strictly on a cost basis without making other changes invites mediocre work and margin stress. Create internal systems to match up agency and client finance representatives, streamline approval processes, clearly define scope, and agree on what you do that adds value. Focus on efficiency, financial transparency, and product quality.
- *Prove you're serious about return on investment (ROI).* Measurement and accountability are no longer hall talk. Agencies and client counterparts must demonstrate the effectiveness of their efforts and benchmark similar work to

compete effectively for budget dollars. As a result, agencies must evolve their own business models and cultures, be accountable—*and merchandise the results!*

- *Consider how you can become eligible for incentive compensation.* If you have done your homework and have ROI measures in place, determine how you can grow your top line through incentive compensation. Suggest a formula based on qualitative performance assessments tied to in-market results. Connect your reward structure to the value your firm has added to your client's success, based on mutually agreed upon goals.
- *Align yourself with how your clients are running their businesses.* Show that what you're doing is what your clients are doing. Demonstrate that you're making data-based decisions, and force the procurement discussion to be pragmatic about costs. For example, if the client wants to review your overhead costs, connect the review to a longer term commitment.
- *Match your people with client peer contacts.* Optimize your relationships. Focus on what you do really well so that, at every point of contact, your team is adding value to the client relationship.

The bottom line? Embrace both the procurement process and the procurement officers with whom you do business. You'll transform challenge into opportunity.

PROFILE 18: ANDY STERN

Chairman, Sunwest Communications
Dallas, Texas

Item: PR Week said he "may just be the most connected PR person in Dallas, considering the charity boards on which he serves and the corporations that seek his help."

Item: From 1975 to 1977, Andy Stern was a staff assistant to President Gerald Ford after serving as press secretary to the mayor of Wilmington, Delaware.

Item: His corporate PR background includes senior level executive positions in two major Dallas corporations. He serves on publicly held corporate boards, while his civic/nonprofit dossier takes in board responsibilities for the likes of the Sixth Floor Museum, Medical City Dallas Hospital, Texas Healthcare Trustees Association, EDS Bryon Nelson Championship PGA tournament, and the Salesmanship Club of Dallas.

Item: Stern started his PR firm in 1982 and managed to lose $82,000 the first year on fee income of $185,000. Today, his firm generates a nicely profitable $3 million fee income annually from a client list that ranges from giants like ExxonMobil to do-it-yourself market leaders such as Liquid Nails.

But when he founded Sunwest Communications, he set up the business financially with a corporate mindset rather than with an agency structure. (No attention to time keeping.) Which he says, "Has worked for us culturally, but may not have been the best structure financially." (See item above regarding the firm's first year's loss.) Now, he's been profitable all except two early years.

Starting over today, he'd, "Find [someone with agency experience] either as a financial person or a consultant for structure." He also recommends that new PR agency principals

Have plenty of capital. Without capital or eventual cash flow, you will end up taking clients you shouldn't take and that can either send you down a path you may not want to go or become a financial liability. Plus, understand that you are running a business, not merely a vehicle to pay the rent.

Chapter 19

Fiscal and Physical Checkups

Put it on your calendar now. At least once a quarter, take the time to examine and evaluate your firm's fiscal and physical progress. Look at your numbers. Are you on target to achieve your annual goals? Check your business plan. (What, you don't have one?) Is it working smoothly or missing on one cylinder? Is your firm moving in the right direction?

Here are some guidelines to help you audit your firm's progress four times a year, starting with the end of a year and looking ahead.

END OF YEAR (PROBABLY DECEMBER)

It's a mixed time of the year. Either you are frantically trying to complete assignments so that they can be billed in this year's client budgets, or you've used up this year's budgets, or your clients are taking holiday vacations and nothing is happening.

Here are some of the things you should be thinking about to get ready for next year:

- What kind of a year has it been? Did we meet our goals? If not, why not? What did we do right or wrong this year? What is the most important thing to change or begin next year?
- Update your long-range business plan, or write a plan if you don't have one. Then, don't stuff it in a file drawer; follow it or change it if it's not working.
- Develop a marketing plan and allocate funds to make it work (1 to 3 percent of your income). Commit at least 25 to 40 percent of your own time to new business development.

doi:10.1300/5561_19

- Develop and promote a unique strategic position for your firm. Decide what you are or what you want your firm to be. And then let prospects know about it.
- Develop a realistic budget for your firm, based on your best income expectations (see Chapter 13); update and adhere to the budget throughout the year. Change your budget if your income projections change.
- Based on your income expectations, plan staff needs for next year. Evaluate your staff, and get rid of the losers now. If you are in a growth mode, promote or hire a competent senior backup person to run client service while you grow the business.
- Vow to achieve at least an 85 percent productivity average next year. Stop fretting about monthly variances; shoot for long-range results.
- Vow to track client profitability monthly. Know when and why profitability on any account drops below where you want it. And do something about it, even if that means resigning the client. Your firm may be profitable overall, but individual problem clients can pull down total profits.

FIRST QUARTER

Okay, now it's the end of the first quarter. Make sure that you are on track to meet year-end financial goals. Ask yourself these questions:

- Do we have a targeted marketing program? Is it working? Are we making the cold contacts with prospects that everyone hates to make? Are we communicating consistently with prospects? Do we know what makes us different? Do we have a well-conceived strategic position? Are the firm's strategic position and special capabilities well understood by prospects? (See Chapter 4.)
- Is our staff in good shape? Do we have the right mix of people to meet unforeseen or likely client needs? Do we have too many, too few people? Do we have the right balance between junior and senior people to meet our clients' needs and generate a solid profit? Is staff productivity (billable hours) high enough? Are we hanging on to poor performers?

- Are our receivables under control? Do we make weekly calls to clients with bills that are more than 30 days old? Should we stop work for clients whose bills are more than 60 days old? Are we getting advance payments on large out-of-pocket expenses? (Don't be afraid to talk money to clients!)
- Are our expenses on budget and in line with projected income? Are salaries too high as a percentage of income? Have we budgeted for salary increases? Is the rent too high? Can we negotiate a lower rate, or should we move to cheaper space? Do we need to tighten controls on expenses?
- Will the first quarter be profitable? If not, why not? Do we know the profit returned by each client? Can we turn unprofitable clients around, or should we consider resigning them?

SECOND QUARTER

It's nearing the end of your second quarter, but there's still time to improve this year's results. Answer these questions:

- Are productivity, income, expenses, and profit in line with projections? If not, why not?
- Are client budgets about half used up? Is there enough money left to do necessary work? Are there any opportunities for new income yet this year?
- Will client budgets hold up? If budget cuts come in the third or fourth quarter, how will we react?
- What are our new business prospects? Are we marketing the firm with discipline and creativity?

THIRD QUARTER

It's autumn. The leaves are falling. Are your hopes for the year falling or rising? By now, there is not much you can do to salvage this year. Starting about Thanksgiving, clients and prospects seem to hibernate until they wake up suddenly on January 2nd with new money to spend. Chances are, most client budgets have been spent or committed by now. Hopefully, you're able to avoid a late-year budget crimp.

Make sure that all scheduled work can be completed within remaining budgets. You don't want to carry this year's agency time or client budgets over to next year. On the other hand, a client may ask you to bill unused-but-budgeted funds in advance and escrow the money for use next year, so this year's budget will appear used up. Clients sometimes fear budgets will be cut the following year if all the money is not spent in a current year. (An agency vice president, finance, on escrow accounts: "It's a mess, but we do it if the client asks. It's better than losing the money.")

Ask vendors to render invoices in time to be billed to clients this year if the project is in this year's budget. If the project won't actually be finished until early next year, but is in this year's budget, get an advance invoice from the vendor for most of the cost.

Most important, begin planning for next year, if you haven't started already. Client budget sources, particularly product managers (whose current year thinking sometimes stops by August), are probably deep into next year's planning by now. If you want budgets approved for next year, submit proposals early.

And start the cycle all over again.

PROFILE 19: MIKE WALKER

President, The Walker Agency
Scottsdale, Arizona

Stung by a 1982 corporate "downsizing," Mike Walker, with wife Mary, jumped into the agency waters. Six weeks later, he had his first client and has been profitable ever since. The firm's first year's income of about $50,000 has grown to about $1.5 million.

The Walker Agency specializes in the outdoor recreation and leisure time products industries, serving such blue chip clients as Yamaha Marine Group and Toyota Motor Sales USA. In addition to media relations, Walker offers Web content provision, e-mail marketing, in-house CD production, Internet distribution of press material, and two media-oriented Web sites. He also syndicates a daily three minute show to 400 radio stations and three times a year sends camera-ready material to 10,000 newspapers. These services feature Walker clients as well as other noncompeting companies.

Although he once sought clients in a variety of fields as a hedge against hard times, his mantra today is "Focus, Focus, Focus!" Walker warns, "If you chase two rabbits, you won't catch either one. Put client service first, last, and always."

Walker admits that previous agency experience would have been helpful before starting his own firm; that he should have broken away earlier from an incompatible partner; should have fired people who needed firing sooner; and should have had "the discipline to make new business a bigger part of my effort."

Advice to other agency principals: "Don't get suckered into debt; hit the road, nothing beats face time; make your word your bond; develop a thick skin and the strongest belief possible in yourself; understand the power of enthusiasm and use it."

Chapter 20

Planning the Future of Your PR Firm

Sooner or later—often the minute they open their doors for the first time, or surely by the time they hit 60—agency owners begin thinking about the future of their firm. (Or they should.) This thinking often includes wistful visions of being acquired by or merging with another firm. Usually, this hallucination includes dollar signs of some magnitude.

Harking back to the turbulent days of the late 1990s, when PR firms, particularly technology specialists, were being gobbled up for big bucks by the multinational holding companies, the owner of a relatively small firm may fantasize about the day big daddy multinational hands him a large chunk of cash in exchange for his firm and he goes off into blissful retirement. It doesn't always go that way.

One of the questions agency owners frequently ask, as they think about the possibility of their firm being acquired, is, "How much is my firm worth?" In many cases, unfortunately, the answer may be, "Not as much as you'd like."

In the following essay, longtime friend, New York management consultant Lee Levitt (LevittLee@cs.com), who specializes in PR firm mergers and acquisitions, outlines the possible and real aspects of agency mergers.

MERGERS AND ACQUISITIONS

Some PR firms are founded by one practitioner, are managed solely by that same person, and go out of business when she or he ceases practice. There is nothing wrong with this.

But many PR firm proprietors want more. They see others build companies that have an existence and a value beyond the

doi:10.1300/5561_20

founder's personal talents. As they grow older and build families, they often want to share the top-management burden with other senior PR practitioners. And they may hope that at some point they will be able to sell the equity they have built up in their firm to someone for a good price.

Some owners expect to achieve this internally. They assume that one or more employees with top-management potential will come along sooner or later. Unfortunately, this rarely happens, especially if the firm is small. Ninety percent of PR firm employees lack the temperament to become top managers and the money to buy into the firm. Even if a suitable-looking candidate appears, the owner often is unable to create an employment package sufficiently attractive to hold the person.

A few firms try to hire a "business manager" from outside the PR profession and groom him or her for top-management responsibility. This usually is an accountant who turns out to have little broad management experience or aptitude.

The best solution for many is to merge with, acquire, or be acquired by another PR firm. Note: There is no sharp distinction between a "merger" and an "acquisition." Either may be total or partial, and the resulting management structure can vary greatly. In the rest of this essay, we use "merger" to mean any deal in which company equity changes hands.

Some Initial Thoughts About Mergers

Mergers have become a normal part of the life-cycle of PR firms. In addition to bolstering top management, they may provide greater opportunity for both parties with minimum risk. Nowadays, involvement in merger discussions usually is a sign of agency strength, not weakness. Almost all professionally managed mergers are at least reasonably successful.

When to Think About Merger

It is never too early to consider merger. You should at least discuss any promising opportunity that comes your way. Such talks can be very educational even if not fruitful. Properly run, they require only a small investment of time, money, and emotion. They never should distract management or disrupt agency operations. They should not be allowed to drag on inconclusively.

If you have reached the age of 55 and your business has leveled off (Assess this realistically.), you should begin to consider merger systematically. Most potential partners want to join forces with a dynamic firm, and (fairly or unfairly) age is a factor in this perception. Each year that passes usually reduces your firm's attractiveness to merger partners.

Don't even think of selling and walking away. At the very least, you probably will have to stay on for several years to fulfill the terms of the merger. Many potential partners will shy away if they suspect that you want out. Numerous PR firm executives have found that once they have unloaded part of the burden of top management, they can become an elder statesman and do the kind of PR work they really enjoy.

Some people seem to believe that you can manage your PR firm in some special way to make it more attractive to merger partners. This is rarely true. What prospects generally want to see are the same things you strive for as an owner: good clients, good staff, good internal management, a proactive new-business program, consistent profitability over a period of several years.

About the only way you can prepare for merger discussions is to make sure you have accurate, sophisticated financial statements that are consistent from one year to the next.

With Whom Can You Merge?

Several types of potential merger partners may be available to your firm, at least in theory:

- *Major communications conglomerates*—Large publicly held holding companies owning ad agencies, PR firms, sales-promotion firms, etc., have made most of the merger news in recent years. These companies usually will consider only PR firms with at least $8 million in annual fee revenue, located in one of the top five geographic markets, and engaged in a currently fashionable line of practice.
- *Mini-conglomerates*—Backed by venture capitalists, a few of these have sprung up in the United States and Canada.

(They are much more common in Great Britain.) Their acquisition policies are less restrictive than those of the majors.

- *Noncommunications corporations*—Purchasing equity in PR firms. These deals are rare in the United States and the results have not been good.
- *Advertising agencies*—From time to time, numerous ad agencies decide to seek or enhance sophisticated PR capability. PR people often find these situations unattractive unless the ad agency has a PR professional in senior management.
- *Independent large and middle-sized PR firms*—These firms have made cautious deals with smaller firms to round out their offerings geographically and/or by type of practice. Some examples: a good-sized firm in a state capital buys several small firms to extend its coverage over the entire state; a high-tech firm in California acquires a small investor-relations firm on the East Coast.
- *Small PR firms*—Small firms generally merge only with other firms in the same geographic market. Many are prospects for "true" or "side-by-side" mergers: fusion of two or more firms via a stock swap. A big advantage of such deals is that neither party has to cough up much money.

How Much Is My Firm Likely to Be Worth?

The standard formula for the value of a PR firm usually is net worth, plus three to six times a weighted average of the firm's imputed net profit before taxes over the preceding three years. The price tends to be low if the firm is in poor condition or specializes in an unfashionable area of practice, higher if the firm is unusually strong or will take the other party into a desirable market in which it previously could not compete.

"Net worth" means cash, receivables, deposits, and the liquidation value of furniture and equipment—minus debts. You may choose to retain assets not needed by the business (e.g., a car or paintings), in which case the net worth at the time of merger is reduced accordingly.

"Imputed" means after adding back to reported profits any compensation or perquisites taken by the owner that would not have been paid to an ordinary employee doing the owner's job.

Opinion may differ regarding the portion of the owner's takings that should be thought of as salary; obviously, the higher the salary, the lower the profits. If you are going to work for the combined firm, the salary you demand in that capacity (see below) may suggest the figure that should be used when calculating imputed profit.

"Weighted" means that the most recent year's performance is given greater weight in the calculation than earlier years.

Payment of a purchase price usually is spread over two to five years. It usually is at least partially conditioned—upward as well as downward—upon revenues actually realized from the clients turned over to the combined firm. The definition of "clients turned over" may include certain prospective accounts as well as those actually on the books at time of merger.

Because salaries and consulting fees are immediately deductible as business expenses for a buyer, while payments for assets may not be, it is common to disguise payments for a PR firm as bonuses or consulting fees.

You probably will go to work for the combined entity at a reasonable salary under an employment contract of two to five years. This real salary should be thought of as entirely separate from any capital payments made in the guise of salary. If you demand a high salary, you can expect the other party to advocate use of a high salary figure in calculating imputed profit to determine the value of your firm (see above). The real salary may have escalators based upon the amount of business you sell and/or manage during employment.

You may receive the same or more liberal benefits as an employee of the combined firm. If you have a tax-sheltered fund in your firm, it often can be rolled over into a partner's fund without tax penalty. If you had certain perquisites in your firm (e.g., a car), the combined firm may guarantee to continue these.

How Is the Deal Structured?

There is no standard formula for merger and no authority to whom one can appeal. The needs and preferences of parties can vary widely; ingenuity in accommodating these often is the key to successful negotiation. Parties frequently change their perspective as negotiations proceed. Often attorneys, accountants, or other counselors have a voice.

Since capital payments usually are disguised as salary or consulting fees and since the combined firm's possession of clients can be ensured via a "restrictive covenant," there usually is no necessity for the combined firm legally to acquire your company. The whole deal can be handled via an employment contract. You retain the shell of your company and are responsible for collecting receivables from clients up to the day of closure. Thereafter, the clients are billed by the combined firm (but often under a close variant of the old name, so the clients may scarcely realize that there has been a change).

Once the terms of the employment contract have been fulfilled, you can quit or the combined company can discharge you. In practice, the relationship often changes sooner than that: you may rise in the hierarchy of the combined firm or leave early by mutual agreement. Your employment contract usually contains a "restrictive covenant" hampering you from departing with accounts served by the combined firm; but this often is negotiable, and some people go back into business on their own several years after merging their firm.

The combined firm usually hires your employees at their prevailing salaries. This ensures continuity of service to your clients. In many cases, the merger offers new opportunities to your employees, and it should be presented to them in this light.

PR firms almost never lose clients as a result of merger. Most clients are utterly incurious regarding such deals if their relationships remain unchanged. Some may be impressed if the merger seems to make additional capability available to the client.

Who Should Manage Negotiations?

Some deals have been negotiated by PR firm principals without help. All too often, however, such discussions degenerate into an endless series of friendly lunches, or terminate unnecessarily because one party says in all innocence something which offends the other. The involvement of a third party often makes agreement more likely by lowering the emotional temperature of negotiations and keeping things moving.

Lawyers and accountants inevitably will be involved in their special capacities when merger discussions become serious. Some also believe they are qualified to initiate and manage negotiations. However, they often tend to think of a merger as a strictly financial matter, which among PR firms is never the case.

An independent consultant specializing in the PR field often can find and develop good merger prospects and help parties negotiate a mutually advantageous deal.

ON THE OTHER HAND

Here's the decision made by the 50-year-old owner of a successful Midwest boutique after being wooed by several very large firms:

> After much analysis, I've decided that the rewards for selling are not that great right now. While our financial picture is really strong, it doesn't translate to a big payoff for me—and the loss of independence requires a big payoff. I hope that's a wise decision, but there are risks whether we sell or stay independent, so I guess I'm choosing the risks that I know and feel I have more control over.

There's also good likelihood that the owner's younger minority partner will decide to buy out the majority partner, which will probably be the best deal for both of them.

PROFILE 20: BOB WALT

President, Walt & Company
Santa Clara, California

Award-winning client service, in-depth knowledge of consumer technology and financial services industries, and a droll sense of humor—combined with surviving the late 1990s dot-com crash—define Walt & Company.

To scratch an entrepreneurial itch, after a long stretch as an executive of several international firms, Bob Walt founded his tech-based firm in 1991. Fee income that first year hit $500,000 income and by 2004 was back up to $2.5 million after a tech bubble high of nearly $5 million. (It's called "survival of the fittest"!)

Adding financial services to his technology base, Walt & Company serves such clients as Epson America, Sonic Solutions, National Retirement Planning Coalition, and National Association for Variable Annuities.

Says Walt, "We approach new opportunities differently than our competitors. We think in terms of solving problems, not just generating publicity. We develop programs that build marketplace value for our clients."

Walt says his international agency P&L responsibility taught him the importance of paying attention to every bottom-line detail while at the same time driving the top line. "Until the dot-com bust, we never did any proactive marketing," Walt admits. "Had we developed and maintained a marketing program from the beginning, I believe we would have had an easier time rebuilding our book of business over the last several years."

Walt urges agency principals to "maintain a good balance between your role as a CEO and your role as a PR professional. Both are critical. Too much of one or the other could spell disaster."

About that droll sense of humor: the firm's Web site (www.walt .com) offers interviews with several employees' pets and an employee's description of the "Ten similarities between snowboarding and PR."

Chapter 21

And In Conclusion:
New Year's Resolutions

In case you're late coming up with your own this year, or need a bright light to guide you through the night, here are ten New Year's Resolutions designed especially for counseling firm principals. They can be applied at any time during the year. Now is not too soon or too late.

1. I resolve not to lose my head when all around me are losing theirs and when, in reality, all seems lost. Instead, I will step into the hall, blow a mighty blast on the police whistle I keep in my desk for such occasions, and yell "Stop the Presses" at the top of my lungs. (A lady account supervisor at Ketchum PR in Pittsburgh used to do just this. Seemed to work fine for her.)

2. I resolve to take no more lip than absolutely necessary from crabby clients. Instead, I will subsidize their treatment in an attitude adjustment class. Or, if that fails, I will insist that we do such good work and provide such excellent service to every one of our clients that they will all become sugar tongued and will no longer beat up on their account executives and other fragile souls.

3. I resolve to be kind to freelance writers, photographers, artists, and all other vendors and suppliers; to always give them careful and complete instructions and plenty of time in which to complete assignments; and to, always, always pay them promptly (within ten days, if possible).

4. I resolve to hold technology close to my heart and checkbook; to spend the bread to buy good cutting-edge hardware and sophisticated software that combines timekeeping, accounting, billing, budgeting, profitability, and productivity tracking and

doi:10.1300/5561_21

pumps out an information-packed plethora of reports. I will retain one typewriter to address an occasional envelope and as a reminder that once upon a time "cut and paste" could not be accomplished with a couple key strokes.

5. I resolve to pay attention to all the little things that motivate employees and make them eager to come to work. This includes such niceties as (A) saying "Thanks," "Great job," and "The client loves you"; (B) walking the halls frequently with a smile on my lips and a spark in my eyes; (C) letting people know exactly where they stand through regular candid and comprehensive performance reviews; (D) not forcing people to ask for a raise, but making sure that everyone knows what our compensation policies are; and (E) remembering that my replacement may be among my junior staff today.

6. I resolve to challenge and inspire employees by providing the training they need to grow; by encouraging them to become involved in professional organizations and activities; and by pushing them to climb mountains that they may believe are too steep and treacherous.

7. I resolve to remember that there is life outside the agency business and that people, especially younger members of the staff, may not be as fervently devoted to the health and future of this agency as I am.

8. I resolve to remember that not everyone can or will write or perform tasks exactly the way I do or would and that this is not necessarily bad. I resolve to delegate both responsibility and authority to competent people; and to be patient and learn to tell the difference between an employee's approach to a task that is merely different from mine and one that is a threat to the agency.

9. I resolve to encourage people, particularly younger staff members, to have the judgment and confidence in their own ability to stop work on a project before they have invested more time than the client will be willing to pay for. And to remember that clients deserve and are very willing to pay for excellence but they are not willing to pay for perfection.

10. I resolve to remember that excellent client service is vital to this firm's success. But that, for the firm to truly succeed, I

must be as good a business executive as I am a public relations counselor.

And in conclusion: The words you have just read (I assume that you have just read them. Otherwise, what are you doing way back here?) are the distillation of things learned during 25 years in three very good public relations agencies and 18 years counseling PR agency principals on a myriad of marketing and management problems and opportunities.

There is really only one more thing that should be said to ensure that your time as a public relations firm principal is mightily successful. Have fun! If you've been paying attention through these pages, you now know how to run a growing and profitable PR firm. And that's a heck of a lot of fun.

Index

Page numbers followed by the letter "t" indicate tables.

doi:10.1300/5561_22

Order a copy of this book with this form or online at:
http://www.haworthpress.com/store/product.asp?sku=5561

MANAGING A PUBLIC RELATIONS FIRM FOR GROWTH AND PROFIT
Second Edition

_____in hardbound at $59.95 (ISBN-13: 978-0-7890-2864-8; ISBN-10: 0-7890-2864-6)

_____in softbound at $39.95 (ISBN-13: 978-0-7890-2865-5; ISBN-10: 0-7890-2865-4)

Or order online and use special offer code HEC25 in the shopping cart.

COST OF BOOKS_____

POSTAGE & HANDLING_____
*(US: $4.00 for first book & $1.50
for each additional book)*
*(Outside US: $5.00 for first book
& $2.00 for each additional book)*

SUBTOTAL_____

IN CANADA: ADD 7% GST_____

STATE TAX_____
*(NJ, NY, OH, MN, CA, IL, IN, PA, & SD
residents, add appropriate local sales tax)*

FINAL TOTAL_____
*(If paying in Canadian funds,
convert using the current
exchange rate, UNESCO
coupons welcome)*

☐ **BILL ME LATER:** (Bill-me option is good on
US/Canada/Mexico orders only; not good to
jobbers, wholesalers, or subscription agencies.)
☐ Check here if billing address is different from
shipping address and attach purchase order and
billing address information.

Signature_____

☐ **PAYMENT ENCLOSED: $_____**

☐ **PLEASE CHARGE TO MY CREDIT CARD.**

☐ Visa ☐ MasterCard ☐ AmEx ☐ Discover
☐ Diner's Club ☐ Eurocard ☐ JCB

Account # _____

Exp. Date_____

Signature_____

Prices in US dollars and subject to change without notice.

NAME_____

INSTITUTION_____

ADDRESS_____

CITY_____

STATE/ZIP_____

COUNTRY_____ COUNTY (NY residents only)_____

TEL_____ FAX_____

E-MAIL_____

May we use your e-mail address for confirmations and other types of information? ☐ Yes ☐ No
We appreciate receiving your e-mail address and fax number. Haworth would like to e-mail or fax special
discount offers to you, as a preferred customer. **We will never share, rent, or exchange your e-mail address
or fax number.** We regard such actions as an invasion of your privacy.

Order From Your Local Bookstore or Directly From
The Haworth Press, Inc.
10 Alice Street, Binghamton, New York 13904-1580 • USA
TELEPHONE: 1-800-HAWORTH (1-800-429-6784) / Outside US/Canada: (607) 722-5857
FAX: 1-800-895-0582 / Outside US/Canada: (607) 771-0012
E-mail to: orders@haworthpress.com

For orders outside US and Canada, you may wish to order through your local
sales representative, distributor, or bookseller.
For information, see http://haworthpress.com/distributors

(Discounts are available for individual orders in US and Canada only, not booksellers/distributors.)
PLEASE PHOTOCOPY THIS FORM FOR YOUR PERSONAL USE.
http://www.HaworthPress.com   BOF06